100 °°
EN/XN

24 Vols

943

THE WORKS OF
THEODORE ROOSEVELT

MEMORIAL EDITION

PREPARED UNDER THE AUSPICES OF

THE ROOSEVELT MEMORIAL ASSOCIATION
HERMANN HAGEDORN, EDITOR

THIS EDITION, PRINTED FROM TYPE WHICH HAS
BEEN DISTRIBUTED, IS STRICTLY LIMITED TO ONE
THOUSAND AND FIFTY SETS, OF WHICH ONE THOUSAND
ARE FOR SALE AND FIFTY ARE FOR PRESENTATION

THIS IS NO. *677* #94

Edith Kermit Roosevelt

THE WORKS OF
THEODORE ROOSEVELT

MEMORIAL EDITION

VOLUME I

Theodore Roosevelt

HUNTING TRIPS OF A RANCHMAN

GAME SHOOTING IN THE WEST

GOOD HUNTING

BY

THEODORE ROOSEVELT

NEW YORK

CHARLES SCRIBNER'S SONS

MCMXXIII

EDITOR'S FOREWORD

In the production of any pageant, the stage is for the actors. The pageant master belongs behind the scenes in his tower high over the stage. It is his part to see that the successive episodes of the pageant he is directing are shown in due order, and by skilful stage-management rather than words to make them reveal most clearly their own significance and, scene by scene, unfold the meaning of the whole.

The editor of the collected works of any great man is in a similar position and, though at the close of the performance it may be appropriate for him to express a word of appreciation of those who have given him aid and counsel, at the beginning he is wise if he says little. Prologues are out of date; the audience is impatient for the action to commence. A few words concerning the arrangement of the diverse and voluminous material represented in Mr. Roosevelt's writings is, however, necessary.

Four main interests dominated Mr. Roosevelt's life —the world of outdoors, history, politics (using the word in its largest sense), and his own human relationships. His writings, therefore, naturally fall into four major groups. The first group includes what have been loosely called his "books of adventure"—a term which is adequate only if recognition is given to the fact that to him the study and recording of the phenomena of the great outdoors represented one of the most exhilarating varieties of adventure—his narrations of frontier life, of hunting and of the habits of wild creatures in many lands, of romantic wanderings in strange places, of arduous exploration afar and joyous communion with nature's children at home. The books covering this field fill the first six volumes.

Mr. Roosevelt's achievement as an historian has been dimmed inevitably by his achievements as a politician, a statesman, and a spiritual leader. It is therefore worth recalling that "The Naval War of 1812" and "The Winning of the West" remain, after a generation or more, the authorities in the domains which they cover. The one has long been accepted by British students of naval warfare as the wisest record of a war which, on sea if not on land, brought glory to both combatants; the other is regarded by the people whose story it tells as the noblest monument yet created to the memory of their heroic forefathers. With the "Hero Tales from American History," the story of the Rough Riders, a brief history of the city of his birth and three studies of striking figures which peculiarly appealed to his imagination, these historical writings fill Volumes VII to XIII.

The succeeding eight volumes (XIV to XXI) contain Mr. Roosevelt's literary, moral, and political essays and addresses. Their arrangement has offered more than one fascinating and complicated problem. The main difficulty has lain not so much in the amazing breadth of Mr. Roosevelt's intellectual field (though that presents problems enough) as in the fact that, from different angles, he expounded certain fundamental themes throughout the course of his life. To bring together all the discussions of the same subject seemed as inevitable and simple in theory as it proved difficult in practice.

There are certain obvious ways in which a statesman's speeches and fugitive papers may be arranged. The chronological way is the simple way which most editors of such collections have followed. It is a very orderly way, indeed, but, like many other manifestations of that austere spirit which Schiller designated as the fairest daughter of Heaven, it makes for dulness. The inevitable juxtaposition of papers associated with each other by no similarity of content or aim, but only by the accidental fact that they happened to come before the public at approximately the same time, casts a blighting effect on the attention. The reader, interested in the address on the control of corporations which he has been reading, turns page on page, skimming impatiently over discussions of military preparedness, the Ninth Commandment, reciprocity with Cuba, the Panama Canal, citizenship, or the duties of motherhood, and takes refuge at last in the Index, only to be confronted by an assemblage of references so extensive and so detailed as to be utterly discouraging to all except the student on a journey to a thesis. Fortunately we have an example of what the chronological method of arrangement can do even to material as lively, as direct, as incisive, as Mr. Roosevelt's essays and speeches. Shortly after Mr. Roosevelt left the Presidency, a collection of his utterances on public questions, strangely interspersed with occasional articles on matters as foreign to Congress as the Ancient Irish Sagas, was published in eight volumes. They are singularly forbidding volumes. To the Gentle Reader—a person with whom Mr. Roosevelt himself had the liveliest sympathy—they stretch out like that bad lands of literature, a source-book, a region for prospecting, perhaps, but not for recreation except for the most intrepid.

EDITOR'S FOREWORD

A consistent arrangement of the material by subject-matter presented difficulties of another sort. Such an arrangement would have necessitated a ruthless disregard of certain collections made at different times by Mr. Roosevelt himself and the elimination of titles which have become dear to many readers and have, in fact, their place in political as well as literary history. It would, furthermore, have added a new element of confusion in bringing into too close relation papers separated in their conception by the profound gulf that separates the consulship of Chester A. Arthur from the consulship of Woodrow Wilson. The wise solution of the puzzle seemed to lie in a compromise by which the original collections were, as far as seemed feasible, kept intact, and augmented with material naturally akin. The editor has dared to lay hand at all on the volumes of essays only because of his conviction that a number of them had not, in the first place, been conceived as units, being rather collections of separate papers, each conceived and executed independently of the others and not resting on any particular juxtaposition for their effect. With the inevitable limitations already described, the editor has as far as possible endeavored from the mass of material published and unpublished to bring together what seemed by nature to belong together. In doing this he has carefully refrained from applying too rigidly any theory of his own and from following too dutifully any accepted convention. He has, in fact, tried to free himself from any theories, and to pursue one aim, regardless of theories, of convention, and even of consistency. That aim has been to arrange the material in a way that would make it as easy as possible for the reader to find out what Mr. Roosevelt's convictions were on any given subject; or haply just to browse in the green fields of his stimulating discourse.

So much for the third group of volumes. There remain Volumes XXII to XXIV, which contain Mr. Roosevelt's autobiography, his "Letters to His Children," and Mr. Joseph Bucklin Bishop's "Theodore Roosevelt and His Time, Shown in His Own Letters." These books tell much of the events of his crowded life, but even more of the human relationships which enriched that life immeasurably. The letters—and particularly the letters to his children—have already taken their place among the classics of epistolary literature. It is safe to assume that they will have a profound effect on American family life.

No further word is necessary. The Introductions to the separate volumes, which distinguished friends of Mr. Roosevelt have contributed, tell, far better than this pen could, of the incisive speech, the learning, the wisdom, the force, the originality, the enduring vitality, the beauty, the deep humanity, which characterize the writings here collected.

HERMANN HAGEDORN.

New York,
August, 1923.

INTRODUCTION*

By George Bird Grinnell

THE varied aspects of Theodore Roosevelt's full life must be discussed by different men. They will tell of his grasp of the things in which he was interested, the great information he brought to bear on whatever came before him, and the readiness with which he adjusted himself to diverse situations. These characteristics, with his democracy, his courage, and his devotion to the welfare of his fellow Americans, are some of the qualities that endeared him to his countrymen.

The side of his life which is least generally understood is that dealing with his devotion to outdoor life and what goes with that life. I shall recall some things about Roosevelt as an outdoor man.

His sojourns in the West, his study of nature and his hunting and fondness of sport, not only had a great influence in forming his character, but were always among his deepest interests—those to which he clung closest up to the end of his life. To many of his old friends it seems strange that this phase of his life, which meant so much to him, should have been so generally ignored, or should have been alluded to only casually by the many who have written of his different activities. An effort was made just after his death to bring forth and fitly emphasize these features, but their importance was not then fully understood.

It was the writing of a review of "Hunting Trips of a Ranchman" that brought me into intimate contact

INTRODUCTION

with Theodore Roosevelt. I had known him casually
as a young man carrying on at Albany a fight for good
politics, which commanded wide sympathy, and as
interested in the cattle business in Dakota, in which,
at the same time, I also was interested in another
Territory; but I had seen little of him until the appearance of this first book of his on hunting and Western life.

Its freshness, its spontaneity, and its enthusiasm
made the book delightful reading. Its English was
good, but above all it was the spirit of the volume
that was charming. Here was a young writer who,
going out into a new country and seeing many new
things, enjoyed them so much that he wished to tell
others all about them—his every impression.

The "Hunting Trips" suggested to me two books,
written nearly forty years before by other writers
wholly new to the West, who saw with young eyes
many of the things that Theodore Roosevelt saw, and
told of them in the same fresh and delightful way.
The similarity of mental attitude of the three seemed
remarkable.

The two books are Parkman's "The California and
Oregon Trail" and Garrard's "Wahtoyah, or the Taos
Trail." Written in 1846 or 1847, describing quite
different countries, and by young men neither of whom
was much more than twenty years of age, these were
interesting and striking literary productions, and
chiefly because of their delightful simplicity and nat-
uralness. Another book of about the same period,
which has something of the same quality but which bears
also some evidence of literary dressing up, is Ruxton's
"Adventures in Mexico and the Rocky Mountains."

I greatly liked "Hunting Trips of a Ranchman,"

but found in it some things that were open to criticism. My experience in the West had begun a dozen or fifteen years before that of Theodore Roosevelt, and I had travelled over much country and seen much of the native life between the Missouri River and the Pacific coast. His experience of two or three years had extended over but a limited area in western Dakota and eastern Montana. What he saw he reported faithfully and accurately, but he had the youthful—and common—tendency to generalize from his own observations and to conclude that certain aspects of nature were always and in all places as he had found them in one place. Moreover, he was inclined to accept as fact some statements made in books, and others by men with whom he had talked, who were either bad observers or careless talkers. These things were pointed out in the notice of the book I had written.

At that rather early day there were not many active writers who had seen so much of the West as I, and who in travelling through it had also given the same careful attention to the ways of the wild creatures. I had checked up my own observations by those of other men—white hunters as well as Indians, and Indians are excellent observers of facts. I knew enough of Theodore Roosevelt—if only from his course in the New York Legislature—to feel that in all that he wrote he wanted to know the truth and to tell it.

Not long after the review was printed, Mr. Roosevelt called at the office of *Forest and Stream*, of which I was then the editor, and we talked freely about the book, and took up at length some of its statements. He at once saw my point of view, and after we had discussed the book and the habits of the animals he had described, we passed on to the broader subject of

INTRODUCTION

hunting in the West, which was still to some extent
unexplored and unhunted, and to the habits of the
animals as modified by their surroundings. I told him
something about game destruction in Montana for the
hides, which, so far as small game was concerned,
had begun in the West only a few years before that,
though the slaughter of buffalo for their skins had been
going on much longer and by this time their extermination had been substantially completed. Straggling
animals were occasionally killed for some years after
this, but the last of the big herds had disappeared.

Roosevelt called often at my office to discuss the
broad country that we both loved, and we came to
know each other extremely well. Though chiefly interested in big game and its hunting, and telling interestingly of events that had occurred on his own hunting
trips, Roosevelt enjoyed hearing of the birds, the small
mammals, the Indians, and the incidents of travel of
early expeditions on which I had gone. He was always
fond of natural history, having begun, as so many boys
have done, with birds; but as he saw more and more
of outdoor life his interest in the subject broadened and
later it became a passion with him.

Besides these subjects we had this in common, that
we were both familiar with life on a cow-ranch, and
that the glamour of the cowboy's life—which to those
who had only read of it seemed so romantic—had quite
worn off, and we knew this life for what it was—the
hardest kind of work.

Eight or ten years before this I had travelled through
Montana and the Yellowstone Park, as naturalist of
Colonel William Ludlow's reconnoissance from Carrol,
Montana, to the Yellowstone Park and return, and
had seen much of the skin-hunting which had then

just begun in that territory. I had reported on this to Colonel Ludlow and the report had been published in 1876 by the War Department. This was one of the early protests against killing big game in the West for profit, though in the same year Doctor J. A. Allen had suggested setting aside a reservation where the buffalo might be protected from destruction by the hide-hunters. My account of big-game destruction much impressed Roosevelt, and gave him his first direct and detailed information about this slaughter of elk, deer, antelope, and mountain-sheep. No doubt it had some influence in making him the ardent game protector that he later became, just as my own experiences had started me along the same road.

We talked of these things at length, and in a vague way foresaw the dangers that already threatened big game in many parts of the West as soon as a point should be reached where their products could be turned into dollars. This meant available transportation, for as soon as the skins could be brought to a market the animals that yielded them would be killed. Destruction had already taken place near the railroads, but though we felt that in time it would follow everywhere, we did not comprehend its imminence and the impending completeness of the extermination. It was a thing impossible to be understood at the time, for no one then realized how swiftly the steel plough would follow the iron horse. Neither had we any comprehension of the attempts that would at once be made to turn into money all our natural things, whether big game, birds, or forests. Those who were concerned to protect native life were still uncertainly trying to find out what they could most effectively do, how they could do it, and what dangers it was necessary to fight first.

INTRODUCTION

We regretted the unnecessary destruction of game animals, but we did not know all it meant, nor had we the vision to look forward and imagine what it portended. So, though we discussed in a general way the preservation of game, it must be confessed—in the light of later events—that we were talking of things about which we knew very little. We wanted the game preserved, but chiefly with the idea that it should be protected in order that there might still be good hunting which should last for generations.

It was somewhat later than this, perhaps in the autumn of 1887, that Roosevelt suggested the establishment of a club of amateur riflemen, an organization which should be made up of good sportsmen who were also good big-game hunters. The project seemed one that might do good, and he became enthusiastic about it, and in December, 1887, invited a dozen men to dine with him at his house on Madison Avenue, and there proposed the formation of the club. Of the men present at that dinner only three are now living.

The club, named for Boone and for Crockett, was founded in December, 1887, and Roosevelt became the first president. The purposes, as expressed in the constitution, show fairly well the attitude of the more advanced sportsmen of the time. These purposes were to promote (1) manly sport with the rifle, (2) travel and exploration in this country, (3) the preservation of our large game, (4) inquiry into and the recording of observations on the natural history of wild animals, and (5) to bring about interchange of opinions and ideas on hunting, travel, and exploration in game localities.

The Boone and Crockett Club was the first club of its kind perhaps in any country. It has performed valuable services for conservation, and has set up standards which have been followed by other associations. The list of its members, living and dead, includes many men who have done much for science, for nature study, for exploration, and for wild-life preservation. Some part of the work done by the club, and thus due directly or indirectly to Roosevelt's efforts and influence, has been recorded in the club's publications, to which he made many contributions.

A few years after the founding of the Boone and Crockett Club it was determined that a volume on hunting should be published, made up of contributions by the members. An editorial committee was appointed consisting of Theodore Roosevelt and myself, and he served as chairman of that committee until he became president eight or ten years later. Then, at his suggestion, his name was omitted from the title-page of subsequent volumes.

Roosevelt's services to science and to conservation were many, but perhaps no single thing that he did for conservation has had so far-reaching an effect as the establishment of the Boone and Crockett Club. Its members were men selected for their good sportsmanship or for their accomplishments in science, in exploration, or in the preservation of native wild life, and most of the names carried weight. The constitution specified clearly, and in order, certain desirable objects, which all good sportsmen recognized as worthy. Before very long, in the United States and in England, other clubs and associations were formed on the same model; so that in founding the club he organized, Roosevelt was directly responsible for the good work of each of these. Aside from what has been accomplished directly by the Boone and Crockett Club, a brief history of which I have written, the clubs more recently established have also performed services of incalculable value by influencing legislation in behalf of conservation, and, above all, by gradually educating the public to understand and to value the importance to public economics, recreation, and health of those natural things most of which we have already destroyed and now are beginning to try to restore.

Roosevelt was thus a great leader in the field of conservation, as he was in the field of sport, and for that reason the country owes him a debt which, as time passes, will be more generally appreciated. He was a leader, and a leader in pioneer times, when, above all, leadership counts.

When Roosevelt went into the West, inhabitants there were few. The old-time independent spirit still prevailed, and one man was just as good as another. That an individual was paid for work did not make him a servant, nor did it make him amenable to orders. One who hired another to work for him expected also to work—to do his share. If a man working for hire was ordered to do something he considered menial, he was likely to express his frank opinion of his employer and to discharge himself forthwith. On the other hand, if the employer asked him to perform the same work and helped him do it, the hired man made no objection and pitched in with a good heart. Roosevelt recognized this attitude of mind—which at first must have astonished him, as it did other Eastern men of the time—and he described it entertainingly in one or two of his Western books. He sympathized with the independent spirit and adjusted himself at once to the situations which it constantly brought up. He used to tell of a very successful hunting trip he had made where the man he took along to help him proved worthless, besides having some whiskey cached in the packs. Roosevelt made his trip and took his man along, but himself did practically all the work. All day he hunted, and at night and morning did the cooking, packed the wood, and wrangled the horses. It was hard and disagreeable, of course, but, like many other hard and disagreeable things, it was good medicine for a youngster to take. His refusal to be beaten by circumstances showed his determination even then.

Like many other outdoor men of early days, Roosevelt enjoyed hunting alone, or with a single comrade. An early instance of this was his trip in western Montana and Idaho, when in company with John Willis of Thompson Falls he set out to secure white goats and covered a considerable area in western Montana and southern Idaho. The trip was full of interest and he was rewarded with success. He made himself agreeable as usual, and preached so effectively the doctrine of game preservation that he wholly converted Willis, who up to this time had been a skin and meat hunter, considering game animals valuable only for the dollars they yielded the hunter. Roosevelt was constantly doing such individual useful work in conservation matters.

His Western experience, coming at an age when his character was just forming, taught him many lessons which later in life were of the greatest value. It was through those experiences, I believe, that he learned his first lessons in real democracy, for he was constantly associating with men of various classes and types, each one of whom was in his own estimation as good as any one else. It was in this, then free and more or less uncontrolled society, that he learned how to meet and get along with men, and how to see and to use the good that is to be found in each one. The association served him as a practical preparatory school for the political activities in which he took part in later years, and in a measure accounts for his great political success.

His experience in ranch life, in association with his fellows, and in hunting, taught him, besides a knowledge of men, good judgment, readiness of adaptation to a variety of conditions, and promptness of decision on the course of action to be followed. From the mistakes he may have made he learned lessons he never forgot. Thus his first Western sojournings went far toward providing the actual groundwork for his then unsuspected future.

It was his life in the West and his acquaintance with the country formerly occupied by some of the Western tribes that gave him an interest in Indians, especially those of the plains. This knowledge, together with the sympathy he always felt for the "under dog" in a fight and, above all, for those who were being imposed on by the stronger, led him more than once to take vigorous action where Indians were threatened with injustice and needed help to secure their rights.

In the year 1902 complaints were received in Washington that the Indian Bureau had leased to cattlemen in North Dakota a large area of the lands of the Standing Rock Sioux on the Missouri River, including not a few Indian dwellings and crop-fields. The Indians were greatly alarmed. In imagination they could already hear the tramp of the advancing herds and the rattle of their horns as they crowded forward to invade and destroy the little homes and gardens that the changing Sioux were slowly and painfully trying to improve. The friends of the Indians were equally alarmed.

INTRODUCTION

The complaints filtered through the Indian Bureau to the Secretary of the Interior, and finally reached Roosevelt. Meantime, men not connected with the government had been appealed to, and some of these were his friends. The statements made by the Indians and the missionaries absolutely contradicted those of the Secretary of the Interior, the Commissioner of Indian Affairs, and the agent of the Standing Rock Sioux, and it seemed impossible to find out which were true. The natural thing to expect was that the President would support his subordinates.

In the midst of the excitement, George Kennan and Doctor C. Hart Merriam appealed to the President, and after much discussion they suggested to him that he should send me out to Standing Rock to get the facts and report directly to him. He asked me to go. Before starting I saw Roosevelt and asked him frankly just what he wanted, telling him that if I went out to find facts I must report what I found, and that if my findings did not agree with the beliefs of his Secretary of the Interior and his Indian Commissioner I should say so. He replied that he wanted the facts, no matter whom they affected, and a settlement of the difficulty on terms that were just.

A few days spent in racing about over the Standing Rock Reservation and in talking with the people there gave me a fairly clear idea of the situation; after that it was merely a question of a little common sense, tact, and persuasion to arrange matters so that a plan was found by which the cattlemen and the Indians alike were satisfied. After many councils and much talk an agreement was reached, and the Indians sent me away with messages of gratitude and affection to the President. The Indians and their friends felt that justice had been done and that it was to the President that they owed this justice.

On more than one occasion when Indian delegations of people whom I knew well were in Washington I took them to see the President, and he always gave them good advice and whole-hearted encouragement. They did not always understand the words he addressed to them, but they did feel in their hearts the sympathy which his tones expressed.

Roosevelt's interest in natural history began early in life, for when a sophomore in college he made, with H. D. Minot, a list of the summer birds of the Adirondacks, which covered ninety-seven species. He once told me that as a very small boy—before it had been learned that he was near-sighted and required glasses—he used to see the birds in the trees near him only as more or less indistinct shapes, without color. He then supposed that every one else saw things just as he saw them, and it was only after the defect in his vision had been discovered and he had begun to wear glasses that he came to understand how wide a world there was all about him, of which before he had known nothing. I have sometimes wondered if his eagerness to find out all the details of this hitherto dimly seen world was not the motive that led him to try to learn all he could about the birds, and then carried him on to that broader nature field that later he studied so interestedly and usefully. As time passed on he had many close friends who were deeply interested in scientific pursuits, and his devotion to science grew to be a very important part of his life, so that he became one of the best of our field naturalists.

His devotion to scientific truth and his impatience of pretense and ignorance led him to denounce the writers of natural-history fiction as "nature fakirs," a characterization that was so apt that the term was caught up and sprang into general use, and did much to discourage the evil it described.

It was this devotion that made him active in the establishment of the New York Zoological Society, which grew out of the appointment by him of a Committee of the Boone and Crockett Club, headed by Madison Grant, to promote the enterprise. The same feeling, in connection with an understanding of the economic importance of the forests, led him strongly to support wise plans for their preservation and for the development and strengthening of the service that cared for them. He earnestly advocated, also, the proposal to establish game refuges in the forest reservations, not merely that the game might be protected and increased, but because to make game abundant was for the advantage of all, especially of the average man. He often declared that men of wealth, by the establishing of private preserves, could provide game for themselves, but that this was not within the power of men of small means, and so he insisted on game protection, because it is only by making game more abundant that the poor man may have the opportunity to indulge his fondness for sport.

As a part of his interest in wild life, while President he established many bird reservations and set on foot a bird-reservation policy that has been followed by other Presidents.

Roosevelt was deeply interested in the care and protection of the Yellowstone Park. The original attempt by a certain group of men to secure for their own profit control of all the important attractions of the park had been defeated before I knew him well, but as soon as he understood about the conditions in Yellowstone Park, he gave time and thought to considering its protection. In New York as police commissioner, and later during his residence in Washington as civil service commissioner, he was one of its most effective friends and, with William Hallett Phillips and others, was instrumental in securing the passage of the law of May 7, 1894, which made the administration of the Yellowstone Park a practical thing.

The objects of the Boone and Crockett Club, as expressed in its constitution, show clearly an aspect of Roosevelt's ambitions and interests at that time, and to these same interests he held all through his life. Always a hunter and always interested in natural history and in helping forward the increase of knowledge, these tastes led him to take charge of the expedition to Africa, by which our information about the fauna of that continent was greatly increased, and later, in collaboration with Edmund Heller, he wrote chapters of great value on the life histories of many of its mammals. The same incentive took him to South America on the exploration that led to his death. After his return he knew that his travels were at an end. A year or two before his death he told me that he could never again do any real outdoor work.

Roosevelt had formulated a noble creed, which he lived up to in a noble way. "Do the best you can and do it all the time" was the principle he worked on. When he took hold of a piece of work he toiled at it hard and earnestly until it was accomplished, and then turned his mind to something else, at which he worked equally hard. I do not believe that he started out in life with a greater mind than many others, but he had the fine intelligence and the strong will to make the very best use of his mind. In the creed just given lies the secret of his towering success. Most of us now and then do, or try to do, the best we can—for a little while—but we do it by spurts and spasms. The genius that Roosevelt possessed consisted in this, that he never stopped doing his best, and the reason he never stopped doing his best was that he used his will to keep himself always at work. After a time this became habit and ceased to be effort.

I hope that, before too long, some one will perform a great service for this country by describing in detail Roosevelt's early life. This must be written so interestingly that it will be enjoyed, and so plainly that it will be understood, by the boys and young men who read it. If properly told, the story will stir the ambition and emulation of every youth, and, once comprehended, will carry a great lesson. It will point out to each one what he may do to help himself, and what results he may attain by persistent self-mastery in behalf of worthy motives. Traced step by step Roosevelt's early life offers to boys a splendid example.

From an ordinary youngster—much like what we all were as boys—Roosevelt developed to what he finally became because of two things—his standards and his will-power. Inheritance and training had given him standards, but he possessed also a will the exercise of which held him to the mark and enabled him to follow straight on the course he had marked out. Cannot our boys be stimulated to adopt like worthy standards and to cultivate the will?

Only a short time before his death Roosevelt wrote me a letter which referred to the passing of the years and which again expressed his faith. He said: "You and I and the rest of our generation are now getting

INTRODUCTION

within range of the rifle-pits. We all of us have to face the same fate a few years earlier or a few years later, and I think that what really matters is that according to our lights we shall have borne ourselves well and rendered what service we were able to, as long as we could do so."

CONTENTS

VOLUME I

HUNTING TRIPS OF A RANCHMAN

AN ACCOUNT OF THE BIG GAME OF
THE UNITED STATES AND ITS CHASE
WITH HORSE, HOUND, AND RIFLE

TO THAT
KEENEST OF SPORTSMEN
AND
TRUEST OF FRIENDS
MY BROTHER
ELLIOTT ROOSEVELT

BIBLIOGRAPHICAL NOTE

HUNTING TRIPS OF A RANCHMAN. Sketches of sport on the northern cattle plains. By Theodore Roosevelt, author of "History of the Nava War of 1812." Illustrated by A. B. Frost, R. Swain Gifford, J. C. Beard, Fannie E. Gifford, Henry Sandham. New York and London. G. P. Putnam's Sons. The Knickerbocker Press, 1885.

xvi, 318 pp., illus., 4to, khaki buckram

This work did not appear serially but was first published in book form, as above, on large paper and limited to 500 copies. It has been frequently reprinted. It appeared as the first part of BIG-GAME HUNTING in 1899; and as the first part of HUNTING TALES OF THE WEST, a four-volume set published in 1907. In HUNTING TALES OF THE WEST and in five editions of Roosevelt's works, HUNTING TRIPS OF A RANCHMAN is divided into two parts, the second part with the title: HUNTING TRIPS ON THE PRAIRIE AND IN THE MOUNTAINS.

CONTENTS

HUNTING TRIPS OF A RANCHMAN

CHAPTER I

RANCHING IN THE BAD LANDS

HE great middle plains of the United States, parts of which are still scantily peopled by men of Mexican parentage, while other parts have been but recently won from the warlike tribes of Horse Indians, now form a broad pastoral belt, stretching in a north and south line from British America to the Rio Grande. Throughout this great belt of grazing-land almost the only industry is stock-raising, which is here engaged in on a really gigantic scale; and it is already nearly covered with the ranches of the stockmen, except on those isolated tracts (often themselves of great extent) from which the red men look hopelessly and sullenly out upon their old hunting-grounds, now roamed over by the countless herds of long-horned cattle. The northern portion of this belt is that which has been most lately thrown open to the whites; and it is with this part only that we have to do.

The Northern cattle plains occupy the basin of the Upper Missouri; that is, they occupy all of the land drained by the tributaries of that river, and by the river itself, before it takes its long trend to the south-east. They stretch from the rich wheat-farms of central Dakota to the Rocky Mountains, and southward to the Black Hills and the Bighorn chain, thus including all of Montana, northern Wyoming, and extreme western Dakota. The character of this rolling, broken, plains country is everywhere much the same. It is a high, nearly treeless region, of light rainfall, crossed by streams which are sometimes rapid torrents and sometimes merely strings of shallow pools. In places, it stretches out into deserts of alkali and sagebrush or into nearly level prairies of short grass, extending many miles without a break; elsewhere there are rolling hills, sometimes of considerable height; and in other places the ground is rent and broken into the most fantastic shapes, partly by volcanic action and partly by the action of water in a dry climate. These latter portions form the famous Bad Lands. Cottonwood-trees fringe the streams or stand in groves on the alluvial bottoms of the rivers; and some of the steep hills and canyon sides are clad with pines or stunted cedars. In the early spring, when the young blades first sprout, the land looks green and bright; but during the rest of the year there is no such appearance of freshness, for the short bunch-grass is almost brown, and the gray-green sage-bush, bitter and withered-looking, abounds everywhere, and gives a peculiarly barren aspect to the landscape.

It is but little over half a dozen years since these lands were won from the Indians. They were their only remaining great hunting-grounds, and toward the end of the last decade all of the Northern plains tribes went on the war-path in a final desperate effort to preserve them. After bloody fighting and protracted campaigns, they were defeated, and the country thrown open to the whites, while the building of the Northern Pacific Railroad gave immigration an immense impetus. There were great quantities of game, especially buffalo, and the hunters who thronged in to pursue the huge herds of the latter were the rough forerunners of civilization. No longer dreading the Indians and having the railway on which to transport the robes, they followed the buffalo in season and out, until, in 1883, the herds were practically destroyed. But, meanwhile, the cattlemen formed the vanguard of the white settlers. Already the hardy Southern stockmen had passed up with their wild-looking herds to the very border of the dangerous land, and even into it, trusting to luck and their own prowess for their safety; and the instant the danger was even partially removed, their cattle swarmed northward along the streams. Some Eastern men, seeing the extent of the grazing country, brought stock out by the railroad, and the short-horned beasts became almost as plenty as the wilder-looking Southern steers. At the present time, indeed, the cattle of these Northern ranges show more shorthorn than longhorn blood.

Cattle-raising on the plains, as now carried on, started in Texas, where the Americans had learned it from the Mexicans whom they dispossessed. It has only become a prominent feature of Western life during the last score of years. When the Civil War was raging, there were hundreds of thousands of bony, half-wild steers and cows in Texas, whose value had hitherto been very slight; but toward the middle of the struggle they became a most important source of food-supply to both armies, and when the war had ended, the profits of the business were widely known and many men had gone into it. At first, the stock-raising was all done in Texas, and the beef-steers, when ready for sale, were annually driven north along what became a regular cattle-trail. Soon the men of Kansas and Colorado began to start ranches, and Texans who were getting crowded out moved their herds north into these lands, and afterward into Wyoming. Large herds of yearling steers also were, and still are, driven from the breeding ranches of the South to some Northern range, there to be fattened for three years before selling. The cattle-trail led through great wastes, and the scores of armed cowboys who, under one or two foremen, accompanied each herd, had often to do battle with bands of hostile Indians; but this danger is now a thing of the past, as, indeed, will soon be the case with the cattle-trail itself, for year by year the grangers press steadily westward into it, and when they have once settled in a place, will not permit the cattle to be driven across it.

In the Northern country, the ranches vary greatly in size: on some there may be but a few hundred head, on others ten times as many thousand. The land is still in great part unsurveyed, and is hardly anywhere fenced in, the cattle roaming over it at will. The small ranches are often quite close to one another, say within a couple of miles; but the home-ranch of a big outfit will not have another building within ten or twenty miles of it, or, indeed, if the country is dry, not within fifty. The ranch-house may be only a mud dugout, or a "shack" made of logs stuck upright in the ground; more often, it is a fair-sized, well-made building of hewn logs, divided into several rooms. Around it are grouped the other buildings—log stables, cow sheds, and hay-ricks, an outhouse in which to store things, and, on large ranches, another house in which the cowboys sleep. The strongly made, circular horse corral, with a snubbing-post in the middle, stands close by; the larger cow corral, in which the stock is branded, may be some distance off. A small patch of ground is usually enclosed as a vegetable-garden, and a very large one, with water in it, as a pasture to be used only in special cases. All the work is done on horseback, and the quantity of ponies is thus of necessity very great, some of the large outfits numbering them by hundreds; on my own ranch there are eighty. Most of them are small, wiry beasts, not very speedy, but with good bottom, and able to pick up a living under the most adverse circumstances. There are usually a few large, fine horses kept for the special use of the ranchman or foreman. The best are those from Oregon; most of them come from Texas, and many are bought from the Indians. They are broken in a very rough manner, and many are in consequence vicious brutes with the detestable habit of bucking. Of this habit I have a perfect dread, and, if I can help it, never get on a confirmed bucker. The horse puts his head down between his forefeet, arches his back, and with stiff legs gives a succession of jarring jumps, often "changing ends" as he does so. Even if a man can keep his seat, the performance gives him about as uncomfortable a shaking up as can be imagined.

The cattle rove free over the hills and prairies, picking up their own living even in winter, all the animals of each herd having certain distinctive brands on them. But little attempt is made to keep them within definite bounds, and they wander whither they wish, except that the ranchmen generally combine to keep some of their cowboys riding lines to prevent them straying away altogether. The missing ones are generally recovered in the annual round-ups, when the calves are branded. These round-ups, in which many outfits join together, and which cover hundreds of miles of territory, are the busiest periods of the year for the stockmen, who then, with their cowboys, work from morning till night. In winter, little is done except a certain amount of line-riding.

The cowboys form a class by themselves, and are now quite as typical representatives of the wilder side of Western life as were a few years ago the skin-clad hunters and trappers. They are mostly of native birth, and although there are among them wild spirits from every land, yet the latter soon become undistinguishable from their American companions, for these plainsmen are far from being so heterogeneous as is commonly supposed. On the contrary, all have a curious similarity to each other; existence in the West seems to put the same stamp upon each and every one of them. Sinewy, hardy, self-reliant, their life forces them to be both daring and adventurous, and the passing over their heads of a few years leaves printed on their faces certain lines which tell of dangers quietly fronted and hardships uncomplainingly endured. They are far from being as lawless as they are described; though they sometimes cut queer antics when, after many months of lonely life, they come into a frontier town in which drinking and gambling are the only recognized forms of amusement, and where pleasure and vice are considered synonymous terms. On the round-ups, or when a number get together, there is much boisterous, often foul-mouthed, mirth; but they are rather silent, self-contained men when with strangers, and are frank and hospitable to a degree. The Texans are perhaps the best at the actual cowboy work. They are absolutely fearless riders and understand well the habits of the half-wild cattle, being unequalled in those most trying times when, for instance, the cattle are stampeded by a thunder-storm at night, while in the use of the rope they are only excelled by the Mexicans. On the other hand, they are prone to drink, and, when drunk, to shoot. Many Kansans, and others from the Northern States, have also taken up the life of late years, and though these scarcely reach, in point of skill and dash, the standard of the Southerners, who may be said to be born in the saddle, yet they are to the full as resolute and even more trustworthy. My own foremen were originally Eastern backwoodsmen.

The cowboy's dress is both picturesque and serviceable, and, like many of the terms of his pursuit, is partly of Hispano-Mexican origin. It consists of a broad felt hat, a flannel shirt, with a bright silk handkerchief loosely knotted round the neck, trousers tucked into high-heeled boots, and a pair of leather "chaps" (*chaparejos*), or heavy riding overalls. Great spurs and a large-caliber revolver complete the costume. For horse-gear there is a cruel curb bit, and a very strong, heavy saddle with high pommel and cantle. This saddle seems needlessly weighty, but the work is so rough as to make strength the first requisite. A small pack is usually carried behind it; also saddle-pockets, or small saddle-bags; and there are strings wherewith to fasten the loops of the rawhide lariat. The pommel has to be stout, as one end of the lariat is twisted around it when work is to be done, and the strain upon it is tremendous when a vigorous steer has been roped, or when, as is often the case, a wagon gets stuck and the team has to be helped out by one of the riders hauling from the saddle. A ranchman or foreman dresses precisely like the cowboys, except that the materials are finer, the saddle leather being handsomely carved, the spurs, bit, and revolver silver-mounted, the chaps of sealskin, etc. The revolver was formerly a necessity, to protect the owner from Indians and other human foes; this is still the case in a few places, but, as a rule, it is now carried merely from habit, or to kill rattlesnakes, or on the chance of falling in with a wolf or coyote, while not unfrequently it is used to add game to the cowboy's not too varied bill of fare.

A cowboy is always a good and bold rider, but his seat in the saddle is not at all like that of one of our Eastern or Southern fox-hunters. The stirrups are so long that the man stands almost erect in them, from his head to his feet being a nearly straight line. It is difficult to compare the horsemanship of a Western plainsman with that of an Eastern or Southern cross-country rider. In following hounds over fences and high walls, on a spirited horse needing very careful humoring, the latter would certainly excel; but he would find it hard work to sit a bucking horse like a cowboy, or to imitate the headlong dash with which one will cut out a cow marked with his own brand from a herd of several hundred others, or will follow at full speed the twistings and doublings of a refractory steer over ground where an Eastern horse would hardly keep its feet walking.

My own ranches, the Elkhorn and the Chimney Butte, lie along the eastern border of the cattle country, where the Little Missouri flows through the heart of the Bad Lands. This, like most other plains rivers, has a broad, shallow bed, through which in times of freshets runs a muddy torrent that neither man nor beast can pass; at other seasons of the year it is very shallow, spreading out into pools, between which the trickling water may be but a few inches deep. Even

10

then, however, it is not always easy to cross, for the bottom is filled with quicksands and mud-holes. The river flows in long sigmoid curves through an alluvial valley of no great width. The amount of this alluvial land enclosed by a single bend is called a bottom, which may be either covered with cottonwood-trees or else be simply a great grass meadow. From the edges of the valley the land rises abruptly in steep high buttes, whose crests are sharp and jagged. This broken country extends back from the river for many miles, and has been called always, by Indians, French voyageurs, and American trappers alike, the "Bad Lands," partly from its dreary and forbidding aspect and partly from the difficulty experienced in travelling through it. Every few miles it is crossed by creeks which open into the Little Missouri, of which they are simply repetitions in miniature, except that during most of the year they are almost dry, some of them having in their beds here and there a never-failing spring or muddy alkaline-water hole. From these creeks run coulées, or narrow, winding valleys, through which water flows when the snow melts; their bottoms contain patches of brush, and they lead back into the heart of the Bad Lands. Some of the buttes spread out into level plateaus, many miles in extent; others form chains, or rise as steep, isolated masses. Some are of volcanic origin, being composed of masses of scoria; the others, of sandstone or clay, are worn by water into the most fantastic shapes. In coloring they are as bizarre as in form. Among the level, parallel strata which make up the land are some of coal. When a coal vein gets on fire it makes what is called a burning mine, and the clay above it is turned into brick; so that where water wears away the side of a hill sharp streaks of black and red are seen across it, mingled with the grays, purples, and browns. Some of the buttes are overgrown with gnarled, stunted cedars, or small pines, and they are all cleft through and riven in every direction by deep narrow ravines, or by canyons with perpendicular sides.

In spite of their look of savage desolation, the Bad Lands make a good cattle country, for there is plenty of nourishing grass and excellent shelter from the winter storms. The cattle keep close to them in the cold months, while in the summer-time they wander out on the broad prairies stretching back of them, or come down to the river-bottoms.

My home-ranch stands on the river brink. From the low, long veranda, shaded by leafy cottonwoods, one looks across sand-bars and shallows to a strip of meadowland, behind which rises a line of sheer cliffs and grassy plateaus. This veranda is a pleasant place in the summer evenings when a cool breeze stirs along the river and blows in the faces of the tired men, who loll back in their rocking-chairs (what true American does not enjoy a rocking-chair?), book in hand — though they do not often read the books, but rock gently to and fro, gazing sleepily out at the weird-looking buttes opposite, until their sharp lines grow indistinct and purple in the afterglow of the sunset. The story-high house of hewn logs is clean and neat, with many rooms, so that one can be alone if one wishes to. The nights in summer are cool and pleasant, and there are plenty of bearskins and buffalo-robes, trophies of our own skill, with which to bid defiance to the bitter cold of winter. In summer-time, we are not much within doors, for we rise before dawn and work hard enough to be willing to go to bed soon after nightfall.

The long winter evenings are spent sitting round the hearthstone, while the pine logs roar and crackle, and the men play checkers or chess, in the firelight. The rifles stand in the corners of the room or rest across the elk-antlers which jut out from over the fireplace. From the deer-horns ranged along the walls and thrust into the beams and rafters hang heavy overcoats of wolfskin or coonskin, and otter-fur or beaver-fur caps and gantlets. Rough board shelves hold a number of books, without which some of the evenings would be long indeed. No ranchman who loves sport can afford to be without Van Dyke's "Still Hunter," Dodge's "Plains of the Great West," or Caton's "Deer and Antelope of America"; and Coues's "Birds of the Northwest" will be valued if he cares at all for natural history. A Western plainsman is reminded every day, by the names of the prominent landmarks among which he rides, that the country was known to men who spoke French long before any of his own kinsfolk came to it, and hence he reads with a double interest Parkman's histories of the early Canadians. As for Irving, Hawthorne, Cooper, Lowell, and the other standbys, I suppose no man, East or West, would willingly be long without them; while for lighter reading there are dreamy Ik Marvel, Burroughs's breezy pages, and the quaint, pathetic character-sketches of the Southern writers—Cable, Craddock, Macon, Joel Chandler Harris, and sweet Sherwood Bonner. And when one is in the Bad Lands he feels as if they somehow *look* just exactly as Poe's tales and poems *sound*.

By the way, my books have some rather unexpected foes, in the shape of the pack-rats. These are larger than our house rats, with soft gray fur, big eyes, and bushy tails, like a squirrel's; they are rather pretty

13

beasts and very tame, often coming into the shacks and log cabins of the settlers. Woodmen and plainsmen, in their limited vocabulary, make great use of the verb "pack," which means to carry, more properly to carry on one's back; and these rats were christened pack-rats on account of their curious and inveterate habit of dragging off to their holes every object they can possibly move. From the hole of one, underneath the wall of a hut, I saw taken a small revolver, a hunting-knife, two books, a fork, a small bag, and a tin cup. The little shack mice are much more common than the rats, and among them there is a wee pocket-mouse, with pouches on the outside of its little cheeks.

In the spring when the thickets are green, the hermit-thrushes sing sweetly in them; when it is moonlight, the voluble, cheery notes of the thrashers or brown thrushes can be heard all night long. One of our sweetest, loudest songsters is the meadow-lark; this I could hardly get used to at first, for it looks exactly like the Eastern meadow-lark, which utters nothing but a harsh disagreeable chatter. But the plains air seems to give it a voice, and it will perch on the top of a bush or tree and sing for hours in rich, bubbling tones. Out on the prairie there are several kinds of plains sparrows which sing very brightly, one of them hovering in the air all the time, like a bobolink. Sometimes, in the early morning, when crossing the open, grassy plateaus, I have heard the prince of them all, the Missouri skylark. The skylark sings on the wing, soaring overhead and mounting in spiral curves until it can hardly be seen, while its bright, tender strains never cease for a moment. I have sat on my horse and listened to one singing for a quarter of an hour at a time without stopping. There is another bird, also, which sings on the wing, though I have not seen the habit put down in the books. One bleak March day, when snow covered the ground and the shaggy ponies crowded about the empty corral, a flock of snow-buntings came familiarly round the cow-shed, clambering over the ridge-pole and roof. Every few moments one of them would mount into the air, hovering about with quivering wings and warbling a loud, merry song, with some very sweet notes. They were a most welcome little group of guests, and we were sorry when, after loitering around a day or two, they disappeared toward their breeding haunts.

In the still fall nights, if we lie awake, we can listen to the clanging cries of the water-fowl, as their flocks speed southward; and in cold weather the coyotes occasionally come near enough for us to hear their uncanny wailing. The larger wolves, too, now and then join in, with a kind of deep, dismal howling; but this melancholy sound is more often heard when out camping than from the ranch-house.

The charm of ranch life comes in its freedom and the vigorous open-air existence it forces a man to lead. Except when hunting in bad ground, the whole time away from the house is spent in the saddle, and there are so many ponies that a fresh one can always be had. These ponies are of every size and disposition, and rejoice in names as different as their looks. Hacka-more, Wire Fence, Steel Trap, War Cloud, Pinto, Buckskin, Circus, and Standing Jimmie are among those that, as I write, are running frantically around the corral in the vain effort to avoid the rope, wielded by the dexterous and sinewy hand of a broad-hatted cowboy.

A ranchman is kept busy most of the time, but his

hardest work comes during the spring and fall round-ups, when the calves are branded or the beeves gathered for market. Our round-up district includes the Beaver and Little Beaver creeks (both of which always contain running water, and head up toward each other) and as much of the river, nearly two hundred miles in extent, as lies between their mouths. All the ranches along the lines of these two creeks and the river space between join in sending from one to three or four men to the round-up, each man taking eight ponies; and for every six or seven men there will be a four-horse wagon to carry the blankets and mess-kit. The whole, including perhaps forty or fifty cowboys, is under the head of one first-class foreman, styled the captain of the round-up. Beginning at one end of the line, the round-up works along clear to the other. Starting at the head of one creek, the wagons and the herd of spare ponies go down ten or twelve miles, while the cowboys, divided into small parties, scour the neighboring country, covering a great extent of territory, and in the evening come into the appointed place with all the cattle they have seen. This big herd, together with the pony herd, is guarded and watched all night, and driven during the day. At each home-ranch (where there is always a large corral fitted for the purpose) all the cattle of that brand are cut out from the rest of the herd, which is to continue its journey; and the cows and calves are driven into the corral, where the latter are roped, thrown, and branded. In throwing the rope from horseback, the loop, held in the right hand, is swung round and round the head by a motion of the wrist; when on foot, the hand is usually held by the side, the loop dragging on the ground. It is a pretty sight to see a man who knows how to use the rope; again and again an expert will catch fifty animals by the leg without making a misthrow. But unless practice is begun very young, it is hard to become really proficient.

Cutting out cattle, next to managing a stampeded herd at night, is that part of the cowboy's work needing the boldest and most skilful horsemanship. A young heifer or steer is very loath to leave the herd, always tries to break back into it, can run like a deer, and can dodge like a rabbit; but a thorough cattle-pony enjoys the work as much as its rider, and follows a beast like a four-footed fate through every double and turn. The ponies for the cutting-out or afternoon work are small and quick; those used for the circle-riding in the morning have need rather to be strong and rangey.

The work on a round-up is very hard, but although the busiest it is also the pleasantest part of a cowboy's existence. His food is good, though coarse, and his sleep is sound indeed; while the work is very exciting, and is done in company under the stress of an intense rivalry between all the men, both as to their own skill and as to the speed and training of their horses. Clumsiness and, still more, the slightest approach to timidity expose a man to the roughest and most merciless raillery; and the unfit are weeded out by a very rapid process of natural selection. When the work is over for the day the men gather round the fire for an hour or two to sing songs, talk, smoke, and tell stories; and he who has a good voice, or, better still, can play a fiddle or banjo, is sure to receive his meed of most sincere homage.

Though the ranchman is busiest during the round-up, yet he is far from idle at other times. He rides round among the cattle to see if any are sick, visits any outlying camp of his men, hunts up any bands of ponies which may stray—and they are always straying—superintends the haying, and, in fact, does not often find that he has too much leisure on his hands. Even in winter he has work which must be done. His ranch supplies milk, butter, eggs, and potatoes, and his rifle keeps him, at least intermittently, in fresh meat; but coffee, sugar, flour, and whatever else he may want has to be hauled in, and this is generally done when the ice will bear. Then fire-wood must be chopped; or, if there is a good vein of coal, as on my ranch, the coal must be dug out and hauled in. Altogether, though the ranchman will have time enough to take shooting trips, he will be very far from having time to make shooting a business, as a stranger who comes for nothing else can afford to do.

There are now no Indians left in my immediate neighborhood, though a small party of harmless Grosventres occasionally passes through; yet it is but six years since the Sioux surprised and killed five men in a log station just south of me, where the Fort Keogh trail crosses the river; and, two years ago, when I went down on the prairies toward the Black Hills, there was still danger from Indians. That summer the buffalo-hunters had killed a couple of Crows, and while we were on the prairie a long-range skirmish occurred near us between some Cheyennes and a number of cowboys. In fact, we ourselves were one day scared by what we thought to be a party of Sioux; but, on riding toward them, they proved to be half-breed Crees who were more afraid of us than we were of them.

During the past century a good deal of sentimental

nonsense has been talked about our taking the Indians' land. Now, I do not mean to say for a moment that gross wrong has not been done the Indians, both by government and individuals, again and again. The government makes promises impossible to perform, and then fails to do even what it might toward their fulfilment; and where brutal and reckless frontiersmen are brought into contact with a set of treacherous, revengeful, and fiendishly cruel savages a long series of outrages by both sides is sure to follow. But as regards taking the land, at least from the Western Indians, the simple truth is that the latter never had any real ownership in it at all. Where the game was plenty, there they hunted; they followed it when it moved away to new hunting-grounds, unless they were prevented by stronger rivals, and to most of the land on which we found them they had no stronger claim than that of having a few years previously butchered the original occupants. When my cattle came to the Little Missouri, the region was only inhabited by a score or so of white hunters; their title to it was quite as good as that of most Indian tribes to the lands they claim; yet nobody dreamed of saying that these hunters owned the country. Each could eventually have kept his own claim of 160 acres, and no more. The Indians should be treated in just the same way that we treat the white settlers. Give each his little claim; if, as would generally happen, he declined this, why, then let him share the fate of the thousands of white hunters and trappers who have lived on the game that the settlement of the country has exterminated, and let him, like these whites, who will not work, perish from the face of the earth which he cumbers.

The doctrine seems merciless, and so it is; but it is

just and rational for all that. It does not do to be merciful to a few at the cost of justice to the many. The cattlemen at least keep herds and build houses on the land; yet I would not for a moment debar settlers from the right of entry to the cattle country, though their coming in means in the end the destruction of us and our industry.

For we ourselves and the life that we lead will shortly pass away from the plains as completely as the red and white hunters who have vanished from before our herds. The free, open-air life of the ranchman, the pleasantest and healthiest life in America, is from its very nature ephemeral. The broad and boundless prairies have already been bounded and will soon be made narrow. It is scarcely a figure of speech to say that the tide of white settlement during the last few years has risen over the West like a flood; and the cattlemen are but the spray from the crest of the wave, thrown far in advance, but soon to be overtaken. As the settlers throng into the lands and seize the good ground, especially that near the streams, the great fenceless ranches, where the cattle and their mounted herdsmen wandered unchecked over hundreds of thousands of acres, will be broken up and divided into corn land, or else into small grazing farms where a few hundred head of stock are closely watched and taken care of. Of course the most powerful ranches, owned by wealthy corporations or individuals, and already firmly rooted in the soil, will long resist this crowding; in places, where the ground is not suited to agriculture, or where, through the old Spanish land-grants, the title has been acquired to a great tract of territory, cattle ranching will continue for a long time, though in a greatly modified form; elsewhere, I doubt if it lasts

out the present century. Immense sums of money
have been made at it in the past, and it is still fairly
profitable; but the good grounds (aside from those re-
served for the Indians) are now almost all taken up,
and it is too late for new men to start at it on their
own account, unless in exceptional cases or where an
Indian reservation is thrown open. Those that are
now in will continue to make money; but most of
those who hereafter take it up will lose.

The profits of the business are great; but the chances
for loss are great also. A winter of unusual severity
will work sad havoc among the young cattle, especially
the heifers; sometimes a disease, like the Texas cattle-
fever, will take off a whole herd; and many animals
stray and are not recovered. In fall, when the grass
is like a mass of dry and brittle tinder, the fires do
much damage, reducing the prairies to blackened deserts as far as the eye can see, and destroying feed which
would keep many thousand head of stock during winter. Then we hold in about equal abhorrence the
granger who may come in to till the land and the
sheep-owner who drives his flocks over it. The former
will gradually fill up the country to our own exclusion,
while the latter's sheep nibble the grass off so close to
the ground as to starve out all other animals.

Then we suffer some loss—in certain regions, very
severe loss—from wild beasts, such as cougars, wolves,
and lynxes. The latter, generally called "bobcats,"
merely make inroads on the hen-roosts (one of them
destroyed half my poultry, coming night after night
with most praiseworthy regularity), but the cougars
and wolves destroy many cattle.

The wolf is not very common with us; nothing like
as plentiful as the little coyote. A few years ago both

wolves and coyotes were very numerous on the plains,
and as Indians and hunters rarely molested them, they
were then very unsuspicious. But all this is changed
now. When the cattlemen came in they soon perceived in the wolves their natural foes, and followed
them unrelentingly. They shot at and chased them
on all occasions, and killed great numbers by poisoning; and, as a consequence, the comparatively few
that are left are as wary and cunning beasts as exist
anywhere. They hardly ever stir abroad by day, and
hence are rarely shot or indeed seen. During the last
three years these brutes have killed nearly a score of
my cattle, and in return we have poisoned six or eight
wolves and a couple of dozen coyotes; yet in all our
riding we have not seen so much as a single wolf, and
only rarely a coyote. The coyotes kill sheep and, occasionally, very young calves, but never meddle with
anything larger. The stockman fears only the large
wolves.

According to my experience, the wolf is rather solitary. A single one or a pair will be found by themselves, or possibly with one or more well-grown young
ones, and will then hunt over a large tract where no
other wolves will be found; and as they wander very
far, and as their melancholy howlings have a most ventriloquial effect, they are often thought to be much
more plentiful than they are. During the daytime
they lie hid in caves or in some patch of bush, and will
let a man pass right by them without betraying their
presence. Occasionally, somebody runs across them
by accident. A neighboring ranchman to me once
stumbled, while riding an unshod pony, right into the
midst of four wolves, who were lying in some tall, rank
grass, and shot one with his revolver and crippled an-

other before they could get away. But such an accident as this is very rare; and when, by any chance, the wolf is himself abroad in the daytime he keeps such a sharp lookout, and is so wary, that it is almost impossible to get near him, and he gives every human being a wide berth. At night it is different. The wolves then wander far and wide, often coming up round the outbuildings of the ranches; I have seen in light snow the tracks of two that had walked round the house within fifty feet of it. I have never heard of an instance where a man was attacked or threatened by them, but they will at times kill every kind of domestic animal. They are fond of trying to catch young foals, but do not often succeed, for the mares and foals keep together in a kind of straggling band, and the foal is early able to run at good speed for a short distance. When attacked the mare and foal dash off toward the rest of the band, which gathers together at once, the foals pressing into the middle and the mares remaining on the outside, not in a ring with their heels out, but moving in and out, and forming a solid mass into which the wolves do not venture. Full-grown horses are rarely molested, while a stallion becomes himself the assailant.

In early spring, when the cows are beginning to calve, the wolves sometimes wait upon the herds as they did of old on the buffalo, and snap up any calf that strays away from its mother. When hard pressed by hunger, they will kill a steer or a heifer, choosing the bitterest and coldest night to make the attack. The prey is invariably seized by the haunch or flank, and its entrails afterward torn out; while a cougar, on the contrary, grasps the neck or throat. Wolves have very strong teeth and jaws and inflict a most severe bite. They will in winter come up to the yards and carry away a sheep, pig, or dog, without much difficulty; I have known one which had tried to seize a sheep, and been prevented by the sheep-dogs, to canter off with one of the latter instead. But a spirited dog will always attack a wolf. On the ranch next below mine there was a plucky bull-terrier, weighing about twenty-five pounds, who lost his life owing to his bravery. On one moonlight night three wolves came round the stable, and the terrier sallied out promptly. He made such a quick rush as to take his opponents by surprise, and seized one by the throat; nor did he let go till the other two tore him almost asunder across the loins. Better luck attended a large mongrel, called a sheep-dog by his master, but whose blood was apparently about equally derived from collie, Newfoundland, and bulldog. He was a sullen but very intelligent and determined brute, powerfully built and with strong jaws, and, though neither as tall nor as heavy as a wolf, he had yet killed two of these animals single-handed. One of them had come into the farmyard at night, and taken a young pig, whose squeals roused everybody. The wolf loped off with his booty, the dog running after him and overtaking him in the darkness. The struggle was short, for the dog had seized the wolf by the throat and the latter could not shake him off, though he made the most desperate efforts, rising on his hind legs and pressing the dog down with his fore paws. This time the victor escaped scathless, but in his second fight, when he strangled a still larger wolf, he was severely punished. The wolf had seized a sheep, when the dog, rushing on him, caused him to leave his quarry. Instead of running, he turned to bay at once, taking off one of the assailant's ears with a rapid snap. The dog did not get a good hold, and the wolf scored him across the shoulders and flung him off. They then faced each other for a minute and at the next dash the dog made good his throat hold, and throttled the wolf, though the latter contrived to get his foe's fore leg into his jaws and broke it clear through. When I saw the dog he had completely recovered, although pretty well scarred.

On another neighboring ranch there is a most ill-favored hybrid, whose mother was a Newfoundland and whose father was a large wolf. It is stoutly built, with erect ears, pointed muzzle, rather short head, short bushy tail, and of a brindled color; funnily enough, it looks more like a hyena than like either of its parents. It is familiar with people and a good cattle-dog, but rather treacherous; it both barks and howls. The parent wolf carried on a long courtship with the Newfoundland. He came round the ranch regularly and boldly every night, and she would at once go out to him. In the daylight he would lie hid in the bushes at some little distance. Once or twice his hiding-place was discovered, and then the men would amuse themselves by setting the Newfoundland on him. She would make at him, but when they were a good way from the men he would turn round and wait for her and they would go romping off together, not to be seen again for several hours.

The cougar is hardly ever seen round my ranch; but toward the mountains it is very destructive both to horses and horned cattle. The ranchmen know it by the name of mountain-lion; and it is the same beast that in the East is called panther or "painter." The cougar is the same size and build as the Old World leopard, and with very much the same habits. One will generally lie in wait for the heifers or young steers as they come down to water, and, singling out an animal, reach it in a couple of bounds and fasten its fangs in the throat or neck. I have seen quite a large cow that had been killed by a cougar; and on another occasion, while out hunting over light snow, I came across a place where two bucks, while fighting, had been stalked up to by a cougar, which pulled down one and tore him in pieces. The cougar's gait is silent and stealthy, to an extraordinary degree; the look of the animal when creeping up to his prey has been wonderfully caught by the sculptor Kemeys in his bronzes: "The Still Hunt" and "The Silent Footfall."

I have never myself killed a cougar, though my brother shot one in Texas, while still-hunting some deer which the cougar itself was after. It never attacks man, and even when hard pressed and wounded turns to bay with extreme reluctance, and at the first chance again seeks safety in flight. This was certainly not the case in old times, but the nature of the animal has been so changed by constant contact with rifle-bearing hunters, that timidity toward them has become a hereditary trait deeply ingrained in its nature. When the continent was first settled, and for long afterward, the cougar was quite as dangerous an antagonist as the African or Indian leopard, and would even attack men unprovoked. An instance of this occurred in the annals of my mother's family. Early in the present century, one of my ancestral relatives, a Georgian, moved down to the wild and almost unknown country bordering on Florida. His plantation was surrounded by jungles in which all kinds of wild beasts swarmed. One of his negroes had a sweetheart on another plantation, and in visiting her, instead of going by the road, he took a short cut through the swamps, heedless of the wild beasts and armed only with a long knife—for he was a man of colossal strength, and of fierce and determined temper. One night he started to return late, expecting to reach the plantation in time for his daily task on the morrow. But he never reached home, and it was thought he had run away. However, when search was made for him his body was found in the path through the swamp, all gashed and torn, and but a few steps from him, the body of a cougar, stabbed and cut in many places. Certainly, that must have been a grim fight, in the gloomy, lonely recesses of the swamp, with no one to watch the midnight death-struggle between the powerful, naked man and the ferocious brute that was his almost unseen assailant.

When hungry, a cougar will attack anything it can master. I have known of their killing wolves and large dogs. A friend of mine, a ranchman in Wyoming, had two grizzly-bear cubs in his possession at one time, and they were kept in a pen outside the ranch. One night two cougars came down, and after vain efforts to catch a dog which was on the place, leaped into the pen and carried off the two young bears!

Two or three powerful dogs, however, will give a cougar all he wants to do to defend himself. A relative of mine in one of the Southern States had a small pack of five bloodhounds, with which he used to hunt the cane-brakes for bear, wildcats, etc. On one occasion they ran across a cougar, and after a sharp chase treed him. As the hunters drew near, he leaped from the tree and made off, but was overtaken by the hounds and torn to pieces after a sharp struggle, in which one or two of the pack were badly scratched.

Cougars are occasionally killed by poisoning, and they may be trapped much more easily than a wolf. I have never known them to be systematically hunted in the West, though now and then one is accidentally run across and killed with the rifle while the hunter is after some other game.

As already said, ranchmen do not have much idle time on their hands, for their duties are manifold, and they need to be ever on the watch against their foes, both animate and inanimate. Where a man has so much to do, he cannot spare a great deal of time for any amusement; but a good part of that which the ranchman can spare he is very apt to spend in hunting. His quarry will be one of the seven kinds of plains game—bear, buffalo, elk, bighorn, antelope, blacktail or whitetail deer. Moose, caribou, and white goat never come down into the cattle country; and it is only on the Southern ranches near the Rio Grande and the Rio Colorado that the truculent peccary and the great spotted jaguar are found.

Until recently, all sporting on the plains was confined to army officers, or to men of leisure who made extensive trips for no other purpose; leaving out of consideration the professional hunters who trapped and shot for their livelihood. But with the incoming of the cattlemen, there grew up a class of residents, men with a stake in the welfare of the country and with a regular business carried on in it, many of whom were keenly devoted to sport—a class whose members were in many respects closely akin to the old Southern planters. In this book I propose to give some description of the kind of sport that can be had by the average ranchman who is fond of the rifle. Of course no man with a regular business can have such opportunities as fall to the lot of some who pass their lives in hunting only; and we cannot pretend to equal the achievements of such men, for with us it is merely a pleasure, to be eagerly sought after when we have the chance, but not to be allowed to interfere with our business. No ranchmen have time to make such extended trips as are made by some devotees of sport who are so fortunate as to have no every-day work to which to attend. Still, ranch life undoubtedly offers more chances to a man to get sport than is now the case with any other occupation in America, and those who follow it are apt to be men of game spirit, fond of excitement and adventure, who perforce lead an open-air life, who must needs ride well, for they are often in the saddle from sunrise to sunset, and who naturally take kindly to that noblest of weapons, the rifle. With such men hunting is one of the chief of pleasures; and they follow it eagerly when their work will allow them. And with some of them it is at times more than a pleasure. On many of the ranches—on my own, for instance—the supply of fresh meat depends mainly on the skill of the riflemen, and so, both for pleasure and profit, most ranchmen do a certain amount of hunting each season. The buffalo are now gone forever, and the elk are rapidly sharing their fate; but antelope and deer are still quite plenty, and will remain so for some years; and these are the common game of the plainsman. Nor is it likely that the game will disappear much before ranch life itself is a thing of the past. It is a phase of American life as fascinating as it is evanescent, and one well deserving an historian. But in these pages I propose to dwell on only one of its many pleasant sides, and to give some idea of the game-shooting which forms perhaps the chief of the cattleman's pleasures, aside from those more strictly connected with his actual work. I have to tell of no unusual adventures, but merely of just such hunting as lies within reach of most of the sport-loving ranchmen whose cattle range along the waters of the Powder and the Bighorn, the Little Missouri and the Yellowstone.

Of course I have never myself gone out hunting under the direction of a professional guide or professional hunter, unless it was to see one of the latter who was reputed a crack shot; all of my trips have been made either by myself or else with one of my cowboys as a companion. Most of the so-called hunters are not worth much. There are plenty of men hanging round the frontier settlements who claim to be hunters, and who bedizen themselves in all the traditional finery of the craft, in the hope of getting a job at guiding some "tenderfoot"; and there are plenty of skin-hunters, or meat-hunters, who, after the Indians have been driven away and when means of communication have been established, mercilessly slaughter the game in season and out, being too lazy to work at any regular trade, and keeping on hunting until the animals become too scarce and shy to be taken without more skill than they possess; but these are all mere temporary excrescences, and the true old Rocky Mountain hunter and trapper, the plainsman, or mountain man, who, with all his faults, was a man of iron nerve and will, is now almost a thing of the past. In the place of these heroes of a bygone age, the men who were clad in buckskin and who carried long rifles, stands, or rather rides, the bronzed and sinewy cowboy, as picturesque and self-reliant, as dashing and resolute as the saturnine Indian fighters whose place he has taken; and—alas that it should be written!—he in his turn must at no distant time share the fate of the men he has displaced. The ground over which he so gallantly rides his small, wiry horse will soon know him no more, and in his stead there will be the plodding grangers and husbandmen. I suppose it is right and for the best that the great cattle country, with its broad extent of fenceless land, over which the ranchman rides as free as the game that he follows or the horned herds that he guards, should be in the end broken up into small patches of fenced farm-land and grazing-land; but I hope against hope that I myself shall not live to see this take place, for when it does one of the pleasantest and freest phases of Western American life will have come to an end.

The old hunters were a class by themselves. They penetrated, alone or in small parties, to the farthest and wildest haunts of the animals they followed, leading a solitary, lonely life, often never seeing a white face for months and even years together. They were skilful shots, and were cool, daring, and resolute to the verge of recklessness. On anything like even terms, they very greatly overmatched the Indians by whom they were surrounded, and with whom they waged constant and ferocious war. In the government expeditions against the plains tribes they were of absolutely invaluable assistance as scouts. They rarely had regular wives or white children, and there are none to take their places, now that the greater part of them have gone. For the men who carry on hunting as a business where it is perfectly safe have all the vices of their prototypes, but, not having to face the dangers that beset the latter, so neither need nor possess the stern, rough virtues that were required in order to meet and overcome them. The ranks of the skin-hunters and meat-hunters contain some good men; but, as a rule, they are a most unlovely race of beings, not excelling even in the pursuit which they follow because they are too shiftless to do anything else; and the sooner they vanish the better.

A word as to weapons and hunting-dress. When I first came to the plains I had a heavy Sharps rifle, 45–120, shooting an ounce and a quarter of lead, and a 50-caliber, double-barrelled English express. Both of these, especially the latter, had a vicious recoil; the former was very clumsy; and, above all, they were neither of them repeaters; for a repeater or magazine-gun is as much superior to a single or double barrelled breech-loader as the latter is to a muzzle-loader. I threw them both aside, and have instead a 40–90 Sharps for very long-range work; a 50–115 6-shot Ballard express, which has the velocity, shock, and low trajectory of the English gun; and, better than either, a 45–75 half-magazine Winchester. The Winchester, which is stocked and sighted to suit myself, is by all odds the best weapon I ever had, and I now use it almost exclusively, having killed every kind of game with it, from a grizzly bear to a bighorn. It is as handy to carry, whether on foot or on horseback, and comes up to the shoulder as readily as a shotgun; it is absolutely sure, and there is no recoil to jar and disturb the aim, while it carries accurately quite as far as a man can aim with any degree of certainty; and the bullet, weighing three-quarters of an ounce, is plenty large enough for anything on this continent. For shooting the very large game (buffalo, elephants, etc.) of India and South Africa, much heavier rifles are undoubtedly necessary; but the Winchester is the best gun for any game to be found in the United

States, for it is as deadly, accurate, and handy as any, stands very rough usage, and is unapproachable for the rapidity of its fire and the facility with which it is loaded.

Of course every ranchman carries a revolver, a long 45 Colt or Smith & Wesson, by preference the former. When after game a hunting-knife is stuck in the girdle. This should be stout and sharp, but not too long, with a round handle. I have two double-barrelled shot-guns: a No. 10 choke-bore for ducks and geese, made by Thomas of Chicago; and a No. 16 hammerless, built for me by Kennedy of St. Paul, for grouse and plover. On regular hunting trips, I always carry the Winchester rifle, but in riding round near home, where a man may see a deer and is sure to come across ducks and grouse, it is best to take the little ranch gun, a double-barrel No. 16, with a 40–70 rifle underneath the shotgun barrels.

As for clothing, when only off on a day's trip the ordinary ranchman's dress is good enough: flannel shirt and overalls tucked into alligator boots, the latter being of service against the brambles, cacti, and rattlesnakes. Such a costume is good in warm weather. When making a long hunting trip where there will be much rough work, especially in the dry cold of fall and winter, there is nothing better than a fringed buckskin tunic or hunting-shirt (held in at the waist by the cartridge-belt), buckskin trousers, and a fur cap, with heavy moccasins for use in the woods, and light alligator-hide shoes if it is intended to cross rocks and open ground. Buckskin is most durable, keeps out wind and cold, and is the best possible color for the hunter—no small point in approaching game. For wet, it is not as good as flannel, and it is hot in warm weather. On very

33

cold days, fur gloves and either a coonskin overcoat
or a short riding-jacket of fisher's fur may be worn.
In cold weather, if travelling light with only what can
be packed behind the horse, I sleep in a big buffalo-
robe, sewed up at the sides and one end into the form
of a bag, and very warm. When, as is sometimes the
case, the spirit in the thermometer sinks to −60°–65°
Fahrenheit, it is necessary to have more wraps and
bedding, and we use beaver-robes and bearskins. An
oilskin "slicker" or water-proof overcoat and a pair of
chaps keep out the rain almost completely.

Where most of the hunting is done on horseback the
hunting-pony is a very important animal. Many people seem to think that any broken-down pony will do
to hunt, but this seems to me a very great mistake.
My own hunting-horse, Manitou, is the best and most
valuable animal on the ranch. He is stoutly built and
strong, able to carry a good-sized buck behind his rider
for miles at a lope without minding it in the least; he
is very enduring and very hardy, not only picking up
a living but even growing fat when left to shift for
himself under very hard conditions; and he is perfectly
sure-footed and as fast as any horse on the river.
Though both willing and spirited, he is very gentle,
with an easy mouth, and will stay grazing in one spot
when left, and will permit himself to be caught without difficulty. Add to these virtues the fact that he
will let any dead beast or thing be packed on him, and
will allow a man to shoot off his back or right by him
without moving, and it is evident that he is as nearly
perfect as can be the case with hunting-horseflesh.
There is a little sorrel mare on the ranch, a perfect little pet, that is almost as good, but too small. We
have some other horses we frequently use, but all have

faults. Some of the quiet ones are slow, lazy, or tire easily; others are gun-shy; while others plunge and buck if we try to pack any game on their backs. Others cannot be left standing untied, as they run away; and I can imagine few forms of exercise so soul-harrowing as that of spending an hour or two in running, in chaps, top-boots, and spurs, over a broken prairie, with the thermometer at 90°, after an escaped horse. Most of the hunting-horses used by my friends have one or more of these tricks, and it is rare to find one, like Manitou, who has none of them. Manitou is a treasure, and I value him accordingly. Besides, he is a sociable old fellow, and a great companion when off alone, coming up to have his head rubbed or to get a crust of bread, of which he is very fond.

To be remarkably successful in killing game, a man must be a good shot; but a good target-shot may be a very poor hunter, and a fairly successful hunte rmay be only a moderate shot. Shooting well with the rifle is the highest kind of skill, for the rifle is the queen of weapons; and it is a difficult art to learn. But many other qualities go to make up the first-class hunter. He must be persevering, watchful, hardy, and with good judgment; and a little dash and energy at the proper time often help him immensely. I myself am not, and never will be, more than an ordinary shot; for my eyes are bad and my hand not oversteady; yet I have killed every kind of game to be found on the plains, partly because I have hunted very perseveringly, and partly because by practice I have learned to shoot about as well at a wild animal as at a target. I have killed rather more game than most of the ranchmen who are my neighbors, though at least half of them are better shots than I am.

Time and again I have seen a man who had, as he deemed, practised sufficiently at a target, come out "to kill a deer" hot with enthusiasm; and nine out of ten times he has gone back unsuccessful, even when deer were quite plenty. Usually, he has been told by the friend who advised him to take the trip, or by the guide who inveigled him into it, that "the deer were so plenty you saw them all round you," and, this not proving quite true, he lacks perseverance to keep on; or else he fails to see the deer at the right time; or else, if he does see it, he misses it, making the discovery that to shoot at a gray object, not overdistinctly seen, at a distance merely guessed at, and with a background of other gray objects, is very different from firing into a target brightly painted and a fixed number of yards off. A man must be able to hit a bull's-eye eight inches across every time to do good work with deer or other game; for the spot around the shoulders that is fatal is not much bigger than this; and a shot a little back of that merely makes a wound which may in the end prove mortal, but which will in all probability allow the animal to escape for the time being. It takes a good shot to hit a bull's-eye offhand several times in succession at a hundred yards, and if the bull's-eye was painted the same color as the rest of the landscape, and was at an uncertain distance, and, moreover, was alive, and likely to take to its heels at any moment, the difficulty of making a good shot would be greatly enhanced. The man who can kill his buck right along at a hundred yards has a right to claim that he is a good shot. If he can shoot offhand standing up, that is much the best way, but I myself always drop on one knee, if I have time, unless the animal is very close. It is curious to hear the nonsense that is talked, and to see the nonsense that is written, about the distance at which game is killed. Rifles now carry with deadly effect the distance of a mile, and most middle-range hunting-rifles would at least kill at half a mile; and in war firing is often begun at these ranges. But in war there is very little accurate aiming, and the fact that there is a variation of thirty or forty feet in the flight of the ball makes no difference; and, finally, a thousand bullets are fired for every man that is killed—and usually many more than a thousand. How would that serve for a record on game? The truth is that three hundred yards is a very long shot, and that even two hundred yards is a long shot. On looking over my game-book I find that the average distance at which I have killed game on the plains is less than a hundred and fifty yards. A few years ago, when the buffalo would stand still in great herds half a mile from the hunter, the latter, using a long-range Sharps rifle, would often, by firing a number of shots into the herd at that distance, knock over two or three buffalo; but I have hardly ever known single animals to be killed six hundred yards off, even in antelope-hunting, the kind in which most long-range shooting is done; and at half that distance a very good shot, with all the surroundings in his favor, is more apt to miss than to hit. Of course old hunters—the most inveterate liars on the face of the earth—are all the time telling of their wonderful shots at even longer distances, and they do occasionally, when shooting very often, make them, but their performances, when actually tested, dwindle amazingly. Others, amateurs, will brag of their rifles. I lately read in a magazine about killing antelopes at eight hundred yards with a Winchester express, a weapon which cannot be depended upon at over two hundred, and is wholly inaccurate at over three hundred, yards.

The truth is that in almost all cases the hunter merely guesses at the distance, and, often perfectly honestly, just about doubles it in his own mind. Once a man told me of an extraordinary shot by which he killed a deer at four hundred yards. A couple of days afterward we happened to pass the place, and I had the curiosity to step off the distance, finding it a trifle over a hundred and ninety. I always make it a rule to pace off the distance after a successful shot, whenever practicable—that is, when the animal has not run too far before dropping—and I was at first both amused and somewhat chagrined to see how rapidly what I had supposed to be remarkably long shots shrank under actual pacing. It is a good rule always to try to get as near the game as possible, and in most cases it is best to risk startling it in the effort to get closer rather than to risk missing it by a shot at long range. At the same time, I am a great believer in powder-burning, and, if I cannot get near, will generally try a shot anyhow, if there is a chance of the rifle's carrying to it. In this way a man will now and then, in the midst of many misses, make a very good long shot, but he should not try to deceive himself into the belief that these occasional long shots are to be taken as samples of his ordinary skill. Yet it is curious to see how a really truthful man will forget his misses and his hits at close quarters, and, by dint of constant repetition, will finally persuade himself that he is in the habit of killing his game at three or four hundred yards. Of course in different kinds of ground the average range for shooting varies. In the Bad Lands most shots will be obtained much closer

than on the prairie, and in the timber they will be
nearer still.

Old hunters, who are hardy, persevering, and well
acquainted with the nature of the animals they pursue, will often kill a great deal of game without being
particularly good marksmen; besides, they are careful
to get up close, and are not flurried at all, shooting as
well at a deer as they do at a target. They are, as a
rule, fair shots; that is, they shoot a great deal better
than Indians or soldiers or than the general run of
Eastern amateur sportsmen—but I have never been out
with one who has not missed a great deal, and the
"Leatherstocking" class of shooting stories are generally untrue, at least to the extent of suppressing part
of the truth; that is, the number of misses. Beyond
question, our Western hunters are, as a body, to the
full as good marksmen as, and probably much better
than, any other body of men in the world, not even
excepting the Dutch Boers or Tyrolese Jägers, and a
certain number of them who shoot a great deal at
game, and are able to squander cartridges very freely,
undoubtedly become crack shots, and perform really
wonderful feats. As an instance, there is old "Vic," a
former scout and Indian fighter, and concededly the
best hunter on the Little Missouri; probably there are
not a dozen men in the West who are better shots or
hunters than he is, and I have seen him do most skilful work. He can run the muzzle of his rifle through
a board so as to hide the sights and yet do quite good
shooting at some little distance; he will cut the head
off a chicken at eighty or ninety yards, shoot a deer
running through brush at that distance, kill grouse on
the wing early in the season, and knock over antelopes
when they are so far off that I should not dream of

39

shooting. He firmly believes, and so do most men that speak of him, that he never misses. Yet I have known him make miss after miss at game, and some that were not especially difficult shots either. One secret of his success is his constant practice. He is firing all the time, at marks, small birds, etc., and will average from fifty to a hundred cartridges a day; he certainly uses nearly twenty thousand a year, while a man who only shoots for sport, and that occasionally, will, in practising at marks and everything else, hardly get through with five hundred. Besides, he was cradled in the midst of wild life, and has handled a rifle and used it against both brute and human foes almost since his infancy; his nerves and sinews are like iron, and his eye is naturally both quick and true.

"Vic" is an exception. With practice an amateur will become nearly as good a shot as the average hunter; and, as I said before, I do not myself believe in taking out a professional hunter as a shooting companion. If I do not go alone I generally go with one of my foremen, Merrifield, who himself came from the East but five years ago. He is a good-looking fellow, daring and self-reliant, a good rider and a first-class shot, and a very keen sportsman. Of late years he has been my *fidus Achates* of the hunting-field. I can kill more game with him than I can alone; and in hunting on the plains there are many occasions on which it is almost a necessity to have a companion along.

It frequently happens that a solitary hunter finds himself in an awkward predicament from which he could be extricated easily enough if there were another man with him. His horse may fall into a washout or may get stuck in a mud-hole or quicksand in such a manner that a man working by himself will have great difficulty in getting it out; and two heads often prove better than one in an emergency, especially if a man gets hurt in any way. The first thing that a Western plainsman has to learn is the capacity for self-help, but at the same time he must not forget that occasions may arise when the help of others will be most grateful.

CHAPTER II

WATER–FOWL

ONE cool afternoon in the early fall, while sitting on the veranda of the ranch-house, we heard a long way off the ha-ha-honk, ha-honk, of a gang of wild geese; and shortly after they came in sight, in a V-shaped line, flying low and heavily toward the south, along the course of the stream. They went by within a hundred yards of the house, and we watched them for some minutes as they flew up the valley, for they were so low in the air that it seemed certain that they would soon alight; and alight they did when they were less than a mile past us. As the ground was flat and without much cover where they had settled, I took the rifle instead of a shotgun and hurried after them on foot. Wild geese are very watchful and wary, and as I came toward the place where I thought they were I crept along with as much caution as if the game had been a deer. At last, peering through a thick clump of bulberry bushes, I saw them. They were clustered on a high sand-bar in the middle of the river which here ran in a very wide bed between low banks. The only way to get at them was to crawl along the river-bed, which was partly dry, using the patches of rushes and the sand hillocks and driftwood to shield myself from their view. As it was already late and the sun was just sinking, I hastily retreated a few paces, dropped over the bank, and began to creep along on my hands and knees through the sand and gravel. Such work is always tiresome, and is especially so when done against time. I kept in line with a great log washed up on the shore, which was some seventy-five yards from the geese. On reaching it and looking over I was annoyed to find that in the fading light I could not distinguish the birds clearly enough to shoot, as the dark river-bank was behind them. I crawled quickly back a few yards, and went off a good bit to the left into a hollow. Peeping over the edge I could now see the geese, gathered into a clump with their necks held straight out, sharply outlined against the horizon; the sand flats stretching out on either side, while the sky above was barred with gray and faint crimson. I fired into the thickest of the bunch, and as the rest flew off, with discordant clamor, ran forward and picked up my victim, a fat young wild goose (or Canada goose), the body badly torn by the bullet.

On two other occasions I have killed geese with the rifle. Once while out riding along the river-bottoms, just at dawn, my attention was drawn to a splashing and low cackling in the stream, where the water deepened in a wide bend which swept round a low bluff. Leaving my horse where he was, I walked off toward the edge of the stream, and lying on the brink of the bank looked over into the water of the bend. Only a faint streak of light was visible in the east, so that objects on the water could hardly be made out; and the little wreaths of mist that rose from the river made the difficulty even greater. The birds were some distance above me, where the water made a long straight stretch through a sandy level. I could not see them, but could plainly hear their low murmuring and splashing, and once one of them, as I judged by the sound, stood up on end and flapped its wings vigorously. Pretty soon a light puff of wind blew the thin mist aside, and I caught a glimpse of them; as I had supposed, they were wild geese, five of them, swimming slowly, or rather resting on the water, and being drifted down with the current. The fog closed over them again, but it was growing light very rapidly, and in a short time I knew they would be in the still water of the bend just below me, so I rose on my elbows and held my rifle ready at poise. In a few minutes, before the sun was above the horizon, but when there was plenty of light by which to shoot, another eddy in the wind blew away the vapor and showed the five geese in a cluster, some thirty yards off. I fired at once, and one of the geese, kicking and flapping frantically, fell over, its neck half cut from the body, while the others, with laborious effort, got under way. Before they could get their heavy bodies fairly off the water and out of range, I had taken three more shots, but missed. Waiting till the dead goose drifted in to shore, I picked it up and tied it on the saddle of my horse to carry home to the ranch. Being young and fat, it was excellent eating.

The third goose I killed with the rifle was of a different kind. I had been out after antelopes, starting before there was any light in the heavens, and pushing straight out toward the rolling prairie. After two or three hours, when the sun was well up, I neared where a creek ran in a broad, shallow valley. I had seen no game, and before coming up to the crest of the divide beyond which lay the creek bottom, I dismounted and crawled up to it, so as to see if any animal had come down to drink. Field-glasses are almost always carried while hunting on the plains, as the distances at which one can see game are so enormous. On looking over the crest with the glasses the valley of the creek for about a mile was stretched before me. At my feet the low hills came closer together than in other places, and shelved abruptly down to the bed of the valley, where there was a small grove of box-alders and cottonwoods. The beavers had, in times gone by, built a large dam at this place across the creek, which must have produced a great back-flow and made a regular little lake in the times of freshets. But the dam was now broken, and the beavers, or most of them, gone, and in the place of the lake was a long green meadow. Glancing toward this my eye was at once caught by a row of white objects stretched straight across it, and another look showed me that they were snow-geese. They were feeding, and were moving abreast of one another slowly down the length of the meadow toward the end nearest me, where the patch of small trees and brushwood lay. A goose is not as big game as an antelope; still I had never shot a snow-goose, and we needed fresh meat, so I slipped back over the crest and ran down to the bed of the creek, round a turn of the hill, where the geese were out of sight. The creek was not an entirely dry one, but there was no depth of water in it except in certain deep holes; elsewhere it was a muddy ditch with steep sides, difficult to cross on horseback because of the quicksands. I walked up to the trees without any special care, as they screened me from view, and looked cautiously out from behind them. The geese were acting just as our tame geese act in feeding on a common, moving along with their necks stretched out before them, nibbling and jerking at the grass as they tore it up by mouthfuls. They were very watchful, and one or the other of them had its head straight in the air looking sharply round all the time. Geese will not come near any cover in which foes may be lurking if they can help it, and so I feared that they would turn before coming near enough to the brush to give me a good shot. I therefore dropped into the bed of the creek, which wound tortuously along the side of the meadow, and crept on all fours along one of its banks until I came to where it made a loop out toward the middle of the bottom. Here there was a tuft of tall grass which served as a good cover, and I stood upright, dropping my hat, and looking through between the blades. The geese, still in a row, with several yards' interval between each one and his neighbor, were only sixty or seventy yards off, still feeding toward me. They came along quite slowly, and the ones nearest, with habitual suspicion, edged away from the scattered tufts of grass and weeds which marked the brink of the creek. I tried to get two in line, but could not. There was one gander much larger than any other bird in the lot, though not the closest to me; as he went by just opposite my hiding-place, he stopped still, broadside to me, and I aimed just at the root of the neck—for he was near enough for any one firing a rifle from a rest to hit him about where he pleased. Away flew the others, and in a few minutes I was riding along with the white gander dangling behind my saddle.

The beaver meadows spoken of above are not common, but, until within the last two or three years, beavers themselves were very plentiful, and there are still a good many left. Although only settled for so short a period, the land has been known to hunters for half a century, and throughout that time it has at intervals been trapped over by whites or half-breeds. If fur was high and the Indians peaceful quite a number of trappers would come in, for the Little Missouri

Bad Lands were always famous both for fur and game; then if fur went down or an Indian war broke out or if the beaver got pretty well thinned out, the place would be forsaken and the animals would go unmolested for perhaps a dozen years, when the process would be repeated. But the incoming of the settlers and the driving out of the Indians have left the ground clear for the trappers to work over unintermittently, and the extinction of the beaver throughout the plains country is a question of but a short time. Excepting an occasional otter or mink, or a few muskrats, it is the only fur-bearing animal followed by the Western plains trapper; and its large size and the marked peculiarities of its habits, together with the accessibility of its haunts on the plains, as compared with its haunts in the deep woods and mountains, render its pursuit and capture comparatively easy. We have trapped (or occasionally shot) on the ranch during the past three years several score of beaver; the fur is paler and less valuable than in the forest animal. Those that live in the river do not build dams all across it, but merely extending up some distance against the current, so as to make a deep pool or eddy, beside which are the burrows and houses. It would seem to be a simple feat to break into a beaver house, but in reality it needs no little toil with both spade and axe, for the house has very thick roof and walls, made of clay and tough branches, twisted together into a perfect mat, which, when frozen, can withstand anything but the sharpest and best of tools. At evening beaver often come out to swim, and by waiting on the bank perfectly quietly for an hour or so a close shot can frequently be obtained.

Beaver are often found in the creeks, not only in

those which always contain running water, but also in the dry ones. Here they build dams clean across, making ponds which always contain water, even if the rest of the bed is almost dry; and I have often been surprised to find fresh traces of beaver in a pond but a few feet across, a mile away from any other body of water. On one occasion I was deer-hunting in a rough, broken country, which was little more than a tangle of ravines and clefts, with very steep sides rising into sharp hills. The sides of the ravines were quite densely overgrown with underbrush and young trees, and through one or two of them ran, or rather trickled, small streams, but an inch or two in depth, and often less. Directly across one of these ravines, at its narrowest and steepest part, the beaver had built an immense, massive dam, completely stopping the course of a little brooklet. The dam was certainly eight feet high, and strong enough and broad enough to cross on horseback; and it had turned back the stream until a large pond, almost a little lake, had been formed by it. This was miles from any other body of water, but, judging from the traces of their work, it had once held a large colony of beavers; when I saw it they had all been trapped out, and the pond had been deserted for a year and over. Though clumsy on dry ground, and fearing much to be caught upon it, yet beaver can make, if necessary, quite long overland journeys, and that at a speed with which it will give a man trouble to keep up.

As there are few fish in the plains streams, otters are naturally not at all common, though occasionally we get one. Muskrats are quite plenty in all the pools of water. Sometimes a little pool out on the prairie will show along its edges numerous traces of animal life;

for, though of small extent and a long distance from other water, it may be the home of beavers and musk-rats, the breeding-place of different kinds of ducks, and the drinking-place for the denizens of the dry country round about, such as wolves, antelopes, and badgers.

Although the plains country is in most places very dry, yet there are here and there patches of prairie land where the reverse is true. One such is some thirty miles distant from my ranch. The ground is gently rolling, in some places almost level, and is crossed by two or three sluggish, winding creeks, with many branches, always holding water, and swelling out into small pools and lakelets wherever there is a hollow. The prairie round about is wet, at times almost marshy, especially at the borders of the great reedy slews. These pools and slews are favorite breeding-places for water-fowl, especially for mallard, and a good bag can be made at them in the fall, both among the young flappers (as tender and delicious birds for the table as any I know) and among the flights of wild duck that make the region a stopping-place on their southern migration. In these small pools with little cover round the edges, the poor flappers are at a great disadvantage; we never shoot them unless we really need them for the table. But quite often, in August or September, if near the place, I have gone down to visit one or two of the pools, and have brought home half a dozen flappers, killed with the rifle if I had been out after large game, or with the revolver if I had merely been among the cattle—each duck, in the latter case, representing the expenditure of a vast number of cartridges.

Later in the fall, when the young ducks are grown

and the flocks are coming in from the north, fair shooting may be had by lying in the rushes on the edge of some large pond and waiting for the evening flight of the birds; or else by taking a station on some spot of low ground across which the ducks fly in passing from one sheet of water to another. Frequently quite a bag of mallard, widgeon, and pintail can be made in this manner, although nowhere in the Bad Lands is there any such duck-shooting as is found farther east. Ducks are not very easy to kill, or even to hit, when they fly past. My duck gun, the No. 10 choke-bore, is a very strong and close-shooting piece, and such a one is needed when the strong-flying birds are at any distance; but the very fact of its shooting so close makes it necessary that the aim should be very true; and as a consequence my shooting at ducks has varied from bad to indifferent, and my bags have been always small.

Once I made an unusually successful right and left, however. In late summer and early fall large flocks of both green-winged and blue-winged teal are often seen both on the ponds and on the river, flying up and down the latter. On one occasion while out with the wagon we halted for the midday meal on the bank of the river. Travelling across the plains in company with a wagon, especially if making a long trip, as we were then doing, is both tiresome and monotonous. The scenery through the places where the wagon must go is everywhere much the same, and the pace is very slow. At lunch-time I was glad to get off the horse which had been plodding along at a walk for hours, and stretch my muscles; and noticing a bunch of teal fly past and round a bend in the river, I seized the chance for a little diversion, and, taking my double-barrel, followed them on foot. The banks were five or six feet high, edged with a thick growth of cottonwood saplings; so the chance to creep up was very good. On getting round the bend I poked my head through the bushes, and saw that the little bunch I was after had joined a great flock of teal, which was on a sand-bar in the middle of the stream. They were all huddled together, some standing on the bar, and others in the water right by it, and I aimed for the thickest part of the flock. At the report they sprang into the air, and I leaped to my feet to give them the second barrel, when, from under the bank right beneath me, two shoveller or spoonbill ducks rose, with great quacking, and, as they were right in line, I took them instead, knocking both over. When I had fished out the two shovellers, I waded over to the sand-bar and picked up eleven teal, making thirteen ducks with the two barrels.

On one occasion my brother and myself made a short wagon trip in the level, fertile farming country whose western edge lies many miles to the east of the Bad Lands around my ranch. There the land was already partially settled by farmers, and we had one or two days' quite fair duck-shooting. It was a rolling country of mixed prairie land and rounded hills, with small groves of trees and numerous little lakes in the hollows. The surface of the natural prairie was broken in places by great wheat-fields, and when we were there the grain was gathered in sheaves and stacks among the stubble. At night-time we either put up at the house of some settler, or, if there were none round, camped out.

One night we had gone into camp among the dense timber fringing a small river, which wound through the prairie in a deep narrow bed with steep banks. Until people have actually camped out themselves it is difficult for them to realize how much work there is in making or breaking camp. But it is very quickly done if every man has his duties assigned to him and starts about doing them at once. In choosing camp there are three essentials to be looked to—wood, water, and grass. The last is found everywhere in the Eastern prairie land, where we were on our duck-shooting trip, but in many places on the great dry plains farther west, it is either very scanty or altogether lacking; and I have at times been forced to travel half a score miles farther than I wished to get feed for the horses. Water, again, is a commodity not by any means to be found everywhere on the plains. If the country is known and the journeys timed aright, water can easily be had, at least at the night camps, for on a pinch a wagon can be pushed along thirty miles or so at a stretch, giving the tough ponies merely a couple of hours' rest and feed at midday; but in going through an unknown country it has been my misfortune on more than one occasion to make a dry camp; that is, one without any water either for men or horses, and such camps are most uncomfortable. The thirst seems to be most annoying just after sundown; after one has gotten to sleep and the air has become cool, he is not troubled much by it again until within two or three hours of noon next day, when the chances are that he will have reached water, for of course by that time he will have made a desperate push to get to it. When found it is more than likely to be bad, being either from a bitter alkaline pool or from a hole in a creek so muddy that it can only be called liquid by courtesy. On the great plains wood is even scarcer, and at least half the time the only material from which to make a

fire will be buffalo chips and sage-brush; the long roots
of the latter if dug up make a very hot blaze. Of
course when wood is so scarce the fire is a small one,
used merely to cook by, and is not kept up after the
cooking is over.

When a place with grass, wood, and water is found,
the wagon is driven up to the windward side of where
the beds are to be laid, and the horses are unhitched,
watered, and turned out to graze freely until bedtime,
when a certain number of them are picketed or hob-
bled. If danger from white or red horse-thieves is
feared, a guard is kept over them all night. The
ground is cleared of stones and cacti where the beds
are to be placed and the blankets and robes spread.
Generally we have no tent, and the wagon-cover is
spread over all to keep out rain. Meanwhile some one
gathers the wood and starts a fire. The coffee-pot is
set among the coals, and the frying-pan with bacon
and whatever game has been shot is placed on top.
Like Eastern backwoodsmen, all plainsmen fry about
everything that they can get hold of to cook; for my
own use I always have a broiler carried along in the
wagon. One evening in every three or four is employed in baking bread in the Dutch oven; if there is
no time for this, biscuits are made in the frying-pan.
The food carried along is very simple, consisting of
bacon, flour, coffee, sugar, baking-powder, and salt; for
all else we depend on our guns. On a long trip every
old hand carries a water-proof canvas bag, containing his few spare clothes and necessaries; on a short trip
a little oilskin one for the tooth-brush, soap, towel, etc.,
will do.

On the evening in question our camping-ground was
an excellent one; we had no trouble about anything,

except that we had to bring water to the horses in pails, for the banks were too steep and rotten to get them down to the river. The beds were made under a great elm, and in a short time the fire was roaring in front of them, while the tender grouse were being roasted on pointed sticks. One of the pleasantest times of camping out is the period immediately after supper, when the hunters lie in the blaze of the firelight, talking over what they have done during the day and making their plans for the morrow. And how soundly a man who has worked hard sleeps in the open, none but he who has tried it knows.

Before we had risen in the morning, when the blackness of the night had barely changed to gray, we were roused by the whistle of wings, as a flock of ducks flew by along the course of the stream, and lit in the water just above the camp. Some kinds of ducks in lighting strike the water with their tails first, and skitter along the surface for a few feet before settling down. Lying in our blankets we could plainly hear all the motions: first of all, the whistle-whistle of their wings; then a long-drawn splash-h-h—plump; and then a low, conversational quacking. It was too dark to shoot, but we got up and ready, and strolled down along the brink of the river opposite where we could hear them; and as soon as we could see we gave them four barrels and picked up half a dozen scaup-ducks. Breakfast was not yet ready, and we took a turn out on the prairie before coming back to the wagon. In a small pool, down in a hollow, were a couple of little dipper ducks or buffleheads; they rose slowly against the wind, and offered such fair marks that it was out of the question to miss them.

The evening before we had lain among the reeds

near a marshy lake and had killed quite a number of
ducks, mostly widgeon and teal; and this morning we
intended to try shooting among the corn-fields. By
sunrise we were a good distance off, on a high ridge
across which we had noticed that the ducks flew in
crossing from one set of lakes to another. The flight
had already begun, and our arrival scared off the birds
for the time being; but in a little while, after we had
hidden among the sheaves, stacking the straw up
around us, the ducks began to come back, either flying
over in their passage from the water or else intending
to light and feed. They were for the most part mallards, which are the commonest of the Western ducks,
and the only species customarily killed in this kind of
shooting. They are especially fond of the corn, of
which there was a small patch in the grain-field. To
this flocks came again and again, and fast though they
flew we got many before they left the place, scared by
the shooting. Those that were merely passing from
one point to another flew low, and among them we
shot a couple of gadwall, and also knocked over a redhead from a little bunch that went by, their squat,
chunky forms giving them a very different look from
the longer, lighter-built mallard. The mallards that
came to feed flew high in the air, wheeling round in
gradually lowering circles when they had reached the
spot where they intended to light. In shooting in the
grain-fields there is usually plenty of time to aim, a
snap-shot being from the nature of the sport exceptional. Care must be taken to lie quiet until the ducks
are near enough; shots are most often lost through
shooting too soon. Heavy guns with heavy loads are
necessary, for the ducks are generally killed at long
range; and both from this circumstance as well as from

the rapidity of their flight, it is imperative to hold well ahead of the bird fired at. It has one advantage over shooting in a marsh, and that is that a wounded bird which drops is of course hardly ever lost. Corn-fed mallards are most delicious eating; they rank on a par with teal and redhead, and second only to the canvas-back—a bird, by the way, of which I have killed but one or two individuals in the West.

In going out of this field we got a shot at a gang of wild geese. We saw them a long way off, coming straight toward us in a head-and-tail line. Down we dropped, flat on our faces, remaining perfectly still without even looking up (for wild geese are quick to catch the slightest motion) until the sound of the heavy wing-strokes and the honking seemed directly overhead. Then we rose on our knees and fired all four barrels, into which we had slipped buckshot cartridges. They were away up in the air, much beyond an ordinary gunshot; and we looked regretfully after them as they flew off. Pretty soon one lagged a little behind; his wings beat slower; suddenly his long neck dropped, and he came down like a stone, one of the buckshot having gone clean through his breast.

We had a long distance to make that day, and after leaving the grain-fields travelled pretty steadily, only getting out of the wagon once or twice after prairie-chickens. At lunch-time we halted near a group of small ponds and reedy sloughs. In these were quite a number of teal and wood-duck, which were lying singly, in pairs, or small bunches on the edges of the reeds or where there were thick clusters of lily-pads; and we had half an hour's good sport in "jumping" these little ducks, moving cautiously along the margin of the reeds, keeping as much as possible concealed from view, and shooting four teal and a wood-duck, as, frightened at our near approach, the others sprang into the air and made off. Late in the evening, while we were passing over a narrow neck of land that divided two small lakes, with reedy shores, from each other, a large flock of the usually shy pintail duck passed over us at close range, and we killed two from the wagon, making in all a bag of twenty-one and a half couple of water-fowl during the day, two-thirds falling to my brother's gun. Of course this is a very small bag indeed compared to those made in the Chesapeake, or in Wisconsin and the Mississippi valley; but the day was so perfect, and there were so many varieties of shooting, that I question if any bag, no matter how large, ever gave much more pleasure to the successful sportsman than did our forty-three ducks to us.

Though ducks fly so fast and need such good shooting to kill them, yet their rate of speed, as compared to that of other birds, is not so great as is commonly supposed. Hawks, for instance, are faster. Once, on the prairie, I saw a mallard singled out of a flock, fairly overtaken, and struck down, by a large, light-colored hawk, which I supposed to be a lanner, or at any rate one of the long-winged falcons; and I saw a duck-hawk, on the coast of Long Island, perform a similar feat with the swift-flying, long-tailed duck—the old squaw, or sou'-sou'-southerly, of the baymen. A more curious instance was related to me by a friend. He was out along a river, shooting ducks as they flew by him, and had noticed a bald eagle perched on the top of a dead tree some distance from him. While looking at it a little bunch of teal flew swiftly by, and to his astonishment the eagle made after them. The little ducks went along like bullets, their wings working so fast that they whistled; flop, flop, came the great eagle after them, with labored-looking flight; and yet he actually gained so rapidly on his seemingly fleeter quarry that he was almost up to them when opposite my friend. Then the five teal went down headlong into the water, diving like so many shot. The eagle kept hovering over the spot, thrusting with its claws at each little duck as it came up; but he was unsuccessful, all of the teal eventually getting into the reeds, where they were safe. In the East, by the way, I have seen the same trick of hovering over the water where a flock of ducks had disappeared, performed by a Cooper's hawk. He had stooped at some nearly grown flappers of the black duck; they all went under water, and he remained just above, grasping at any one that appeared, and forcing them to go under without getting a chance to breathe. Soon he had singled out one, which kept down a shorter and shorter time at each dive; it soon grew exhausted, was a little too slow in taking a dive, and was grasped in the claws of its foe.

In duck-shooting where there are reeds, grass, and water-lilies, the cripples should be killed at once, even at the cost of burning some additional powder, many kinds of water-fowl being very expert at diving. Others, as widgeon, shoveller, and teal, do not dive, merely trying to hide in some hole in the bank; and these are generally birds that fall to the touch of shot much more easily than is the case with their tougher relatives.

There are two or three species of birds, tolerably common over the plains, which we do not often regularly hunt, but which are occasionally shot for the table. These are the curlew, the upland or grass plover, and the golden plover. All three kinds belong to the family of what are called wading-birds; but with us it is rare to see any one of them near water.

The curlew is the most conspicuous; indeed its loud, incessant clamor, its erect carriage, and the intense curiosity which possesses it and which makes it come up to circle around any strange object, all combine to make it in springtime one of the most conspicuous features of plains life. At that time curlews are seen in pairs or small parties, keeping to the prairies and grassy uplands. They are never silent, and their discordant noise can be heard half a mile off. Whenever they discover a wagon or a man on horseback, they fly toward him, though usually taking good care to keep out of gunshot. They then fly over and round the object, calling all the time, and sometimes going off to one side, where they will light and run rapidly through the grass; and in this manner they will sometimes accompany a hunter or traveller for miles, scaring off all game. By the end of July or August they have reared their young; they then go in small flocks, and are comparatively silent, and are very good eating. I have never made a practice of shooting them, though I have fired at them sometimes with the rifle, and in this way have now and then killed one; twice I have hit them on the wing with this weapon, while they were soaring slowly about above me, occasionally passing pretty near.

The grass-plover is found in the same places as the curlew, and, like it, breeds with us. Its flesh is just as good, and it has somewhat the same habits, but is less wary, noisy, and inquisitive. The golden plover is only found during the migrations, when large flocks may sometimes be seen. They are delicious eating;

the only ones I have ever shot have been killed with the little ranch gun, when riding round the ranch, or travelling from one point to another.

Like the grouse and other ground-nesting birds, the curlews and plovers during breeding-time have for their chief foes the coyotes, badgers, skunks, and other flesh-eating prowlers; and as all these are greatly thinned off by the cattlemen, with their firearms and their infinitely more deadly poison, the partial and light settlement of the country that accompanies the cattle industry has had the effect of making all these birds more plentiful than before; and, most unlike the large game, game-birds bid fair to increase in numbers during the next few years.

The skunks are a nuisance in more ways than one. They are stupid, familiar beasts, with a great predilection for visiting camps, and the shacks or huts of the settlers, to pick up any scraps of meat that may be lying round. I have time and again known a skunk to actually spend several hours of the night in perseveringly digging a hole underneath the logs of a hut, so as to get inside among the inmates. The animal then hunts about among them, and of course no one will willingly molest it; and it has often been known to deliberately settle down upon and begin to eat one of the sleepers. The strange and terrible thing about these attacks is that in certain districts and at certain times the bite of the skunk is surely fatal, producing hydrophobia; and many cowmen, soldiers, and hunters have annually died from this cause. There is no wild beast in the West, no matter what its size and ferocity, so dreaded by our plainsmen as this seemingly harmless little beast.

I remember one rather ludicrous incident connected

with a skunk. A number of us, among whom was a huge, happy-go-lucky Scotchman, who went by the name of Sandy, were sleeping in a hut when a skunk burrowed under the logs and got in. Hearing it moving about among the tin pans Sandy struck a light, was much taken by the familiarity of the pretty black-and-white little animal, and, as it seemed in his eyes a curiosity, took a shot at it with his revolver. He missed; the skunk, for a wonder, retired promptly without taking any notice of the attack; and the rest of the alarmed sleepers, when informed of the cause of the shot, cursed the Scotchman up hill and down dale for having so nearly brought dire confusion on them all. The latter took the abuse very philosophically, merely remarking: "I'm glad a did na kill him mysel'; he seemed such a dacent wee beastie." The sequel proved that neither the skunk nor Sandy had learned any wisdom by the encounter, for half an hour later the "dacent wee beastie" came back, and this time Sandy fired at him with fatal effect. Of course the result was a frantic rush of all hands from the hut, Sandy exclaiming with late but sincere repentance: "A did na ken 't wad cause such a tragadee."

Besides curlew and plover, there are, at times, especially during the migrations, a number of species of other waders to be found along the streams and pools in the cattle region. Yellowlegs, yelper, willet, marlin, dough-bird, stilt, and avocet are often common, but they do not begin to be as plentiful as they are in the more fertile lands to the eastward, and the ranchmen never shoot at them or follow them as game-birds.

A more curious bird than any of these is the plains plover, which avoids the water and seems to prefer the barren plateaus and almost desert-like reaches of sage-brush and alkali. Plains plovers are pretty birds, and not at all shy. In fall they are fat and good eating, but they are not plentiful enough to be worth going after. Sometimes they are to be seen in the most seemingly unlikely places for a wader to be. Last spring one pair nested in a broken piece of Bad Lands near my ranch, where the ground is riven and twisted into abrupt, steep crests and deep canyons. The soil is seemingly wholly unfitted to support bird life, as it is almost bare of vegetation, being covered with fossil plants, shells, fishes, etc.—all of which objects, by the way, the frontiersman, who is much given to broad generalization, groups together under the startling title of "stone clams."

CHAPTER III

THE GROUSE OF THE NORTHERN CATTLE PLAINS

To my mind, there is no comparison between sport with the rifle and sport with the shotgun. The rifle is the freeman's weapon. The man who uses it well in the chase shows that he can at need use it also in war with human foes. I would no more compare the feat of one who bags his score of ducks or quail with that of him who fairly hunts down and slays a buck or bear than I would compare the skill necessary to drive a buggy with that required to ride a horse across country; or the dexterity acquired in handling a billiard-cue with that shown by a skilful boxer or oarsman. The difference is not one of degree; it is one of kind.

I am far from decrying the shotgun. It is always pleasant as a change from the rifle, and in the Eastern States it is almost the only firearm which we now have a chance to use. But out in the cattle country it is the rifle that is always carried by the ranchman who cares for sport. Large game is still that which is sought after, and most of the birds killed are either simply slaughtered for the pot, or else shot for the sake of variety while really after deer or antelope; though every now and then I have taken a day with the shotgun after nothing else but prairie-fowl.

The sharp-tailed prairie-fowl is much the most plentiful of the feathered game to be found on the northern cattle plains, where it replaces the common prairie-chicken so abundant on the prairies to the east and

63

southeast of the range of our birds. In habits, it is much like the latter, being one of the grouse which keep to the open, treeless tracts, though it is far less averse to timber than is its nearest relative, and often is found among the cottonwood-trees and thick brush which fringe the streams. I have never noticed that its habits, when pursued, differ much from those of the common prairie-chicken, though it is perhaps a little more shy, and is certainly much more apt to light on a tree, like the ruffed grouse. It is, however, essentially a bird of the wilds, and it is a curious fact that it is seen to retreat before civilization, continually moving westward as the wheat-fields advance, while its place is taken by the common form, which seems to keep pace with the settlement of the country. Like the latter bird, and unlike the ruffed grouse and blue grouse which have white meat, its flesh is dark, and it is very good eating from about the middle of August to the middle of November, after which it is a little tough.

As already said, the ranchmen do not often make a regular hunt after these grouse. This is partly because most of them look with something akin to contempt upon any firearm but the rifle or revolver, and partly because it is next to impossible to keep hunting-dogs very long on the plains. The only way to check, in any degree, the ravages of the wolves is by the most liberal use of strychnine, and the offal of any game killed by a cattleman is pretty sure to be poisoned before being left, while the "wolfer," or professional wolf-killer, strews his bait everywhere. It thus comes about that any dog who is in the habit of going any distance from the house is almost sure to run across and eat some of the poisoned meat, the effect of which is almost certain death.   The only time I have ever shot sharp-tailed prairie-fowl over dogs was during a trip to the eastward with my brother, which will be described farther on.   Out on the plains, I have occasionally taken a morning with the shotgun after them, but more often have either simply butchered them for the pot, when out of meat or else have killed a few with the rifle when I happened to come across them while after deer or antelope.

Occasions frequently arise, in living a more or less wild life, when a man has to show his skill in shifting for himself; when, for instance, he has to go out and make a foray upon the grouse, neither for sport nor yet for a change of diet, but actually for food.   Under such circumstances he, of course, pays no regard to the rules of sport which would govern his conduct on other occasions.   If a man's dinner for several consecutive days depends upon a single shot, he is a fool if he does not take every advantage he can.   I remember, for instance, one time when we were travelling along the valley of the Powder River, and got entirely out of fresh meat, owing to my making a succession of ludicrously bad misses at deer.   Having had my faith in my capacity to kill anything whatever with the rifle a good deal shaken, I started off one morning on horseback with the shotgun.   Until nearly noon I saw nothing; then, while riding through a barren-looking bottom, I happened to spy some prairie-fowl squatting close to the ground underneath a sage-brush.   It was some minutes before I could make out what they were, they kept so low and so quiet, and their color harmonized so well with their surroundings.   Finally, I was convinced that they were grouse, and rode my horse slowly by them.   When opposite, I reined him in and fired, killing the whole bunch of five birds. Another time, at the ranch our supply of fresh meat gave out entirely, and I sallied forth with the ranch gun, intent, not on sport, but on slaughter. It was late fall, and as I rode along in the dawn (for the sun was not up) a small pack of prairie-fowl passed over my head and lit on a dead tree that stood out some little distance from a grove of cottonwoods. They paid little attention to me, but they are so shy at that season that I did not dare to try to approach them on foot, but let the horse jog on at the regular cow-pony gait—a kind of single-foot pace, between a walk and a trot—and as I passed by, fired into the tree and killed four birds. Now, of course, I would not have dreamed of taking either of these shots had I been out purely for sport, and neither needed any more skill than would be shown in killing hens in a barnyard; but, after all, when one is hunting for one's dinner he takes an interest in his success which he would otherwise lack, and on both occasions I felt a most unsportsmanlike glee when I found how many I had potted.

The habits of this prairie-fowl vary greatly at different seasons of the year. It is found pretty much everywhere within moderate distance of water, for it does not frequent the perfectly dry wastes where we find the great sage-cock. But it is equally at home on the level prairie and among the steep hills of the Bad Lands. When on the ground it has rather a comical look, for it stands very high on its legs, carries its sharp little tail cocked up like a wren's, and when startled stretches its neck out straight; altogether, it gives one the impression of being a very angular bird. Of course it crouches, and moves about when feeding, like any other grouse.

THE GROUSE OF THE PLAINS

One of the strangest, and to me one of the most attractive, sounds of the prairie is the hollow booming made by the cocks in spring. Before the snow has left the ground they begin, and at the break of morning their deep resonant calls sound from far and near, for in still weather they can be heard at an immense distance. I hardly know how to describe the call; indeed it cannot be described in words. It has a hollow, vibrant sound like that of some wind-instrument, and would hardly be recognized as a bird note at all. I have heard it at evening, but more often shortly after dawn; and I have often stopped and listened to it for many minutes, for it is as strange and weird a form of natural music as any I know. At the time of the year when they utter these notes the cocks gather together in certain places and hold dancing rings, posturing and strutting about as they face and pass each other.

The nest is generally placed in a tuft of grass or under a sage-brush in the open, but occasionally in the brushwood near a stream. The chicks are pretty little balls of mottled brown and yellow down. The mother takes great care of them, leading them generally into some patch of brushwood, but often keeping them out in the deep grass. Frequently, when out among the cattle, I have ridden my horse almost over a hen with a brood of chicks. The little chicks first attempt to run off in single file; if discovered, they scatter and squat down under clods of earth or tufts of grass. Holding one in my hand near my pocket, it scuttled into it like a flash. The mother, when she sees her brood discovered, tumbles about through the grass as if wounded, in the effort to decoy the foe after her. If she is successful in this, she takes a series of short flights, keeping just out of reach of her pursuer, and when the latter has been lured far enough from the chicks the hen rises and flies off at a humming speed.

By the middle of August the young are well enough grown to shoot, and are then most delicious eating. Different coveys at this time vary greatly in their behavior if surprised feeding in the open. Sometimes they will not permit a very close approach, and will fly off after one or two have been shot; while, again, they will show perfect indifference to the approach of man, and will allow the latter to knock off the heads of five or six with his rifle before the rest take the alarm and fly off. They now go more or less over the open ground, but are especially fond of frequenting the long grass in the bottoms of the coulées and ravines and the dense brush along the edges of the creeks and in the valleys; there they will invariably be found at midday, and will lie till they are almost trodden on before rising.

Late in the month of August one year we had been close-herding a small bunch of young cattle on a bottom about a mile square, walled in by bluffs, and with, as an inlet, a long, dry creek running back many miles into the Bad Lands, where it branched out into innumerable smaller creeks and coulées. We wished to get the cattle accustomed to the locality, for animals are more apt to stray when first brought on new ground than at any later period; so each night we "bedded" them on the level bottom; that is, gathering them together on the plain, one of us would ride slowly and quietly round and round the herd, heading off and turning back into it all beasts that tried to stray off, but carefully avoiding disturbing them or making any unusual noise; and by degrees they would all lie down, close together. This "bedding down" is always done when travelling with a large herd, when, of course, it needs several cowboys to do it; and in such cases some of the cowboys keep guard all the time, walking their horses round the herd, and singing and calling to the cattle all night long. The cattle seem to like to hear the human voice, and it tends to keep them quiet and free from panic. Often when camping near some great cattle outfit I have lain awake at night for an hour or over listening to the wild, not unmusical, calls of the cowboys as they rode round the half-slumbering steers. In the clear, still night air the calls can be heard for a mile and more, and I like to listen to them as they come through the darkness, half-mellowed by the distance, for they are one of the characteristic sounds of plains life. Texan steers often give considerable trouble before they can be bedded, and are prone to stampede, especially in a thunder-storm. But with the little herd we were at this time guarding there was no difficulty whatever, the animals being grade shorthorns of Eastern origin. After seeing them quiet, we would leave them for the night, again riding out early in the morning.

On every occasion when we thus rode out in the morning we saw great numbers of prairie-fowl feeding in the open plain in small flocks, each evidently composed of a hen and her own brood. They would often be right around the cattle, and went indifferently among the sage-brush or out on the short prairie-grass. They flew into the bottom from some distance off about daybreak, fed for a couple of hours, and soon after sunrise again took wing and flew up along the course of the dry creek mentioned above. While on the bottom they were generally quite shy, not permitting anything like a close approach before taking wing. Their habit of crowing or clucking while flying off is very notice-

69

able; it is, by the way, a most strongly characteristic trait of this species. I have been especially struck by it when shooting in Minnesota, where both the sharp-tail and the common prairie-fowl are found; the contrast between the noisiness of one bird and the quiet of the other was very marked. If one of us approached a covey on horseback, the birds would, if they thought they were unobserved, squat down close to the ground; more often they would stand very erect, and walk off. If we came too close to one it would utter a loud kuk-kuk-kuk, and be off, at every few strokes of its wings repeating the sound—a kind of crowing cluck. This is the note they utter when alarmed or when calling to one another. When a flock are together and undisturbed, they keep up a sociable, garrulous cackling.

Every morning, by the time the sun had been up a little while, the grouse had all gone from the bottom, but later in the day, while riding along the creek among the cattle, we often stumbled upon little flocks. We fired at them with our revolvers whenever we were close enough, but the amount we got in this way was very limited, and as we were rather stinted for fresh meat, the cattle taking up so much of our time as to prevent our going after deer, I made up my mind to devote a morning to hunting up the creeks and coulées for grouse, with the shotgun.

Accordingly, the next morning I started, just about the time the last of the flocks were flying away from their feeding-grounds on the bottom. I trudged along on foot, not wanting to be bothered by a horse. The air was fresh and cool, though the cloudless sky boded a hot noon. As I walked by the cattle, they stopped grazing and looked curiously at me, for they were unused to seeing any man not on horseback. But they did not offer to molest me; Texan or even Northern steers bred on the more remote ranges will often follow and threaten a footman for miles. While passing among the cattle, it was amusing to see the actions of the little cow-buntings. They were very familiar little birds, lighting on the backs of the beasts, and keeping fluttering round their heads as they walked through the grass, hopping up into the air all the time. At first, I could not make out what they were doing; but on watching them closely, saw that they were catching the grasshoppers and moths which flew into the air to avoid the cattle's hoofs. They are as tame with horsemen; while riding through a patch of tall grass a flock of buntings will often keep circling within a couple of yards of the horse's head, seizing the insects as they fly up before him.

The valley through which the creek ran was quite wide, bordered by low buttes. After a heavy rainfall the water rushes through the at other times dry bed in a foaming torrent, and it thus cuts it down into a canyon-like shape, making it a deep, winding narrow ditch, with steep sides. Along the edges of this ditch were dense patches, often quite large, of rose-bushes, bullberry bushes, ash, and wild cherry, making almost impenetrable thickets, generally not over breast-high. In the bottom of the valley, along the edges of the stream-bed, the grass was long and coarse, entirely different from the short fine bunch-grass a little farther back, the favorite food of the cattle.

Almost as soon as I had entered the creek, in walking through a small patch of brush I put up an old cock, as strong a flyer as the general run of October birds. Off he went, with a whir, clucking and crowing; I held the little 16-bore fully two feet ahead of

him, pulled the trigger, and down he came into the
bushes. The sharptails fly strongly and steadily,
springing into the air when they rise, and then going
off in a straight line, alternately sailing and giving a
succession of rapid wing-beats. Sometimes they will
sail a long distance with set wings before alighting,
and when they are passing overhead with their wings
outstretched each of the separate wing-feathers can be
seen, rigid and distinct.

Picking up and pocketing my bird, I walked on,
and on turning round a shoulder of the bluffs saw a pair
of sharptails sitting sunning themselves on the top of
a bullberry bush. As soon as they saw me they flew
off a short distance and lit in the bed of the creek.
Rightly judging that there were more birds than those
I had seen, I began to beat with great care the patches
of brush and long grass on both sides of the creek, and
soon was rewarded by some very pretty shooting. The
covey was a large one, composed of two or three broods
of young prairie-fowl, and I had struck on the exact
place, a slight hollow filled with low brush and tall
grass, where they were lying. They lay very close, and
my first notice of their presence was given by one that
I almost trod on, which rose from fairly between my
feet. A young grouse at this season offers an easy
shot, and he was dropped without difficulty. At the
report two others rose and I got one. When I had
barely reloaded, the rest began to get up, singly or two
or three at a time, rising straight up to clear the edge
of the hollow, and making beautiful marks; when the
last one had been put up I had down seven birds of
which I picked up six, not being able to find the other.
A little farther I put up and shot a single grouse which
fell into a patch of briars I could not penetrate. Then

for some time I saw nothing, although beating carefully through every likely looking place. One patch of grass, but a few feet across, I walked directly through without rousing anything; happening to look back, when I had gone some fifty yards, I was surprised to see a dozen heads and necks stretched up, and eying me most inquisitively; their owners were sharptails, a covey of which I had almost walked over without their making a sign. I strode back; but at my first step they all stood up straight with their absurd little tails held up in the air, and at the next step away they went, flying off a quarter of a mile and then scattering in the bushy hollows where a coulée headed up into the buttes. (Grouse at this season hardly ever light in a tree.) I marked them down carefully and tramped all through the place, yet I only succeeded in putting up two, of which I got one and missed the other with both barrels. After that I walked across the heads of the coulées but saw nothing except in a small swale of high grass, where there was a little covey of five, of which I got two with a right and left. It was now very hot, and I made for a spring which I knew ran out of a cliff a mile or two off. There I stayed till long after the shadows began to lengthen, when I started homeward. For some miles I saw nothing, but as the evening came on the grouse began to stir. A small party flew over my head, and though I missed them with both barrels, either because I miscalculated the distance or for some other reason, yet I marked them down very well and when I put them up again got two. Three times afterward I came across coveys, either flying or walking out from the edges of the brushes, and I got one bird out of each, reaching home just after sunset with fifteen sharptails strung over my back. Of course working after grouse on an August day in this manner, without a dog, is very tiring, and no great bag can be made without a pointer or setter.

In September, the sharptails begin to come out from the brushy coulées and creek bottoms, and to wander out among the short grass of the ravines and over the open prairie. They are at first not very shy, and in the early part of the month I have once or twice had good sport with them. Once I took a companion in the buckboard, and drove during the course of the day twenty or twenty-five miles along the edge of the rolling prairie, crossing the creeks and skirting the wooded basins where the Bad Lands began. We came across quite a number of coveys, which in almost all cases waited for us to come up, and as the birds did not rise all together, I got three or four shots at each covey, and came home with ten and a half couple.

A little later the birds become shy and acquire their full strength of wing. They now wander far out on the prairie, and hardly ever make any effort to squat down and conceal themselves in the marvellous way which they have earlier in the season, but, on the contrary, trust to their vigilance and their powers of flight for their safety. On bare ground it is now impossible to get anywhere near them, but if they are among sagebrush or in other low cover they afford fine sport to a good shot with a close-shooting, strong-hitting gun. I remember one evening, while coming over with a wagon team from the headwaters of O'Fallon Creek, across the Big Sandy, when it became a matter of a good deal of interest for us to kill something, as otherwise we would have had very little to eat. We had camped near a succession of small pools, containing one or two teal which I shot; but a teal is a small bird when

74

placed before three hungry men. Sharptails, however, were quite numerous, having come in from round about, as evening came on, to drink. They were in superb condition, stout and heavy, with clean, bright plumage, but very shy; and they rose so far off and flew so strongly and swiftly that a good many cartridges were spent before four of the plump, white-bellied birds were brought back to the wagon in my pockets.

Later than this they sometimes unite into great packs containing hundreds of individuals, and then show a strong preference for the timbered ravines and the dense woods and underbrush of the river-bottoms, the upper branches of the trees being their favorite resting-places. On very cold mornings, when they are feeling numb and chilled, a man can sometimes get very close up to them, but as a rule they are very wild, and the few I have killed at this season of the year have been shot with the rifle, either from a tree or when standing out on the bare hillsides, at a considerable distance. They offer very pretty marks for target practice with the rifle, and it needs a good shot to hit one at eighty or a hundred yards.

But, though the shotgun is generally of no use late in the season, yet last December I had a good afternoon's sport with it. There was a light snow falling, and having been in the house all the morning, I determined to take a stroll out in the afternoon with the shotgun. A couple of miles from the house was a cedar canyon; that is, a canyon one of whose sides was densely wooded with gnarled, stunted evergreens. This had been a favorite resort for the sharptails for some time, and it was especially likely that they would go to it during a storm, as it afforded fine shelter, and also food. The buttes bounding it on the side where the trees were, rose to a sharp crest which extended along, with occasional interruptions, for over a mile, and by walking along near this and occasionally looking out over it, I judged I would get up close to the grouse, while the falling snow and the wind would deaden the report of the gun, and not let it scare all the prairie-fowl out of the canyon at the first fire. It came out as I had planned and expected. I climbed up to the crest near the mouth of the gorge, braced myself firmly, and looked over the top. At once a dozen sharptails, who had perched in the cedar tops almost at my feet, took wing, crossed over the canyon, and as they rose all in a bunch to clear the opposite wall I fired both barrels into the brown, and two of the birds dropped down to the bottom of the ravine. They fell on the snow-covered open ground where I could easily find them again, and as it would have been a great and useless labor to have gone down for them, I left them where they were and walked on along the crest. Before I had gone a hundred yards I had put up another sharptail from a cedar and killed him in fine style as he sailed off below me. The snow and bad weather seemed to make the prairie-fowl disinclined to move. There must have been a good many score of them scattered in bunches among the cedars, and as I walked along I put up a covey or a single bird every two or three hundred yards. They were always started when I was close up to them, and the nature of the place made them offer excellent shots as they went off, while, when killed, they dropped down on the snow-covered canyon bottom where they could be easily recovered on my walk home. When the sharptails had once left the canyon, they scattered among the broken buttes. I tried to creep up to one or two, but they were fully as wild and watchful as deer, and would not let me come within a hundred yards of them; so I turned back, climbed down into the canyon, and walked homeward through it, picking up nine birds on the way, the result of a little over an hour's shooting. Most of them were dead outright; and the two or three who had been only wounded were easily followed by the tracks they made in the telltale snow.

Most of the prairie-fowl I have killed, however, have not been obtained in the course of a day or an afternoon regularly spent after them for the sake of sport, but have simply been shot with whatever weapon came handy, because we actually needed them for immediate use. On more than one occasion I would have gone supperless or dinnerless had it not been for some of these grouse; and one such instance I will give.

One November, about the middle of the month, we had driven in a beef herd (which we wished to ship to the cattle-yards) round the old cantonment building, in which a few years ago troops had been stationed to guard against Indian outbreaks. Having taken care of the beef herd, I determined to visit a little bunch of cattle which was some thirty-five miles down the river, under the care of one of my men—a grizzled old fellow, born in Maine, whose career had been varied to an extent only possible in America, he having successively followed the occupations of seaman, druggist, clerk, buffalo-hunter, and cowboy.

I intended to start about noon, but there was so much business to settle that it was an hour and a half afterward before I put spurs to the smart little cow-pony and loped briskly down the valley. It was a sharp day, the mercury well down toward zero; and the pony, fresh and untired, and impatient of standing in the cold, went along at a good rate; but darkness sets in so early at this season that I had not gone many miles before I began to fear that I would not reach the shack by nightfall. The well-beaten trail followed along the bottoms for some distance and then branched out into the Bad Lands, leading up and down through the ravines and over the ridge crests of some very rough and broken country, and crossing a great level plateau, over which the wind blew savagely, sweeping the powdery snow clean off of the bent blades of short brown grass. After making a wide circle of some twelve miles, the trail again came back to the Little Missouri, and led along the bottoms between the rows of high bluffs, continually crossing and recrossing the river. These crossings were difficult and disagreeable for the horse, as they always are when the ice is not quite heavy enough to bear. The water had not frozen until two or three days before, and the cold snap had not yet lasted long enough to make the ice solid, besides which it was covered with about half an inch of light snow that had fallen, concealing all bad-looking places. The ice, after bearing the cautiously stepping pony for a few yards, would suddenly break and let him down to the bottom, and he would then have to plunge and paw his way through to the opposite shore. Often it is almost impossible to make a pony attempt the crossing under such difficulties; and I have seen ponies which had to be knocked down and pulled across glare ice on their sides. If the horse slips and falls, it is a serious matter to the rider; for a wetting in such cold weather, with a long horseback journey to make, is no joke.

I was still several miles from the hut I was striving to reach when the sun set; and for some time previous

the valley had been in partial darkness, though the
tops of the sombre bluffs around were still lit up. The
pony loped steadily on along the trail, which could be
dimly made out by the starlight. I hurried the willing
little fellow all I could without distressing him, for,
though I knew the road pretty well, yet I doubted if I
could find it easily in perfect darkness; and the clouds
were gathering overhead with a rapidity which showed
that the starlight would last but a short while. The
light snow rendered the hoof-beats of my horse muffled
and indistinct; and almost the only sound that broke
the silence was the long-drawn, melancholy howling of
a wolf, a quarter of a mile off. When we came to the
last crossing the pony was stopped and watered; and
we splashed through over a rapid where the ice had
formed only a thin crust. On the opposite side was a
large patch of cottonwoods, thickly grown up with underbrush, the whole about half a mile square. In this
was the cowboy's shack, but as it was now pitch-dark
I was unable to find it until I rode clean through to
the cow corral, which was out in the open on the other
side. Here I dismounted, groped around till I found
the path, and then easily followed it to the shack.

Rather to my annoyance, the cowboy was away,
having run out of provisions, as I afterward learned;
and, of course, he had left nothing to eat behind him.
The tough little pony was, according to custom, turned
loose to shift for himself; and I went into the low, win-
dowless hut, which was less than twelve feet square.
In one end was a great chimney-place, and it took but
a short time to start a roaring fire which speedily made
the hut warm and comfortable. Then I went down to
the river with an axe and a pail, and got some water;
I had carried a paper of tea in my pocket, and the tea-

kettle was soon simmering away. I should have liked something to eat, but as I did not have it, the tea did not prove such a bad substitute for a cold and tired man.

Next morning I sallied out at break of day with the rifle, for I was pretty hungry. As soon as I stepped from the hut I could hear the prairie-fowl crowing and calling to one another from the tall trees. There were many score—many hundreds would perhaps be more accurate—scattered through the wood. Evidently they had been attracted by the good cover and by the thick growth of choke-cherries and wild plums. As the dawn brightened, the sharptails kept up incessantly their hoarse clucking, and small parties began to fly down from their roosts to the berrybushes. While perched up among the bare limbs of the trees, sharply outlined against the sky, they were very conspicuous. Generally, they crouched close down, with the head drawn in to the body and the feathers ruffled, but when alarmed or restless they stood up straight with their necks stretched out, looking very awkward. Later in the day they would have been wild and hard to approach, but I kept out of their sight, and sometimes got two or three shots at the same bird before it flew off. They offered beautiful marks, and I could generally get a rest for my rifle, while in the gray morning, before sunrise, I was not very conspicuous myself, and could get up close beneath where they were; so I did not have much trouble in killing five, almost all of them shot very nearly where the neck joins the body, one having the head fairly cut off. Salt, like tea, I had carried with me, and it was not long before two of the birds, plucked and cleaned, were split open and roasting before the fire. And to me they seemed most delicious food, although even in November the sharptails, while keeping their game flavor, have begun to be dry and tough, most unlike the tender and juicy young of August and September.

The best day's work I ever did after sharptails was in the course of the wagon trip, already mentioned, which my brother and I made through the fertile farming country to the eastward. We had stopped over night with a Norwegian settler, who had taken and adapted to a farmhouse an old log trading-post of one of the fur companies, lying in the timber which fringed a river, and so stoutly built as to have successfully withstood the assaults of Time. We were travelling in a light, covered wagon, in which we could drive anywhere over the prairie. Our dogs would have made an Eastern sportsman blush, for when roughing it in the West we have to put up with any kind of mongrel makeshift, and the best dog gets pretty well battered after a season or two. I never had a better duck-retriever than a little yellow cur, with hardly a trace of hunting blood in his veins. On this occasion we had a stiff-jointed old pointer with a stub tail, and a wild young setter pup, tireless and ranging very free (a Western dog on the prairies should cover five times the ground necessary for an Eastern one to get over), but very imperfectly trained.

Half of the secret of success on a shooting trip lies in getting up early and working all day; and this at least we had learned, for we were off as soon as there was light enough by which to drive. The ground, of course, was absolutely fenceless, houses being many miles apart. Through the prairie, with its tall grass, in which the sharptails lay at night and during the day, were scattered great grain-fields, their feeding-grounds in the morning and evening. Our plan was to drive from one field to another, getting out at each and letting the dogs hunt it over. The birds were in small coveys and lay fairly well to the dogs, though they rose much farther off from us in the grain-fields than they did later in the day, when we flushed them from the tall grass of the prairie (I call it tall grass in contradistinction to the short bunch-grass of the cattle plains to the westward). Old stubtail, though slow, was very stanch and careful, never flushing a bird, while the puppy, from pure heedlessness and with the best intentions, would sometimes bounce into the midst of a covey before he knew of their presence. On the other hand, he covered twice the ground that the pointer did. The actual killing the birds was a good deal like quail-shooting in the East, except that it was easier, the marks being so much larger. When we came to a field we would beat through it a hundred yards apart, the dogs ranging in long diagonals. When either the setter or the pointer came to a stand, the other generally backed him. If the covey was near enough, both of us—otherwise, whichever was closest—walked cautiously up. The grouse generally flushed before we came up to the dog, rising all together, so as to give only a right and left.

When the morning was well advanced, the grouse left the stubble-fields and flew into the adjoining prairie. We marked down several coveys into one spot, where the ground was rolling and there were here and there a few bushes in the hollows. Carefully hunting over this, we found two or three coveys, and had excellent sport out of each. The sharptails in these places lay very close, and we had to walk them up, when they rose one at a time, and thus allowed us shot after shot; whereas, as already said, earlier in the day we merely got a quick right and left at each covey. At least half the time we were shooting in our rubber overcoats, as the weather was cloudy and there were frequent flurries of rain.

We rested a couple of hours at noon for lunch, and the afternoon's sport was simply a repetition of the morning's, except that we had but one dog to work with; for shortly after midday the stub-tailed pointer, for his sins, encountered a skunk, with which he waged prompt and valiant battle—thereby rendering himself, for the balance of the time, wholly useless as a servant and highly offensive as a companion.

The setter pup did well, ranging very freely, but naturally got tired and careless, flushing his birds half the time; and we had to stop when we still had a good hour of daylight left. Nevertheless, we had in our wagon, when we came in at night, a hundred and five grouse, of which sixty-two had fallen to my brother's gun, and forty-three to mine. We would have done much better with more serviceable dogs; besides, I was suffering all day long from a most acute colic, which was anything but a help to good shooting.

Besides the sharptail, there is but one kind of grouse found in the northern cattle plains. This is the sage-cock, a bird the size of a young turkey, and, next to the Old World capercailzie, or cock-of-the-woods, the largest of the grouse family. It is a handsome bird, with a long pointed tail and black belly, and is a very characteristic form of the regions which it inhabits.

It is peculiarly a desert grouse, for, though sometimes found in the grassy prairies and on the open river-bottoms, it seems really to prefer the dry, arid wastes, where the withered-looking sage-brush and the spiny cactus are almost the only plants to be found, and where the few pools of water are so bitterly alkaline as to be nearly undrinkable. It is pre-eminently the grouse of the plains, and, unlike all of its relatives, is never found near trees; indeed, no trees grow in its haunts.

As is the case with the two species of prairie-fowl, the cocks of this great bird become very noisy in the early spring. If a man happens at that season to be out in the dry plains which are frequented by the sage-fowl, he will hear in the morning before sunrise the deep, sonorous booming of the cocks as they challenge one another or call to their mates. This call is uttered in a hollow bass tone, and can be heard a long distance in still weather; it is difficult to follow up, for it has a very ventriloquial effect.

Unlike the sharptail, the habits and haunts of the sage-fowl are throughout the year the same, except that it grows shyer as the season advances, and occasionally wanders a little farther than formerly from its birthplace. It is only found where the tough, scraggly wild sage abounds, and it feeds for most of the year solely on sage-leaves, varying this diet in August and September by quantities of grasshoppers. Curiously enough, it does not possess any gizzard, such as most gallinaceous birds have, but has in its place a membranous stomach, suited to the digestion of its peculiar food.

The little chicks follow their mother as soon as hatched, and she generally keeps them in the midst of some patch of sage-brush so dense as to be almost impenetrable to man or beast. The little fellows skulk and dodge through the crooked stems so cleverly that it is almost impossible to catch them. Early in August, when the brood is well grown, the mother leads them out, and during the next two months they are more often found out on the grassy prairies than is the case at any other season. They do not form into packs like the prairie-fowl as winter comes on, two broods at the outside occasionally coming together; and they then again retire to the more waste parts of the plains, living purely on sage-leaves, and keeping closely to the best-sheltered hollows until the springtime.

In the early part of the season, the young, and, indeed, their parents also, are tame and unsuspicious to the very verge of stupidity, and at this time are often known by the name of "fool-hens" among the frontiersmen. They grow shyer as the season advances, and after the first of October are difficult to approach, but even then are rarely as wild as the sharptails.

It is commonly believed that the flesh of the sage-fowl is uneatable, but this is very far from being the truth, and, on the contrary, it is excellent eating in August and September, when grasshoppers constitute their chief food, and, if the birds are drawn as soon as shot, is generally perfectly palatable at other seasons of the year. The first time I happened to find this out was in the course of a trip taken with one of my foremen as a companion through the arid plains to the westward of the Little Missouri. We had been gone for two or three days and camped by a mud-hole, which was almost dry, what water it still held being almost as thick as treacle. Our luxuries being limited, I bethought me of a sage-cock which I had shot during the day and had hung to the saddle. I had drawn it as soon as it was picked up, and I made up my mind to try how it tasted. A good deal to our surprise, the meat, though dark and coarse-grained, proved perfectly well flavored, and was quite as good as wild goose, which it much resembled. Some young sage-fowl, shot shortly afterward, proved tender and juicy, and tasted quite as well as sharptails. All of these birds had their crops crammed with grasshoppers, and doubtless the nature of their food had much to do with their proving so good for the table. An old bird, which had fed on nothing but sage, and was not drawn when shot, would, beyond question, be very poor eating. Like the spruce-grouse and the two kinds of prairie-fowl, but unlike the ruffed grouse and blue grouse, the sage-fowl has dark meat.

In walking and running on the ground, sage-fowl act much like common hens, and can skulk through the sage-brush so fast that it is often difficult to make them take wing. When surprised, they will sometimes squat flat down with their heads on the ground, when it is very difficult to make them out, as their upper parts harmonize curiously in color with the surroundings. I have never known of their being shot over a dog, and, indeed, the country where they are found is so dry and difficult that no dog would be able to do any work in it.

When flushed, they rise with a loud whirring, laboring heavily, often clucking hoarsely; when they get fairly under way, they move along in a strong, steady flight, sailing most of the time, but giving, every now and then, a succession of powerful wing-beats, and their course is usually sustained for a mile or over before they light. They are very easy marks, but require hard hitting to bring them down, for they are very tenacious of life. On one occasion, I came upon a flock and shot an old cock through the body with the rifle. He fell over, fluttering and kicking, and I shot a young one before the rest of the flock rose. To my

86

astonishment, the old cock recovered himself and made off after them, actually flying for half a mile before he dropped. When I found him he was quite dead, the ball having gone clean through him. It was a good deal as if a man had run a mile with a large grape-shot through his body.

Most of the sage-fowl I have killed have been shot with the rifle when I happened to run across a covey while out riding, and wished to take two or three of them back for dinner. Only once did I ever make a trip with the shotgun for the sole purpose of a day's sport with these birds.

This was after having observed that there were several small flocks of sage-fowl at home on a great plateau or high plain, crossed by several dry creeks, which was about eight miles from the cow-camp where I was staying; and I concluded that I would devote a day to their pursuit. Accordingly, one morning I started out on horseback with my double-barrel 10-bore and a supply of cartridges loaded with No. 4 shot; one of my cowboys went with me, carrying a rifle so as to be ready if we ran across any antelope. Our horses were fresh, and the only way to find the birds was to cover as much ground as possible; so as soon as we reached the plateau we loped across it in parallel lines till we struck one of the creeks, when we went up it, one on each side, at a good gait, and then crossed over to another, where we repeated the operation. It was nearly noon when, while going up the third creek, we ran into a covey of about fifteen sage-fowl, a much larger covey than ordinary. They were down in the bottom of the creek, which here exhibited a formation very common on the plains. Although now perfectly dry, every series of heavy rainfalls changed it into a foaming torrent, which flowed down the valley in sharp curves, eating away the land into perpendicular banks on the outside of each curve. Thus a series of small bottoms was formed, each fronted by a semicircular bluff, highest in the middle, and rising perfectly sheer and straight. At the foot of these bluffs, which varied from six to thirty feet in height, was the bed of the stream. In many of these creeks there will be a growth of small trees by the stream bed where it runs under the bluffs, and perhaps pools of water will be found in such places even in times of drought. But on the creek where we found the sage-fowl, there were neither trees nor water, and the little bottoms were only covered with stunted sage-brush. Dismounting and leaving my horse with the cowboy, I walked down to the edge of the bottom, which was not more than thirty or forty yards across. The covey retreated into the brush, some of the birds crouching flat down, while the others walked or ran off among the bushes. They were pretty tame, and rose one at a time as I walked on. They had to rise over the low, semicircular bluff in front of them, and, it being still early in the season, they labored heavily as they left the ground. I fired just as they topped the bluff, and as they were so close and large, and were going so slowly, I was able to knock over eight birds, hardly moving from my place during the entire time. On our way back we ran into another covey, a much smaller one, on the side of another creek; of these I got a couple; and I got another out of still a third covey, which we found out in the open, but of which the birds all rose and made off together. We carried eleven birds back, most of them young and tender, and all of them good eating.

In shooting grouse we sometimes run across rabbits.

THE GROUSE OF THE PLAINS

There are two kinds of these. One is the little cotton-tail, almost precisely similar in appearance to the common gray rabbit of the Eastern woods. It abounds in all the patches of dense cover along the river-bottoms and in the larger creeks, and can be quite easily shot at all times, but especially when there is any snow on the ground. It is eatable, but hardly ever killed except to poison and throw out as bait for the wolves.

The other kind is the great jack-rabbit. This is a characteristic animal of the plains; quite as much so as the antelope or prairie-dog. It is not very abundant, but is found everywhere over the open ground, both on the prairie or those river-bottoms which are not wooded, and in the more open valleys and along the gentle slopes of the Bad Lands. Sometimes it keeps to the patches of sage-brush, and in such cases will lie close to the ground when approached; but more often it is found in the short grass, where there is no cover at all to speak of, and relies upon its speed for its safety. It is a comical-looking beast, with its huge ears and long legs, and runs very fast, with a curious lopsided gait, as if it was off its balance. After running a couple of hundred yards it will generally stop and sit up erect on its haunches to look around and see if it is pursued. In winter it turns snow-white, except that the tips of the ears remain black. The flesh is dry, and I have never eaten it unless I could get nothing else.

Jack-rabbits are not plentiful enough nor valuable enough to warrant a man's making a hunting trip solely for their sakes; and the few that I have shot have been killed with the rifle while out after other game. They offer beautiful marks for target practice when they sit upon their haunches. But though hardly worth powder, they afford excellent sport when coursed with greyhounds, being very fleet, and when closely pressed able to double so quickly that the dogs shoot by them. For reasons already given, however, it is difficult to keep sporting-dogs on the plains, though doubtless in the future coursing with greyhounds will become a recognized Western sport.

This finishes the account of the small game of the northern cattle country. The wild turkey is not found with us; but it is an abundant bird farther south, and eagerly followed by the ranchmen in whose neighborhood it exists. And as it is easily the king of all game-birds, and as its pursuit is a peculiarly American form of sport, some account of how it is hunted in the southern plains country may be worth reading. The following is an extract from a letter written to me by my brother, in December, 1875, while he was in Texas, containing an account of some of his turkey-hunting experience in that State. The portion relating how the birds are coursed with greyhounds is especially markworthy; it reminds one of the method of killing the great bustard with gaze-hounds, as described in English sporting-books of two centuries back.

"Here, some hundred miles south and west of Fort McKavett, are the largest turkey-roosts in the world. This beautiful fertile valley, through which the deep, silent stream of the Llano flows, is densely wooded with grand old pecan-trees along its banks; as are those of its minor tributaries which come boiling down from off the immense upland watershed of the staked plains, cutting the sides of the 'divide' into narrow canyons. The journey to this sportsman's paradise was over the long-rolling plains of western Texas. Hour after hour through the day's travel we would drop into the trough of some great plains-wave only to toil on up to the crest of the next, and be met by an endless vista of boundless, billowy-looking prairie. We were following the old Fort Terret trail, its ruts cut so deep in the prairie soil by the heavy supply-wagons that these ten years have not healed the scars in the earth's face. At last, after journeying for leagues through the stunted live-oaks, we saw from the top of one of the larger divides a dark bluish line against the horizon—the color of distant leafless trees—and knew that it meant we should soon open out the valley. Another hour brought us over the last divide, and then our hunting-grounds lay before and below us. All along through the unbroken natural fields the blacktail and prong-horn abound, and feast to their hearts' content all the winter through on the white, luscious, and nutritious mesquite-grass. Through the valley with its flashing silver stream ran the dark line of the famous pecan-tree forests—the nightly resting-place of that king of game-birds, the wild turkey. It would sound like romancing to tell of the endless number and variety of the water-fowl upon the river; while the multitude of game-fish inhabiting the waters make the days spent on the river with the rod rival in excitement and good sport the nights passed gun in hand among the trees in the roosts. Of course, as we are purely out on a turkey-shoot, dur-ing the day no louder sport is permitted than whipping the stream, or taking the greyhounds well back on the plains away from the river to course antelope, jack-rabbit, or maybe even some fine old gobbler himself.

"When, after our journey, we reached the brink of the canyon; to drop down into the valley, pass over the lowlands, and settle ourselves comfortably in camp under the shadow of the old stockade fort by the river, was a matter of but a few hours. There we waited for the afternoon shadows to lengthen and the evening to come, when off we went up the stream for five or six miles to a spot where some mighty forest monarchs with huge, bare, spreading limbs had caught the eye of one of our sporting scouts in the afternoon. Leaving our horses half a mile from the place, we walked silently along the river-bank through the jungle to the roosting-trees, where we scattered, and each man secreted himself as best he could in the underbrush, or in a hollow stump, or in the reeds of the river itself. The sun was setting, and over the hills and from the lowlands came the echoes of the familiar gobble, gobble, gobble, as each strutting, foolishly proud cock headed his admiring family for the roost, after their day's feeding on the uplands. Soon, as I lay close and hushed in my hiding-place, sounds like the clinking of silver, followed by what seemed like a breath of the wind rushing through the trees, struck my ears. I hardly dared breathe, for the sounds were made by the snapping of a gobbler's quills and his rustling feathers; and immediately a magnificent old bird, swelling and clucking, bullying his wives and abusing his weaker children to the last, trod majestically down to the water's edge, and, after taking his evening drink, winged his way to his favorite bough above, where he was joined, one by one, by his family and relations and friends, who came by tens and dozens from the surrounding country. Soon in the rapidly darkening twilight the superb old pecan-trees looked as if they were bending under a heavy crop of the most odd-shaped and lively kind of fruit. The air was filled with the peevish pi-ou! pi-ou! of the sleepy birds. Gradually the noisy fluttering subsided, and the last faint unsettled peep, even, was hushed. Dead silence reigned, and we waited and watched. The moon climbed up, and in another hour, as we looked through the tree-tops, we could make out against the light background of the sky, almost as clearly as by day, the sleeping victims of our guns and rifles. A low soft whistle was passed along from man to man; and the signal given, how different the scene became! A deafening report suddenly rang out into the silent night, a flash of light belched from the gun-muzzle, and a heavy thud followed as twenty pounds of turkey struck the ground. In our silent moccasins we flitted about under the roost, and report after report on all sides told how good the sport was and how excellent the chance that the boys at McKavett would have plenty of turkeys at their Christmas dinner. The turkeys were so surprised by the sudden noise, so entirely unprepared for the visit of the sportsman to their secluded retreat, that they did not know what to make of it, often remaining stupidly on their branch after a companion five feet off had been shot down. With the last bird shot or flown away ended our evening's sport. All the dead birds were gathered together and strapped in bunches by our saddles and on the pack-mules. It does not take many pecan and grass fed turkeys to make a load, and back we trotted to camp, the steel hoofs striking into the prairie soil with a merry ring of triumph over the night's work. The hour was nearly midnight when we sat down to the delicately browned turkey-steaks in the mess tent and realized that we had enjoyed the delights of one of the best sports in Texas—turkey-shooting in the roosts.

"Early in the afternoon following the night's sport we left the fort mounted on fine three-quarter Kentucky thoroughbreds, and, taking the eleven greyhounds, struck off six or eight miles into the plains. Then spreading into line we alternated dogs and horses, and keeping a general direction, beat up the small oak clumps, grass clusters, or mesquite jungles as we went along. Soon, with a loud whir of wings, three or four turkeys rose out of the grass ahead, started up by one of the greyhounds; the rest of the party closed in from all sides, dogs and men choosing each the bird they marked as theirs. The turkey, after towering a bit, with wings set struck off at a pace like a bullet, and with eyes fixed upward the hounds coursed after him. It was whip and spur for a mile, as hard as horse, man, and hound could make the pace. The turkey at last came down nearer and nearer the ground, its small wings refusing to bear the weight of the heavy body. Finally, down he came and began running; then the hounds closed in on him and forced him up again, as is always the case. The second flight was not a strong one, and soon he was skimming ten or even a less number of feet from the ground. Now came the sport of it all; the hounds were bunched and running like a pack behind him. Suddenly old 'Grimbeard,' in the heart of the pack, thought it was time for the supreme effort; with a rush he went to the front, and, as a mighty spring carried him up in the air, he snapped his clean, cruel fangs under the brave old gobbler, who by a great effort rose just out of reach. One after another, in the next twenty-five yards, each hound made his trial and failed. At last the old hound again made his rush, sprang up a wonderful height into the air, and cut the bird down as with a knife.

"The first flight of a turkey when being coursed is rarely more than a mile, and the second about half as long. After that, if it gets up at all again, it is for very short flights, so near the ground that it is soon cut down by any hound. The astonishing springs a greyhound who is an old hand at turkey-coursing will make, are a constant source of surprise and wonder to those fond of the sport. A turkey, after coming down from his first flight, will really perform the feat which fable attributes to the ostrich; that is, will run its head into a clump of bushes and stand motionless as if, since it cannot see its foes, it were itself equally invisible. During the day turkeys are scattered all over the plains, and it is no unusual thing to get in one afternoon's ride eight or ten of them."

CHAPTER IV

THE DEER OF THE RIVER–BOTTOMS

OF all the large game of the United States, the whitetail deer is the best known and the most widely distributed. Taking the Union as a whole, fully ten men will be found who have killed whitetail for one who has killed any other kind of large game. And it is the only ruminant animal which is able to live on in the land even when it has been pretty thickly settled. There is hardly a State wherein it does not still exist, at least in some out-of-the-way corner; and long after the elk and the buffalo have passed away, and when the bighorn and pronghorn have become rare indeed, the whitetail deer will still be common in certain parts of the country.

When, less than five years ago, cattle were first driven on to the northern plains, the whitetail were the least plentiful and the least sought after of all the large game; but they have held their own as none of the others have begun to do, and are already in certain localities more common than any other kind, and indeed in many places are more common than all other kinds put together. The ranchmen along the Powder River, for instance, now have to content themselves with whitetail venison unless they make long trips back among the hills. The same is rapidly getting to be true of the Little Missouri. This is partly because the skin and meat hunters find the chase of this deer to be the most tedious and least remunerative species of hunting, and therefore only turn their attention to

96

it when there is nothing else left to hunt, and partly because the sheep and cattle and the herdsmen who follow them are less likely to trespass on their grounds than on the grounds of other game. The whitetail is the deer of the river-bottoms and of the large creeks, whose beds contain plenty of brush and timber running down into them. It prefers the densest cover, in which it lies hid all day, and it is especially fond of wet, swampy places, where a horse runs the risk of being engulfed. Thus it is very rarely jumped by accident, and when the cattle stray into its haunts, which is but seldom, the cowboys are not apt to follow them. Besides, unlike most other game, it has no aversion to the presence of cattle, and in the morning and evening will come out and feed freely among them.

This last habit was the cause of our getting a fine buck a few days before last Christmas. The weather was bitterly cold, the spirit in the thermometer sometimes going down at night to 50° below zero and never for over a fortnight getting above −10° (Fahrenheit). Snow covered the ground, to the depth, however, of but a few inches, for in the cattle country the snowfall is always light. When the cold is so great it is far from pleasant to be out-of-doors. Still, a certain amount of riding about among the cattle and ponies had to be done, and almost every day was spent by at least one of us in the saddle. We wore the heaviest kind of all-wool underclothing, with flannels, lined boots, and great fur coats, caps, and gantlets or mittens, but yet after each ride one or the other of us would be almost sure to come in with a touch of the frost somewhere about him. On one ride I froze my nose and one cheek, and each of the men froze his ears, fingers, or toes at least once during the fortnight. This generally happened while riding over a plain or plateau with a strong wind blowing in our faces. When the wind was on our backs it was not bad fun to gallop along through the white weather, but when we had to face it, it cut through us like a keen knife. The ponies did not seem to mind the cold much, but the cattle were very uncomfortable, standing humped up in the bushes except for an hour or two at midday, when they ventured out to feed; some of the young stock, which were wintering on the range for the first time, died from the exposure. A very weak animal we would bring into the cow-shed and feed with hay; but this was only done in cases of the direst necessity, as such an animal has then to be fed for the rest of the winter, and the quantity of hay is limited. In the Bad Lands proper, cattle do not wander far, the deep ravines affording them a refuge from the bitter icy blasts of the winter gales; but if by any accident caught out on the open prairie in a blizzard, a herd will drift before it for maybe more than a hundred miles, until it finds a shelter capable of holding it. For this reason it is best to keep more or less of a lookout over all the bunches of beasts, riding about among them every few days and turning back any herd that begins to straggle toward the open plains; though in winter, when weak and emaciated, the cattle must be disturbed and driven as little as possible, or the loss among them will be fearful.

One afternoon, while most of us were away from the ranch-house, one of the cowboys, riding in from his day's outing over the range, brought word that he had seen two whitetail deer, a buck and a doe, feeding with some cattle on the side of a hill across the river, and not much more than half a mile from the house. There was about an hour of daylight left, and one of the foremen, a tall, fine-looking fellow named Ferris, the best rider on the ranch, but not an unusually good shot, started out at once after the deer; for in the late fall and early winter we generally kill a good deal of game, as it then keeps well and serves as a food-supply throughout the cold months; after January we hunt as little as possible. Ferris found the deer easily enough, but they started before he could get a standing shot at them, and when he fired as they ran, he only broke one of the buck's hind legs, just above the ankle. He followed it in the snow for several miles, across the river, and down near the house to the end of the bottom, and then back toward the house. The buck was a cunning old beast, keeping in the densest cover, and often doubling back on its trail and sneaking off to one side as his pursuer passed by. Finally it grew too dark to see the tracks any longer, and Ferris came home.

Next morning, early, we went out to where he had left the trail, feeling very sure from his description of the place (which was less than a mile from the house) that we would get the buck; for when he had abandoned the pursuit the deer was in a copse of bushes and young trees some hundreds of yards across, and in this it had doubtless spent the night, for it was extremely unlikely that, wounded and tired as it was, it would go any distance after finding that it was no longer pursued.

When we got to the thicket we first made a circuit round it to see if the wounded animal had broken cover, but though there were fresh deer tracks leading both in and out of it, none of them were made by a cripple; so we knew he was still within. It would seem to be a very easy task to track up and kill a broken-legged buck in light snow; but we had to go very cautiously, for though with only three legs he could still run a good deal faster than either of us on two, and we were anxious not to alarm him and give him a good start. Then there were several well-beaten cattle trails through the thicket, and, in addition to that, one or two other deer had been walking to and fro within it; so that it was hard work to follow the tracks. After working some little time we hit on the right trail, finding where the buck had turned into the thickest growth. While Ferris followed carefully in on the tracks, I stationed myself farther on toward the outside, knowing that the buck would in all likelihood start up wind. In a minute or two Ferris came on the bed where he had passed the night, and which he had evidently just left; a shout informed me that the game was on foot, and immediately afterward the crackling and snapping of the branches were heard as the deer rushed through them. I ran as rapidly and quietly as possible toward the place where the sounds seemed to indicate that he would break cover, stopping under a small tree. A minute afterward he appeared, some thirty yards off on the edge of the thicket, and halted for a second to look round before going into the open. Only his head and antlers were visible above the bushes which hid from view the rest of his body. He turned his head sharply toward me as I raised the rifle, and the bullet went fairly into his throat, just under the jaw, breaking his neck, and bringing him down in his tracks with hardly a kick. He was a fine buck of eight points, unusually fat, considering that the rutting season was just over. We dressed it at once, and, as the house was so near, determined we would drag it there over the snow ourselves, without going back for a horse. Each took an antler, and the body slipped along very easily; but so intense was the cold that we had to keep shifting sides all the time, the hand which grasped the horn becoming numb almost immediately.

Whitetail are very canny, and know perfectly well what threatens danger and what does not. Their larger, and to my mind nobler, relation, the blacktail, is, if anything, easier to approach and kill, and yet is by no means so apt to stay in the immediate neighborhood of a ranch where there is always more or less noise and confusion. The bottom on which my ranch-house stands is a couple of miles in length, and well wooded; all through last summer it was the home of a number of whitetails, and most of them are on it to this moment. Two fawns in especial were really amusingly tame, at one time spending their days hid in an almost impenetrable tangle of bullberry bushes, whose hither edge was barely a hundred yards from the ranch-house; and in the evening they could frequently be seen from the door as they came out to feed. In walking out after sunset, or in riding home when night had fallen, we would often run across them when it was too dark to make out anything but their flaunting white tails as they cantered out of the way. Yet for all their seeming familiarity they took good care not to expose themselves to danger. We were reluctant to molest them, but one day, having performed our usual weekly or fortnightly feat of eating up about everything there was in the house, it was determined that the two deer (for it was late in autumn and they were then well grown) should be sacrificed. Accordingly one of us sallied out, but found that the sacrifice was not to be consummated so easily, for the should-be victims appeared to distinguish perfectly well between a mere passer-by, whom they regarded with absolute indifference, and any one who harbored sinister designs. They kept such a sharp lookout and made off so rapidly if any one tried to approach them that on two evenings the appointed hunter returned empty-handed, and by the third some one else had brought in a couple of black-tail. After that, no necessity arose for molesting the two "tame deer," for whose sound common sense we had all acquired a greatly increased respect.

When not much molested whitetail feed in the evening or late afternoon; but if often shot at and chased they only come out at night. They are very partial to the water, and in the warm summer nights will come down into the prairie ponds and stand knee-deep in them, eating the succulent marsh plants. Most of the plains rivers flow through sandy or muddy beds with no vegetable growth, and to these, of course, the deer merely come down to drink or refresh themselves by bathing, as they contain nothing to eat.

Throughout the day the whitetails keep in the densest thickets, choosing if possible those of considerable extent. For this reason they are confined to the bottoms of the rivers and the mouths of the largest creeks, the cover elsewhere being too scanty to suit them. It is very difficult to make them leave one of their haunts during the daytime. They lie very close, permitting a man to pass right by them; and the twigs and branches surrounding them are so thick and interlaced that they can hear the approach of any one from a long distance off, and hence are rarely surprised. If they think there is danger that the intruder will discover them, they arise and skulk silently off through the thickest part of the brush. If followed, they keep well ahead, moving perfectly noiselessly through the thicket, often going round in a circle and not breaking cover until hard pressed; yet all the time stepping with such sharp-eyed caution that the pursuing hunter will never get a glimpse of the quarry, though the patch of brush may not be fifty rods across.

At times the whitetail will lie so close that it may almost be trodden on. One June morning I was riding down along the river, and came to a long bottom, crowded with rose-bushes all in bloom. It was crossed in every direction by cattle paths, and a drove of long-horned Texans were scattered over it. A cow-pony gets accustomed to travelling at speed along the cattle trails, and the one I bestrode threaded its way among the twisted narrow paths with perfect ease, loping rapidly onward through a sea of low rose-bushes covered with the sweet, pink flowers. They gave a bright color to the whole plain, while the air was filled with the rich, full songs of the yellow-breasted meadow-larks, as they perched on the topmost sprays of the little trees. Suddenly a whitetail doe sprang up almost from under the horse's feet, and scudded off with her white flag flaunting. There was no reason for harming her and she made a pretty picture as she bounded lightly off among the rose-red flowers, passing without heed through the ranks of the long-horned and savage-looking steers.

Doubtless she had a little spotted fawn not far away. These wee fellows soon after birth grow very cunning and able to take care of themselves, keeping in the densest part of the brush, through which they run and dodge like a rabbit. If taken young, they grow very tame and are most dainty pets. One which we had round the house answered well to its name. It was at first fed with milk, which it lapped eagerly from a saucer, sharing the meal with the two cats, who rather resented its presence and cuffed it heartily when they thought it was greedy and was taking more than its share. As it grew older it would eat bread or potatoes from our hands, and was perfectly fearless. At night it was let go or put in the cow-shed, whichever was handiest, but it was generally round in time for breakfast next morning. A blue ribbon with a bell attached was hung round its neck, so as to prevent its being shot; but in the end it shared the fate of all pets, for one night it went off and never came back again. Perhaps it strayed away of its own accord, but more probably some raw hand at hunting saw it and slaughtered it without noticing the bell hanging from its neck.

The best way to kill whitetail is to still-hunt carefully through their haunts at dusk, when the deer leave the deep recesses in which their day-beds lie and come out to feed in the more open parts. For this kind of hunting, no dress is so good as a buckskin suit and moccasins. The moccasins enable one to tread softly and noiselessly, while the buckskin suit is of a most inconspicuous color, and makes less rustling than any other material when passing among projecting twigs. Care must be taken to always hunt up wind and to advance without any sudden motions, walking close in to the edge of the thickets and keeping a sharp lookout, as it is of the first importance to see the game before the game sees you. The feeding-grounds of the deer may vary. If they are on a bottom studded with dense copses, they move out on the open between them; if they are in a dense wood, they feed along its edges; but, by preference, they keep in the little glades and among the bushes underneath the trees. Wherever they may be found, they are rarely far from thick cover and are always on the alert, lifting up their heads every few bites they take to see if any danger threatens them.   But, unlike the antelope, they seem to rely for safety even more upon escaping observation than upon discovering danger while it is still far off, and so are usually in sheltered places where they cannot be seen at any distance.   Hence, shots at them are generally obtained, if obtained at all, at very much closer range than at any other kind of game; the average distance would be nearer fifty than a hundred yards. On the other hand, more of the shots obtained are running ones than is the case with the same number taken at antelope or blacktail.

If the deer is standing just out of a fair-sized wood, it can often be obtained by creeping up along the edge; if seen among the large trees, it is even more easily still-hunted, as a tree-trunk can be readily kept in line with the quarry and thus prevent its suspecting any approach.   But only a few whitetail are killed by regular and careful stalking; in much the greater number of instances the hunter simply beats, patiently and noiselessly from leeward, carefully through the clumps of trees and bushes, always prepared to see his game, and with his rifle at the ready.   Sooner or later, as he steals round a corner, he either sees the motionless form of a deer, not a great distance off, regarding him intently for a moment before taking flight, or else he hears a sudden crash, and catches a glimpse of the animal as it lopes into the bushes.   In either case, he must shoot quick; but the shot is a close one.

If he is heard or seen a long way off, the deer is very apt, instead of running away at full speed, to skulk off quietly through the bushes.   But when suddenly startled, the whitetail makes off at a great rate, at a rolling gallop, the long, broad tail, pure white, held up in the air.   In the dark or in thick woods, often all that can be seen is the flash of white from the tail. The head is carried low and well forward in running; a buck, when passing swiftly through thick underbrush, usually throws his horns back almost on his shoulders, with his nose held straight in front. Whitetail venison is, in season, most delicious eating, only inferior to the mutton of the mountain-sheep.

Among the places which are most certain to contain whitetails may be mentioned the tracts of swampy ground covered with willows and the like, which are to be found in a few (and but a few) localities through the plains country; there are, for example, several such along the Powder River, just below where the Little Powder empties into it. Here there is a dense growth of slim-stemmed young trees, sometimes almost impenetrable, and in other places opening out into what seem like arched passageways, through which a man must at times go almost on all fours. The ground may be covered with rank shrubbery, or it may be bare mud with patches of tall reeds. Here and there, scattered through these swamps, are pools of water, and sluggish ditches occasionally cut their way deep below the surface of the muddy soil. Game trails are abundant all through them, and now and then there is a large path beaten out by the cattle; while at intervals there are glades and openings. A horse must be very careful in going through such a swamp or he will certainly get mired, and even a man must be cautious about his footing. In the morning or late afternoon a man stands a good chance of killing deer in such a place, if he hunts carefully through it. It is comparatively easy to make but little noise in the mud and among the wet, yielding swamp plants; and by moving cautiously along the trails and through the openings, one can see some little distance ahead; and toward evening the pools should be visited, and the borders as far back as possible carefully examined for any deer that come to drink, and the glades should be searched through for any that may be feeding. In the soft mud, too, a fresh track can be followed as readily as if in snow, and without exposing the hunter to such probability of detection. If a shot is obtained at all, it is at such close quarters as to more than counterbalance the dimness of the light, and to render the chance of a miss very unlikely. Such hunting is, for a change, very pleasant, the perfect stillness of the place, the quiet with which one has to move, and the constant expectation of seeing game keeping one's nerves always on the stretch; but after a while it grows tedious, and it makes a man feel cramped to be always ducking and crawling through such places. It is not to be compared, in cool weather, with still-hunting on the open hills; nevertheless, in the furious heat of the summer sun it has its advantages, for it is not often so oppressingly hot in the swamp as it is on the open prairie in the dry thickets.

The whitetail is the only kind of large game for which the shotgun can occasionally be used. At times in the dense brush it is seen, if seen at all, at such short distances, and the shots have to be taken so hurriedly, that the shotgun is really the best weapon wherewith to attempt its death. One method of taking it is to have trained dogs hunt through a valley and drive the deer to guns stationed at the opposite end. With a single slow hound, given to baying, a hunter can often follow the deer on foot in the method adopted in most of the Eastern States for the capture of both the gray and the red fox. If the dog is slow and noisy, the deer will play round in circles and can be cut off and shot from a stand.

107

Any dog will soon put a deer out of a thicket, or
drive it down a valley; but without a dog it is often
difficult to drive deer toward the runway or place
at which the guns are stationed, for the whitetail will
often skulk round and round a thicket instead of putting out of it when a man enters; and even when started
it may break back past the driver instead of going
toward the guns.

In all these habits whitetail are the very reverse of
such game as antelope. Antelope care nothing at all
about being seen, and indeed rather court observation,
while the chief anxiety of a whitetail is to go unobserved. In passing through a country where there are
antelope, it is almost impossible not to see them; while,
where there are an equal number of whitetail, the odds
are manifold against travellers catching a glimpse of a
single individual. The pronghorn is perfectly indifferent as to whether the pursuer sees him, so long as in his
turn he is able to see the pursuer; and he relies entirely
upon his speed and wariness for his safety; he never
trusts for a moment to eluding observation. Whitetail, on the contrary, rely almost exclusively either upon
lying perfectly still and letting the danger pass by, or
else, upon skulking off so slyly as to be unobserved; it
is only when hard pressed or suddenly startled that
they bound boldly and freely away.

In many of the dense jungles without any opening
the brush is higher than a man's head, and one has then
practically no chance at all of getting a shot on foot
when crossing through such places. But I have known
instances where a man had himself driven in a tall light
wagon through a place like this, and got several snap-
shots at the deer, as he caught momentary glimpses of
them stealing off through the underbrush; and another

method of pursuit in these jungles is occasionally followed by one of my foremen, who, mounted on a quiet horse which will stand fire, pushes through the bushes and now and then gets a quick shot at a deer from horseback. I have tried this method myself, but without success, for, though my hunting-horse, old Manitou, stands as steady as a rock, yet I find it impossible to shoot the rifle with any degree of accuracy from the saddle.

Except on such occasions as those just mentioned, the whitetail is rarely killed while hunting on horseback. This last term, by the way, must not be understood in the sense in which it would be taken by the fox-hunter of the South, or by the Californian and Texan horsemen who course hare, antelope, and wild turkey with their fleet greyhounds. With us, hunting on horseback simply means that the horse is ridden not only to the hunting-grounds, but also through them until the game is discovered; then the hunter immediately dismounts, shooting at once if the animal is near enough and has seen him, or stalking up to it on foot if it is a good distance off and he is still unobserved. Where great stretches of country have to be covered, as in antelope-shooting, hunting on horseback is almost the only way followed; but the haunts and habits of the whitetail deer render it nearly useless to try to kill them in this way, as the horse would be sure to alarm them by making a noise, and even if he did not there would hardly be time to dismount and take a snap-shot. Only once have I ever killed a whitetail buck while hunting on horseback; and at that time I had been expecting to fall in with blacktail.

This was while we had been making a wagon trip to the westward, following the old Keogh trail, which was made by the heavy army wagons that journeyed to Fort Keogh in the old days when the soldiers were, except a few daring trappers, the only white men to be seen on the last great hunting-ground of the Indians. It was abandoned as a military route several years ago, and is now only rarely travelled over, either by the canvas-topped ranch wagon of some wandering cattlemen—like ourselves—or else by a small party of emigrants, in two or three prairie-schooners which contain all their household goods. Nevertheless, it is still as plain and distinct as ever. The two deep parallel ruts, cut into the sod by the wheels of the heavy wagon, stretch for scores of miles in a straight line across the level prairie, and take great turns and doublings to avoid the impassable portions of the Bad Lands. The track is always perfectly plain, for in the dry climate of the Western plains the action of the weather tends to preserve rather than to obliterate it; where it leads downhill, the snow water has cut and widened the ruts into deep gullies, so that a wagon has at those places to travel alongside the road. From any little rising in the prairie the road can be seen, a long way off, as a dark line, which, when near, resolves itself into two sharply defined parallel cuts. Such a road is a great convenience as a landmark. When travelling along it, or one like it, the hunters can separate in all directions, and no matter how long or how far they hunt, there is never the least difficulty about finding camp. For the general direction in which the road lies is, of course, kept in mind, and it can be reached whether the sun is down or not; then a glance tells if the wagon has passed, and all that remains to be done is to gallop along the trail until camp is found.

On the trip in question we had at first very bad

weather.   Leaving the ranch in the morning, two of us, who were mounted, pushed on ahead to hunt, the wagon following slowly, with a couple of spare saddle-ponies leading behind it.   Early in the afternoon, while riding over the crest of a great divide, which separates the drainage-basins of two important creeks, we saw that a tremendous storm was brewing with that marvellous rapidity which is so marked a characteristic of weather changes on the plains.   A towering mass of clouds gathered in the northwest, turning that whole quarter of the sky to an inky blackness.   From there the storm rolled down toward us at a furious speed, obscuring by degrees the light of the sun, and extending its wings toward each side, as if to overlap any that tried to avoid its path.   Against the dark background of the mass could be seen pillars and clouds of gray mist, whirled hither and thither by the wind, and sheets of level rain driven before it.   The edges of the wings tossed to and fro, and the wind shrieked and moaned as it swept over the prairie.   It was a storm of unusual intensity; the prairie-fowl rose in flocks before it, scudding with spread wings toward the thickest cover, and the herds of antelope ran across the plain like race-horses to gather in the hollows and behind the low ridges.

We spurred hard to get out of the open, riding with loose reins for the creek.   The centre of the storm swept by behind us, fairly across our track, and we only got a wipe from the tail of it.   Yet this itself we could not have faced in the open.   The first gust caught us a few hundred yards from the creek, almost taking us from the saddle, and driving the rain and hail in stinging level sheets against us.   We galloped to the edge of a deep washout, scrambled into it at the risk of our necks, and huddled up with our horses underneath the windward bank. Here we remained pretty well sheltered until the storm was over. Although it was August, the air became very cold. The wagon was fairly caught, and would have been blown over if the top had been on; the driver and horses escaped without injury, pressing under the leeward side, the storm coming so level that they did not need a roof to protect them from the hail. Where the centre of the whirlwind struck, it did great damage, sheets of hailstones as large as pigeons' eggs striking the earth with the velocity of bullets; next day the hailstones could have been gathered up by the bushel from the heaps that lay in the bottom of the gullies and ravines. One of my cowboys was out in the storm, during whose continuance he crouched under his horse's belly; coming home he came across some antelope so numb and stiffened that they could barely limp out of the way.

Near my ranch the hail killed quite a number of lambs. These were the miserable remnants of a flock of twelve thousand sheep driven into the Bad Lands a year before, four-fifths of whom had died during the first winter, to the delight of all the neighboring cattlemen. Cattlemen hate sheep because they eat the grass so close that cattle cannot live on the same ground. The sheep-herders are a morose, melancholy set of men, generally afoot, and with no companionship except that of the bleating idiots they are hired to guard. No man can associate with sheep and retain his self-respect. Intellectually, a sheep is about on the lowest level of the brute creation; why the early Christians admired it, whether young or old, is to a good cattleman always a profound mystery.

The wagon came on to the creek, along whose banks

we had taken shelter, and we then went into camp. It rained all night, and there was a thick mist, with continual sharp showers, all the next day and night. The wheeling was, in consequence, very heavy, and, after striking the Keogh trail, we were able to go along it but a few miles before the fagged-out look of the team and the approach of evening warned us that we should have to go into camp while still a dozen miles from any pool or spring. Accordingly, we made what would have been a dry camp had it not been for the incessant downpour of rain, which we gathered in the canvas wagon-sheet and in our oilskin overcoats in sufficient quantity to make coffee, having with infinite difficulty started a smouldering fire just to leeward of the wagon. The horses, feeding on the soaked grass, did not need water. An antelope, with the bold and heedless curiosity sometimes shown by its tribe, came up within two hundred yards of us as we were building the fire; but though one of us took a shot at him, it missed. Our chaps and oilskins had kept us perfectly dry, and as soon as our frugal supper was over, we coiled up among the bundles and boxes inside the wagon and slept soundly until daybreak.

When the sun rose next day, the third we were out, the sky was clear, and we two horsemen at once prepared to make a hunt. Some three miles off to the south of where we were camped, the plateau on which we were sloped off into a great expanse of broken ground, with chains upon chains of steep hills, separated by deep valleys, winding and branching in every direction, their bottoms filled with trees and brushwood. Toward this place we rode, intending to go into it some little distance, and then to hunt along through it near the edge. As soon as we got down near the brushy ravine we rode along without talking, guiding the horses as far as possible on earthy places, where they would neither stumble nor strike their feet against stones, and not letting our rifle-barrels or spurs clink against anything. Keeping outside of the brush, a little up the side of the hill, one of us would ride along each side of the ravine, examining intently with our eyes every clump of trees or brushwood. For some time we saw nothing, but, finally, as we were riding both together round the jutting spur of a steep hill, my companion suddenly brought his horse to a halt, and, pointing across the shelving bend to a patch of trees well up on the opposite side of a broad ravine, asked me if I did not see a deer in it. I was off the horse in a second, throwing the reins over his head. We were in the shadow of the cliff-shoulder, and with the wind in our favor; so we were unlikely to be observed by the game. I looked long and eagerly toward the spot indicated, which was about a hundred and twenty-five yards from us, but at first could see nothing. By this time, however, the experienced plainsman who was with me was satisfied that he was right in his supposition, and he told me to try again and look for a patch of red. I saw the patch at once, just glimmering through the bushes, but should certainly never have dreamed it was a deer if left to myself. Watching it attentively I soon saw it move enough to satisfy me where the head lay; kneeling on one knee and (as it was a little beyond point-blank range) holding at the top of the portion visible, I pulled trigger, and the bright-colored patch disappeared from among the bushes. The aim was a good one, for, on riding up to the brink of the ravine, we saw a fine white-tailed buck lying below us, shot through just behind the shoulder; he was still in the red coat, with his antlers in the velvet.

A deer is far from being such an easy animal to see as the novice is apt to suppose. Until the middle of September he is in the red coat; after that time he is in the gray; but it is curious how each one harmonizes in tint with certain of the surroundings. A red doe lying down is, at a little distance, indistinguishable from the soil on which she is; while a buck in the gray can hardly be made out in dead timber. While feeding quietly or standing still, they rarely show the proud, free port we are accustomed to associate with the idea of a buck, and look rather ordinary, humble-seeming animals, not at all conspicuous or likely to attract the hunter's attention; but once let them be frightened, and as they stand facing the danger or bound away from it, their graceful movements and lordly bearing leave nothing to be desired. The blacktail is a still nobler-looking animal; while an antelope, on the contrary, though as light and quick on its feet as is possible for any animal not possessing wings to be, yet has an angular, goat-like look, and by no means conveys to the beholder the same idea of grace that a deer does.

In coming home, on this wagon trip, we made a long moonlight ride, passing over between sunset and sunrise what had taken us three days' journey on the outward march. Of our riding-horses, two were still in good condition and able to stand a twenty-four hours' jaunt, in spite of hard work and rough usage; the spare ones, as well as the team, were pretty well done up and could get along but slowly. All day long we had been riding beside the wagon over barren sage-brush plains, following the dusty trails made by the beef-herds that had been driven toward one of the Montana shipping towns.

When we halted for the evening meal we came near learning by practical experience how easy it is to start a prairie fire. We were camped by a dry creek on a broad bottom covered with thick short grass, as dry as so much tinder. We wished to burn a good circle clear for the camp-fire; lighting it, we stood round with branches to keep it under. While thus standing a puff of wind struck us; the fire roared like a wild beast as it darted up; and our hair and eyelashes were well singed before we had beaten it out. At one time it seemed as if, though but a very few feet in extent, it would actually get away from us; in which case the whole bottom would have been a blazing furnace within five minutes.

After supper, looking at the worn-out condition of the team, we realized that it would take three more days' travelling at the rate we had been going to bring us in, and as the country was monotonous, without much game, we concluded we would leave the wagon with the driver and, taking advantage of the full moon, push through the whole distance before breakfast next morning. Accordingly, we at nine o'clock again saddled the tough little ponies we had ridden all day and loped off out of the circle of firelight. For nine hours we rode steadily, generally at a quick lope, across the moonlit prairie. The hoof-beats of our horses rang out in steady rhythm through the silence of the night, otherwise unbroken save now and then by the wailing cry of a coyote. The rolling plains stretched out on all sides of us, shimmering in the clear moonlight; and occasionally a band of spectral-looking antelope swept silently away from before our path. Once we went by a drove of Texan cattle, who stared wildly at the intruders; as we passed they charged down by us, the ground rumbling beneath their tread, while their long

116

horns knocked against each other with a sound like the clattering of a multitude of castanets. We could see clearly enough to keep our general course over the trackless plain, steering by the stars where the prairie was perfectly level and without landmarks; and our ride was timed well, for as we galloped down into the valley of the Little Missouri the sky above the line of the level bluffs in our front was crimson with the glow of the unrisen sun.

CHAPTER V

THE BLACKTAIL DEER

FAR different from the low-scudding, brush-loving whitetail is the blacktail deer, the deer of the ravines and the rocky uplands. In general shape and form, both are much alike; but the blacktail is the larger of the two, with heavier antlers of which the prongs start from one another as if each of the tines of a two-pronged pitchfork had bifurcated; and in some cases it looks as if the process had been again repeated. The tail—instead of being broad and bushy as a squirrel's, spreading from the base and pure white to the tip—is round and close-haired, with the end black, though the rest is white. If an ordinary deer is running, its flaunting flag is almost its most conspicuous part; but no one would notice the tail of a blacktail deer.

All deer vary greatly in size; and a small blacktail buck will be surpassed in bulk by many whitetails; but the latter never reaches the weight and height sometimes attained by the former. The same holds true of the antlers borne by the two animals; on the average, those of the blacktail are the heavier, and exceptionally large antlers of this species are larger than any of the whitetail. Bucks of both kinds very often have, when full-grown, more than the normal number of ten points; sometimes these many-pronged antlers will be merely deformities, while in other instances the points are more symmetrical and add greatly to the beauty and grandeur of the head. The venison of the

118

blacktail is said to be inferior in quality to that of the whitetail; but I have never been able to detect much difference, though, perhaps, on the whole, the latter is slightly better.

The gaits of the two animals are widely different. The whitetail runs at a rolling gallop, striking the ground with the forward feet first, the head held forward. The blacktail, on the contrary, holds its head higher up, and progresses by a series of prodigious bounds, striking the earth with all four feet at once, the legs held nearly stiff. It seems like an extraordinary method of running; and the violent exertion tires the deer sooner than does the more easy and natural gait of the whitetail; but for a mile or so these rapidly succeeding bounds enable the blacktail to get over the ground at remarkable speed. Over rough ground, along precipitous slopes and among the boulders of rocky cliffs, it will go with surprising rapidity and surefootedness, only surpassed by the feats of the bighorn in similar localities, and not equalled by those of any other plains game.

One of the noticeable things in Western plains hunting is the different zones or bands of territory inhabited by different kinds of game. Along the alluvial lands of the rivers and large creeks is found the whitetail. Back of those alluvial lands generally comes a broad tract of broken, hilly country scantily clad with brush in some places; this is the abode of the blacktail deer. And where these hills rise highest and where the ground is most rugged and barren, there the bighorn is found. After this hilly country is passed, in travelling away from the river, we come to the broad, level plains, the domain of the antelope. Of course the habitats of the different species overlap at the edges; and this overlapping is most extended in the cases of the bighorn and the blacktail.

The Bad Lands are the favorite haunts of the blacktail. Here the hills are steep and rugged, cut up and crossed in every direction by canyon-like ravines and valleys, which branch out and subdivide in the most intricate and perplexing manner. Here and there are small springs, or pools, marked by the greener vegetation growing round them. Along the bottoms and sides of the ravines there are patches of scrubby undergrowth, and in many of the pockets or glens in the sides of the hills the trees grow to some little height. High buttes rise here and there, naked to the top, or else covered with stunted pines and cedars which also grow in the deep ravines and on the edges of the sheer canyons. Such lands, where the ground is roughest and where there is some cover, even though scattered and scanty, are the best places to find the blacktail. Naturally their pursuit needs very different qualities in the hunter from those required in the chase of the whitetail. In the latter case stealth and caution are the prime requisites; while the man who would hunt and kill the deer of the uplands has more especial need of energy, activity, and endurance, of good judgment and of skill with the rifle. Hunting the blacktail is beyond all comparison the nobler sport. Indeed, there is no kind of plains hunting, except only the chase of the bighorn, more fitted to bring out the best and hardiest of the many qualities which go to make up a good hunter.

It is still a moot question whether it is better to hunt on horseback or on foot; but the course of events is rapidly deciding it in favor of the latter method. Undoubtedly, it is easier and pleasanter to hunt on horseback; and it has the advantage of covering a great deal of ground. But it is impossible to advance with such caution, and it is difficult to shoot as quickly, as when on foot; and where the deer are shy and not very plenty, the most enthusiastic must, slowly and reluctantly but surely, come to the conclusion that a large bag can only be made by the still-hunter who goes on foot. Of course in the plains country it is not as in mountainous or thickly wooded regions, and the horse should almost always be taken as a means of conveyance to the hunting-grounds and from one point to another; but the places where game is expected should, as a rule, be hunted over on foot. This rule is by no means a general one, however. There are still many localities where the advantage of covering a great deal of ground more than counterbalances the disadvantage of being on horseback. About one-third of my hunts are still made on horseback; and in almost all the others I take old Manitou to carry me to and from the grounds and to pack out any game that may be killed. A hunting-horse is of no use whatever unless he will permit a man to jump from his back and fire with the greatest rapidity; and nowhere does practice have more to do with success than in the case of jumping off a horse to shoot at game which has just been seen. The various movements take a novice a good deal of time; while an old hand will be off and firing with the most instantaneous quickness. Manitou can be left anywhere at a moment's warning, while his rider leaps off, shoots at a deer from almost under his head, and perhaps chases the wounded animal a mile or over; and on his return the good old fellow will be grazing away, perfectly happy and contented, and not making a movement to run off or evade being caught.

One method of killing deer on horseback is very ex-

citing. Many of the valleys or ravines extend with
continual abrupt turns and windings for several miles,
the brush and young trees stretching with constant
breaks down the middle of the bottom, and leaving a
space on each side along which a surefooted horse can
gallop at speed. Two men, on swift, hardy horses, can
hunt down such a ravine very successfully at evening,
by each taking a side and galloping at a good speed
the whole length against the wind. The patter of the
unshod hoofs over the turf makes but little noise; and
the turns are so numerous and abrupt, and the horses
go so swiftly, that the hunters come on the deer almost
before the latter are aware of their presence. If it is
so late in the day that the deer have begun to move
they will find the horses close up before they have a
suspicion of danger, while if they are still lying in the
cover the suddenness of the appearance of their foe is
apt so to startle them as to make them break out and
show themselves instead of keeping hid, as they would
probably do if they perceived the approach from afar.
One thus gets a close running shot or if he waits a minute he will generally get a standing shot at some little
distance, owing to a very characteristic habit of the
blacktail. This is its custom of turning round, apparently actuated simply by curiosity, to look at the
object which startled it, after it has run off a hundred
and fifty yards or so. It then stands motionless for a
few seconds, and offers a chance for a steady shot. If
the chance is not improved, no other will offer, for as
soon as the deer has ended its scrutiny it is off again,
and this time will not halt till well out of danger.
Owing to its singular gait, a succession of buck jumps,
the blacktail is a peculiarly difficult animal to hit while
on the run; and it is best to wait until it stops and

122

turns before taking the shot, as, if fired at, the report will generally so alarm it as to make it continue its course without halting to look back. Some of the finest antlers in my possession come from bucks killed by this method of hunting; and it is a most exhilarating form of sport, the horse galloping rapidly over what is often very broken ground, and the senses being continually on the alert for any sign of game. The rush and motion of the horse, and the care necessary to guide it and at the same time be in constant readiness for a shot, prevent the chase having any of the monotony that is at times inseparable from still-hunting proper.

Nevertheless, it is by still-hunting that most deer are killed, and the highest form of hunting craft is shown in the science of the skilful still-hunter. With sufficient practice, any man who possesses common sense, and is both hardy and persevering, can become, to a certain extent, a still-hunter. But the really *good* still-hunter is born rather than made; though, of course, in addition to possessing the gifts naturally, he must also have developed them, by constant practice, to the highest point possible. One of the foremen on my ranch is a really remarkably good hunter and game shot, and another does almost as well; but the rest of us are not, and never will be, anything very much out of the common. By dint of practice, we have learned to shoot as well at game as at a target; and those of us who are fond of the sport hunt continually, and so get a good deal of game at one time or another. Hunting through good localities, up-wind, quietly and perseveringly, we come upon quite a number of animals; and we can kill a standing shot at a fair distance and a running shot close up, and by good luck every now and then kill far off; but to much more than is implied in the description of such modest feats we cannot pretend.

After the disappearance of the buffalo and the thinning out of the elk, the blacktail was, and in most places it still is, the game most sought after by the hunters; I have myself shot as many of them as of all other kinds of plains game put together. But for this very reason it is fast disappearing; and bids fair to be the next animal, after the buffalo and elk, to vanish from the places that formerly knew it. The bighorn and the pronghorn are more difficult to stalk and kill, partly from their greater natural wariness, and partly from the kind of ground on which they are found. But it seems at first sight strange that the blacktail should be exterminated or driven away so much more quickly than the whitetail, when it has sharper ears and nose, is more tenacious of life, and is more wary. The main reason is to be found in the difference in the character of the haunts of the two creatures. The blacktail is found on much more open ground, where the animals can be seen farther off, where it is much easier to take advantage of the direction of the wind and to get along without noise, and where far more country can be traversed in a given time; and though the average length of the shots taken is in one case two or three times as great as in the other, yet this is more than counterbalanced by the fact that they are more often standing ones, and that there is usually much more time for aiming. Moreover, one kind of sport can be followed on horseback, while the other must be followed on foot; and then the chase of the whitetail, in addition, is by far the more tedious and patience-trying. And the blacktail are much the more easily scared or driven out of a locality by persecution or by the encroaching settlements. All these qualities combine to make it less able to hold its own against mankind than its smaller rival. It is the favorite game of the skin-hunters and meat-hunters, and has, in consequence, already disappeared from many places, while in others its extermination is going on at a frightfully rapid rate, owing to its being followed in season and out of season without mercy. Besides, the cattle are very fond of just the places to which it most often resorts; and wherever cattle go the cowboys ride about after them, with their ready six-shooters at their hips. They blaze away at any deer they see, of course, and in addition to now and then killing or wounding one, continually harry and disturb the poor animals. In the more remote and inaccessible districts the blacktail will long hold its own, to be one of the animals whose successful pursuit will redound most to the glory of the still-hunter; but in a very few years it will have ceased entirely to be one of the common game animals of the plains.

Its great curiosity is one of the disadvantages under which it labors in the fierce struggle for existence, compared to the whitetail. The latter, when startled, does not often stop to look round; but, as already said, the former will generally do so after having gone a few hundred feet. The first blacktail I ever killed—unfortunately killed, for the body was not found until spoiled—was obtained owing solely to this peculiarity. I had been riding up along the side of a brushy coulée, when a fine buck started out some thirty yards ahead. Although so close, my first shot, a running one, was a miss; when a couple of hundred yards off, on the very crest of the spur up which he had run, he stopped and turned partially round. Firing again from a rest, the bullet broke his hind leg far up and went into his body. Off he went on three legs, and I after him as fast as the horse could gallop. He went over the spur and down into the valley of the creek from which the coulée branched up, in very bad ground. My pony was neither fast nor surefooted, but of course in half a mile overhauled the three-legged deer, which turned short off and over the side of the hill flanking the valley. Instead of running right up on it I foolishly dismounted and began firing; after the first shot—a miss—it got behind a boulder hitherto unseen, and thence over the crest. The pony meanwhile had slipped its hind leg into the rein; when, after some time, I got it out and galloped up to the ridge, the most careful scrutiny of which my unpractised eyes were capable failed to discover a track on the dry ground, hard as granite. A day or two afterward the place where the carcass lay was made known by the vultures, gathered together from all parts to feed upon it.

When fired at from a place of hiding, deer which have not been accustomed to the report of a gun will often appear confused and uncertain what to do. On one occasion, while hunting in the mountains, I saw an old buck with remarkably large horns, of curious and beautiful shape, more symmetrical than in most instances where the normal form is departed from. The deer was feeding in a wide, gently sloping valley, containing no cover from behind which to approach him. We were in no need of meat, but the antlers were so fine that I felt they justified the death of their bearer. After a little patient waiting, the buck walked out of the valley, and over the ridge on the other side, moving up-wind; I raced after him, and crept up behind a thick growth of stunted cedars which had started up from among some boulders. The deer was about a hundred yards off, down in the valley. Out of breath and overconfident, I fired hastily, overshooting him. The wind blew the smoke back away from the ridge, so that he saw nothing, while the echo prevented his placing the sound. He took a couple of jumps nearer, when he stood still and was again overshot. Again he took a few jumps, and the third shot went below him, and the fourth just behind him. This was too much, and away he went. In despair, I knelt down (I had been firing offhand), took a steady aim well forward on his body, and fired, bringing him down, but with small credit to the shot, for the bullet had gone into his hip, paralyzing his hindquarters. The antlers are the finest pair I ever got, and form a magnificent ornament for the hall; but the shooting is hardly to be recalled with pleasure. Still, though certainly very bad, it was not quite as discreditable as the mere target-shot would think. I have seen many a crack marksman at the target do quite as bad, missing when out in the field, and that not once but again and again.

Of course in those parts of the wilderness where the blacktail are entirely unused to man, they are as easy to approach (from the leeward side) as is any and every other kind of game under like conditions. In lonely spots, to which hunters rarely or never penetrate, deer of this species will stand and look at a hunter without offering to run away till he is within fifty yards of them, if he will advance quietly. In a far-off mountain forest I have more than once shot a young buck at less than that distance as he stood motionless, gazing at me, although but little caution had been used in approaching him.

But a short experience of danger on the part of the

blacktail changes all this; and where hunters are often afoot, he becomes as wild and wary as may be. Then the successful still-hunter shows that he is indeed well up in the higher forms of hunting craft. For the man who can, not once by accident, but again and again as a regular thing, single-handed, find and kill his black-tail, has shown that he is no mere novice in his art; still-hunting the blacktail is a sport that only the skil-ful can follow with good results, and one which implies in the successful sportsman the presence of most of the still-hunter's rarest attributes. All of the qualities which a still-hunter should possess are of service in the pursuit of any kind of game; but different ones will be called into especial play in hunting different kinds of animals. Thus, to be a successful hunter after any-thing, a man should be patient, resolute, hardy, and with good judgment; he should have good lungs and stout muscles; he should be able to move with noiseless stealth; and he should be keen-eyed, and a first-rate marksman with the rifle. But in different kinds of shooting, the relative importance of these qualities varies greatly. In hunting whitetail deer, the two prime requisites are stealth and patience. If the quarry is a bighorn, a man needs especially to be sound in wind and limbs, and to be both hardy and resolute. Skill in the use of the long-range rifle counts for more in antelope-hunting than in any other form of sport; and it is in this kind of hunting alone that good marks-manship is more important than anything else. With dangerous game, cool and steady nerves are of the first consequence; all else comes after. Then, again, in the use of the rifle, the *kind* of skill—not merely the *degree* of skill—required to hunt different animals may vary greatly. In shooting whitetail, it is especially neces-

128

sary to be a good snap-shot at running game; when the distance is close, quickness is an essential. But at antelope there is plenty of time, and what is necessary is ability to judge distance and capacity to hit a small stationary object at long range.

The different degrees of estimation in which the chase of the various kinds of plains game is held depend less upon the difficulty of capture than upon the nature of the qualities in the hunter which each particular form of hunting calls into play. A man who is hardy, resolute, and a good shot, has come nearer to realizing the ideal of a bold and free hunter than is the case with one who is merely stealthy and patient; and so, though to kill a whitetail is rather more difficult than to kill a blacktail, yet the chase of the latter is certainly the nobler form of sport, for it calls into play and either develops or implies the presence of much more manly qualities than does the other. Most hunters would find it nearly as difficult to watch in silence by a salt-lick throughout the night, and then to butcher with a shotgun a whitetail, as it would be to walk on foot through rough ground from morning till evening, and fairly to approach and kill a blacktail; yet there is no comparison between the degree of credit to be attached to one feat and that to be attached to the other. Indeed, if difficulty in killing is to be taken as a criterion, a mink or even a weasel would have to stand as high up in the scale as a deer, were the animals equally plenty.

Ranged in the order of the difficulty with which they are approached and slain, plains game stand as follows: bighorn, antelope, whitetail, blacktail, elk, and buffalo. But, as regards the amount of manly sport furnished by the chase of each, the whitetail should stand at the bottom of the list, and the elk and blacktail abreast of the antelope.

Other things being equal, the length of an animal's stay in the land, when the arch-foe of all lower forms of animal life has made his appearance therein, depends upon the difficulty with which he is hunted and slain. But other influences have to be taken into account. The bighorn is shy and retiring; very few, compared to the whole number, will be killed; and yet the others vanish completely. Apparently, they will not remain where they are hunted and disturbed. With antelope and whitetail this does not hold; they will cling to a place far more tenaciously, even if often harassed. The former, being the more conspicuous and living in such open ground, is apt to be more persecuted; while the whitetail, longer than any other animal, keeps its place in the land in spite of the swinish game-butchers, who hunt for hides and not for sport or actual food, and who murder the gravid doe and the spotted fawn with as little hesitation as they would kill a buck of ten points. No one who is not himself a sportsman and lover of nature can realize the intense indignation with which a true hunter sees these butchers at their brutal work of slaughtering the game, in season and out, for the sake of the few dollars they are too lazy to earn in any other and more honest way.

All game animals rely upon both eyes, ears, and nose to warn them of the approach of danger; but the amount of reliance placed on each sense varies greatly in different species. Those found out on the plains pay very little attention to what they hear; indeed, in the open they can hardly be approached near enough to make of much account any ordinary amount of noise caused by the stalker, especially as the latter is walking over little but grass and soft earth. The buffalo, whose shaggy frontlet of hair falls over his eyes and prevents his seeing at any great distance, depends mainly upon his exquisite sense of smell. The antelope, on the other hand, depends almost entirely on his great bulging eyes, and very little on his nose. His sight is many times as good as that of deer, both species of which, as well as elk, rely both upon sight and hearing but most of all upon their sense of smell, for their safety. The bighorn has almost as keen eyesight as an antelope, while his ears and nose are as sensitive to sound and scent as are those of an elk.

Blacktail, like other members of the deer family, do not pay much attention to an object which is not moving. A hunter who is standing motionless or squatting down is not likely to receive attention, while a bighorn or pronghorn would probably see him and take the alarm at once; and if the blacktail is frightened and running he will run almost over a man standing in plain sight, without paying any heed to him, if the latter does not move. But the very slightest movement at once attracts a deer's attention, and deer are not subject to the panics that at times overtake other kinds of game. The blacktail has much curiosity, which often proves fatal to it, but which with it is, after all, by no means the ungovernable passion that it is with the antelope. The whitetail and the bighorn are neither overafflicted with morbid curiosity nor subject to panics or fits of stupidity; and both these animals, as well as the blacktail, seem to care very little for the death of the leader of the band, going their own ways with small regard for the fate of the chief, while elk will huddle together in a confused group and remain almost motionless when their leader is struck down.

Antelope, and more especially elk, are subject to perfect panics of unreasoning terror, during which they will often put themselves completely in the power of the hunter; while buffalo will frequently show a downright stupidity, almost unequalled.

The blacktail suffers from no such peculiarities. His eyes are good; his nose and ears excellent. He is ever alert and wary; his only failing is his occasional overcuriosity; and his pursuit taxes to the utmost the skill and resources of the still-hunter.

By all means the best coverings for the feet when still-hunting are moccasins, as with them a man can go noiselessly through ground where hobnailed boots would clatter like the hoofs of a horse; but in hunting in winter over the icy buttes and cliffs it is best to have stout shoes, with nails in the soles, and if the main work is done on horseback it is best to wear high boots, as they keep the trousers down. Indeed, in the Bad Lands boots have other advantages, for rattlesnakes abound, and against these they afford perfect protection—unless a man should happen to stumble on a snake while crawling along on all fours. But moccasins are beyond all comparison the best foot-gear for hunting. In very cold weather a fur cap which can be pulled down over the ears is a necessity; but at other times a brimmed felt hat offers better protection against both sun and rain. The clothes should be of some neutral tint—buckskin is on this account excellent—and very strong.

The still-hunter should be well acquainted with, at any rate, certain of the habits of his quarry. There are seasons when the blacktail is found in bands; such is apt to be the case when the rutting-time is over. At this period, too, the deer wander far and wide, making what may almost be called a migration; and in rutting-time the bucks follow the does at speed for miles at a stretch. But except at these seasons each individual blacktail has a certain limited tract of country to which he confines himself unless disturbed or driven away, not, of course, keeping in the same spot all the time, but working round among a particular set of ravines and coulées, where the feed is good, and where water can be obtained without going too far out of the immediate neighborhood.

Throughout the plains country the blacktail lives in the broken ground, seldom coming down to the alluvial bottoms or out on the open prairies and plateaus. But he is found all through this broken ground. Sometimes it is rolling in character, with rounded hills and gentle valleys, dotted here and there with groves of trees; or the hills may rise into high chains, covered with an open pine forest, sending off long spurs, and divided by deep valleys and basins. Such places are favorite resorts of this deer; but it is as plentiful in the Bad Lands proper. There are tracts of these which are in part or wholly of volcanic origin; then the hills are called scoria buttes. They are high and very steep, but with rounded tops and edges, and are covered, as is the ground round about, with scoriac boulders. Bushes, and sometimes a few cedar, grow among them, and though they would seem to be most unlikely places for deer, yet blacktail are very fond of them, and are very apt to be found among them. Often in the cold fall mornings they will lie out among the boulders, on the steep side of such a scoria butte, sunning themselves, far from any cover except a growth of brushwood in the bottom of the dry creeks or coulées. The grass on top of and between these scoria buttes is often very nutritious, and cattle are also fond of it. The higher buttes are choice haunts of the mountain-sheep.

Nineteen-twentieths of the Bad Lands, however, owe their origin not to volcanic action but to erosion and to the peculiar weathering forces always at work in the dry climate of the plains. Geologically, the land is for the most part composed of a set of parallel, perfectly horizontal strata of clay, marl, or sandstone, which, being of different degrees of hardness, offer some more and some less resistance to the action of the weather. The table-lands, peaks, cliffs, and jagged ridges are caused solely by the rains and torrents cutting away the land into channels, which at first are merely wash-outs, and at last grow into deep canyons, winding valleys, and narrow ravines or basins. The sides of these cuts are at first perpendicular, exposing to view the various bands of soil, perhaps of a dozen different colors; the hardest bands resist the action of the weather best and form narrow ledges stretching along the face of the cliff. Peaks of the most fantastic shape are formed in this manner; and where a ridge is worn away on each side its crest may be as sharp as a knife-blade, but all notched and jagged. The peaks and ridges vary in height from a few feet to several hundred; the sides of the buttes are generally worn down in places so as to be steeply sloping instead of perpendicular. The long washouts and the canyons and canyon-like valleys stretch and branch out in every direction; the dryness of the atmosphere, the extremes of intense heat and bitter cold, and the occasional furious rain-storms keep the edges and angles sharp and jagged, and pile up boulders and masses of loose detritus at the foot of the cliffs and great lonely crags. Sometimes the valleys are quite broad, with steep sides and with numerous pockets, separated by spurs jutting out into the bottom from the lateral ridges. Other ravines or clefts taper down to a ditch, a foot or so wide, from which the banks rise at an angle of sixty degrees to the tops of the enclosing ridges.

The faces of the terraced cliffs and sheer crags are bare of all but the scantiest vegetation, and where the Bad Lands are most rugged and broken the bighorn is the only game found. But in most places the tops of the buttes, the sides of the slopes, and the bottoms of the valleys are more or less thickly covered with the nutritious grass which is the favorite food of the blacktail.

Of course the Bad Lands grade all the way from those that are almost rolling in character to those that are so fantastically broken in form and so bizarre in color as to seem hardly properly to belong to this earth. If the weathering forces have not been very active, the ground will look, from a little distance, almost like a level plain, but on approaching nearer, it will be seen to be crossed by straight-sided gullies and canyons, miles in length, cutting across the land in every direction and rendering it almost impassable for horsemen or wagon teams. If the forces at work have been more intense, the walls between the different gullies have been cut down to thin edges, or broken through, leaving isolated peaks of strange shape, while the hollows have been channelled out deeper and deeper; such places show the extreme and most characteristic Bad Lands formation. When the weathering has gone on farther, the angles are rounded off, grass begins to grow, bushes and patches of small trees sprout up, water is found in places, and the still very rugged country becomes the favorite abode of the blacktail.

During the daytime these deer lie quietly in their beds, which are sometimes in the brush and among the matted bushes in the bottoms of the small branching coulées, or heads of the crooked ravines. More often they will be found in the thickets of stunted cedars clothing the brinks of the canyons or the precipitous slopes of the great chasms into which the ground is cleft and rent; or else among the groves of gnarled pines on the sides of the buttes, and in the basins and pockets between the spurs. If the country is not much hunted over, a buck or old doe will often take its mid-day rest out in the open, lying down among the long grass or shrubbery on one of the bare benches at the head of a ravine, at the edge of the dense brush with which its bottom and sides are covered. In such a case, a position is always chosen from which a lookout can be kept all around; and the moment any suspicious object is seen, the deer slips off into the thicket below him. Perhaps the favorite resting-places are the rounded edges of the gorges, just before the sides of the latter break sheer off. Here the deer lies, usually among a few straggling pines or cedars, on the very edge of the straight side-wall of the canyon, with a steep-shelving slope above him, so that he cannot be seen from the summit; and in such places it is next to impossible to get at him. If lying on a cedar-grown spur or ridge-point, the still-hunter has a better chance, for the evergreen needles with which the ground is covered enable a man to walk noiselessly, and, by stooping or going on all fours, he can keep under the branches. But it is at all times hard and unsatisfactory work to find and successfully still-hunt a deer that is enjoying its day rest. Generally, the only result is to find the warm, fresh bed from which the deer has just sneaked off, the blades of grass still slowly rising, after the hasty departure of the weight that has flattened them down; or else, if in dense cover, the hunter suddenly hears a scramble, a couple of crashing bounds through the twigs and dead limbs, and gets a momentary glimpse of a dark outline vanishing into the thicket as the sole reward of his labor. Almost the only way successfully to still-hunt a deer in the middle of the day is to find its trail and follow it up to the resting-places, and such a feat needs an expert tracker and a noiseless and most skilful stalker.

The blacktail prefers to live in the neighborhood of water, where he can get it every twenty-four hours; but he is perfectly willing to drink only every other day, if, as is often the case, he happens to be in a very dry locality. Nor does he stay long in the water or near it, like the whitetail, but moves off as soon as he is no longer thirsty. On moonlight nights he feeds a good deal of the time, and before dawn he is always on foot for his breakfast; the hours around daybreak are those in which most of his grazing is done. By the time the sun has been up an hour he is on his way homeward, grazing as he goes; and he will often stay for some little time longer, if there has been no disturbance from man or other foes, feeding among the scattered scrub-cedars skirting the thicket in which he intends to make his bed for the day. Having once made his bed he crouches very close in it, and is difficult to put up during the heat of the day; but as the afternoon wears on he becomes more restless, and will break from his bed and bound off at much smaller provocation, while if the place is lonely he will wander out into the open hours before sunset. If, however, he is in much danger of being molested, he will keep close to his hiding-place until nearly nightfall, when he ventures out to feed. Owing to the lateness of his evening appearance in localities where there is much hunting, it is a safer plan to follow him in the early morning, being on the ground and ready to start out by the time the first streak of dawn appears. Often have I lost deer when riding home in the evening, because the dusk had deepened so that it was impossible to distinguish clearly enough to shoot.

One day one of my cowboys and myself were returning from an unsuccessful hunt, about nightfall, and were still several miles from the river, when a couple of yearling blacktails jumped up in the bed of the dry creek down which we were riding. Our horses, though stout and swift, were not well trained, and the instant we were off their backs they trotted off. No sooner were we on the ground and trying to sight the deer, one of which was cantering slowly off among the bushes, than we found we could not catch the bead sights of our rifles, the outlines of the animals seeming vague and shadowy, and confounding themselves with the banks and dull-green sage-bushes behind them. Certainly, six or eight shots were fired, we doing our best to aim, but without any effect; and when we gave it up and turned to look for our horses we were annoyed to see them trotting off down the valley half a mile away. We went after at a round pace; but darkness closed in before we had gained at all on them. There was nothing left to do but to walk on down the valley to the bottoms, and then to wade the river; as the latter was quite high, we had to take off our clothes, and it is very uncomfortable to feel one's way across a river at night, in bare feet, with the gun and the bundle of clothes held high overhead. However, when across the

river and half a mile from home, we ran into our horses
—a piece of good luck, as otherwise we should have
had to spend the next day in looking for them.

Almost the only way in which it is possible to aim
after dark is to get the object against the horizon,
toward the light. One of the finest bucks I ever killed
was shot in this way. It was some little time after
the sun had set, and I was hurrying home, riding down
along a winding creek at a gallop. The middle of the
bottom was covered with brush, while the steep, grassy,
rounded hills on each side sent off spurs into the valley, the part between every two spurs making a deep
pocket. The horse's feet were unshod and he made
very little noise, coming down against the wind. While
passing a deep pocket I heard from within it a snort
and stamping of feet, the well-known sounds made by
a startled deer. Pulling up short I jumped off the
horse—it was Manitou—who instantly began feeding
with perfect indifference to what he probably regarded
as an irrational freak of his master; and, aiming as well
as I could in the gathering dusk, held the rifle well
ahead of a shadowy gray object which was scudding
along the base of the hill toward the mouth of the
pocket. The ball struck in front of and turned the
deer, which then started obliquely up the hill. A second shot missed it; and I then (here comes in the good
of having a repeater) knelt down and pointed the rifle
against the sky-line, at the place where the deer seemed
likely to top the bluff. Immediately afterward the
buck appeared, making the last jump with a great
effort which landed him square on the edge, as sharply
outlined as a silhouette against the fading western light.
My rifle bead was just above him; pulling it down I
fired, as the buck paused for a second to recover him-

self from his last great bound, and with a crash the mighty-antlered beast came rolling down the hill, the bullet having broken his back behind the shoulders, afterward going out through his chest.

At times a little caution must be used in approaching a wounded buck, for if it is not disabled it may be a rather formidable antagonist. In my own experience I have never known a wounded buck to do more than make a pass with his horns, or, in plunging when the knife enters his throat, to strike with his forefeet. But one of my men was regularly charged by a great buck which he had wounded and which was brought to bay on the ice by a dog. It seemed to realize that the dog was not the main antagonist, and knocking him over charged straight past him at the man, and as the latter had in his haste not reloaded his rifle, he might have been seriously injured had it not been for the dog, a very strong and plucky one, which caught the buck by the hock and threw him. The buck got up and again came straight at his foe, uttering a kind of grunting bleat, and it was not till after quite a scuffle that the man, by the help of the dog, got him down and thrust the knife in his throat. Twice I have known hounds to be killed by bucks which they had brought to bay in the rutting season. One of these bucks was a savage old fellow with great thick neck and sharp-pointed antlers. He came to bay in a stream, under a bank thickly matted with willows which grew down into the water, guarding his rear and flanks, while there was a small pool in his front across which the hounds had to swim. Backing in among the willows he rushed out at every dog that came near, striking it under water with his forefeet, and then again retreating to his fortress. In this way he kept the whole pack off, and so injured one hound that he had to be killed. Indeed, a full-grown buck with antlers would be a match for a wolf, unless surprised, and could not improbably beat off a cougar if he received the latter's spring fairly on his prong-points.

Bucks fight fiercely among themselves during the rutting season. At that time the blacktail, unlike the whitetail, is found in bands, somewhat like those of the elk but much smaller, and the bucks of each band keep up an incessant warfare. A weak buck promptly gets out of the way if charged by a large one; but when two of equal strength come together the battle is well fought. Instances occasionally occur of a pair of these duellists getting their horns firmly interlocked and thus perishing; but these instances are much rarer, owing to the shape of the antlers, than with the whitetail of which species I have in my own experience come across two or three sets of skulls held together by their interlacing antlers, the bearers of which had doubtless died owing to their inability to break away from each other.

A blacktail buck is one of the most noble-looking of all deer. His branching and symmetrically curved antlers are set on a small head, carried with beautiful pose by the proud, massive neck. The body seems almost too heavy for the slender legs, and yet the latter bear it as if they were rods of springing steel. Every movement is full of alert, fiery life and grace, and he steps as lightly as though he hardly trod the earth. The large, sensitive ears are thrown forward to catch the slightest sound; and in the buck they are not too conspicuous, though they are the only parts of his frame which to any eye can be said to take away from his beauty. They give the doe a somewhat mulish look; at a distance, the head of a doe peering out from among twigs

141

looks like a great black V. To me, however, even in the case of the doe, they seem to set off and strengthen by contrast the delicate, finely moulded look of the head. Owing to these ears the species is called in the books the Mule-Deer, and every now and then a plains-man will speak of it by this title. But all plainsmen know it generally, and ninety-nine out of a hundred know it only, as the Blacktail Deer; and as this is the title by which it is known among all who hunt it or live near it, it should certainly be called by the same name in the books.

But though so grand and striking an object when startled, or when excited whether by curiosity or fear, love or hate, a blacktail is nevertheless often very hard to make out when standing motionless among the trees and brushwood, or when lying down among the boul-ders. A raw hand at hunting has no idea how hard it is to see a deer when at rest. The color of the hair is gray, almost the same tint as that of the leafless branches and tree-trunks; for of course the hunting season is at its height only when the leaves have fallen. A deer standing motionless looks black or gray, accord-ing as the sunlight strikes it; but always looks exactly the same color as the trees around it. It generally stands or lies near some tree-trunks; and the eye may pass over it once or twice without recognizing its real nature. In the brush it is still more difficult, and there a deer's form is often absolutely indistinguishable from the surroundings as one peers through the mass of in-terlacing limbs and twigs. Once an old hunter and myself in walking along the ridge of a scoria butte passed by, without seeing them, three blacktail lying among the scattered boulders of volcanic rock on the hillside, not fifty yards from us. After a little practical experience a would-be hunter learns not to expect deer always, or even generally, to appear as they do when near by or suddenly startled; but on the contrary to keep a sharp lookout on every dull-looking red or yellow patch he sees in a thicket and closely to examine any grayish-looking object observed on the hillsides, for it is just such small patches or obscure-looking objects which are apt, if incautiously approached, to suddenly take to themselves legs and go bounding off at a rate which takes them out of danger before the astonished tyro has really waked up to the fact that they are deer. The first lesson to be learned in still-hunting is the knowledge of how to tell what objects are and what are not deer; and to learn it is by no means as easy a task as those who have never tried it would think.

When he has learned to see a deer, the novice then has to learn to hit it, and this again is not the easy feat it seems. That he can do well with a shotgun proves very little as to a man's skill with the rifle, for the latter carries but one bullet, and can therefore hit but in one place, while with a shotgun, if you hold a foot off your mark you will be nearly as apt to hit as if you held plumb centre. Nor does *mere* practice at a mark avail, though excellent in its way; for a deer is never seen at a fixed and ascertained distance, nor is its outline often clearly and sharply defined, as with a target. Even if a man keeps cool—and for the first shot or two he will probably be flurried—he may miss an absurdly easy shot by not taking pains. I remember on one occasion missing two shots in succession where it seemed really impossible for a man to help hitting. I was out hunting on horseback with one of my men, and on loping round the corner of a brushy valley came suddenly in sight of a buck with certainly more than a dozen points on his great spreading antlers. I jumped off my horse instantly, and fired as he stood facing me not over forty yards off; fired, as I supposed perfectly, coolly, though without dropping on my knee as I should have done. The shot must have gone high, for the buck bounded away unharmed, heedless of a second ball; and immediately his place was taken by another, somewhat smaller, who sprang out of a thicket into almost the identical place where the big buck had stood. Again I fired and missed; again the buck ran off, and was shot at and missed while running—all four shots being taken within fifty yards. I clambered on to the horse without looking at my companion, but too conscious of his smothered disfavor; after riding a few hundred yards, he said with forced politeness and a vague desire to offer some cheap consolation, that he supposed I had done my best; to which I responded with asperity that I'd be damned if I had; and we finished our journey homeward in silence. A man is likely to overshoot at any distance; but at from twenty-five to seventy-five yards he is certain to do so if he is at all careless.

Moreover, besides not missing, a man must learn to hit his deer in the right place; the first two or three times he shoots he will probably see the whole deer in the rifle sights, instead of just the particular spot he wishes to strike; that is, he will aim in a general way at the deer's whole body—which will probably result in a wound not disabling the animal in the least for the time, although insuring its finally dying a lingering and painful death. The most instantaneously fatal places are the brain and any part of the spinal column; but these offer such small marks that it is usually only by accident they are hit. The mark at any part of which one can fire with safety is a patch about eight inches or a foot square, including the shoulder-blades, lungs, and heart. A kidney-shot is very fatal; but a blacktail will go all day with a bullet through his entrails, and in cold weather I have known one to run several miles with a portion of his entrails sticking out of a wound and frozen solid. To break both shoulders by a shot as the deer stands sideways to the hunter brings the buck down in its tracks; but perhaps the best place at which to aim is the point in the body right behind the shoulder-blade. On receiving a bullet in this spot the deer will plunge forward for a jump or two, and then go some fifty yards in a labored gallop; will then stop, sway unsteadily on its legs for a second, and pitch forward on its side. When the hunter comes up he will find his quarry stone-dead. If the deer stands facing the hunter it offers only a narrow mark, but either a throat or chest shot will be fatal.

Good shooting is especially necessary after blacktail, because it is so very tenacious of life; much more so than the whitetail or, in proportion to its bulk, than the elk. For this reason it is of the utmost importance to give an immediately fatal or disabling wound, or the game will almost certainly be lost. It is wonderful to see how far and how fast a seemingly crippled deer will go. Of course a properly trained dog would be of the greatest use in tracking and bringing to bay wounded blacktail; but, unless properly trained to come in to heel, a dog is worse than useless; and, anyhow, it will be hard to keep one, as long as the wolf-hunters strew the ground so plentifully with poisoned bait. We have had several hunting-dogs on our ranch at different times; generally wire-haired deerhounds, foxhounds, or greyhounds, by no means absolutely pure in blood; but they all, sooner or later, succumbed to the effects of eating poisoned meat. Some of them were quite good hunting-dogs, the rough deerhounds being perhaps the best at following and tackling a wounded buck. They were all very eager for the sport, and when in the morning we started out on a hunt the dogs were apparently more interested than the men; but their judgment did not equal their zeal, and lack of training made them on the whole more bother than advantage.

But much more than good shooting is necessary before a man can be called a good hunter. Indians, for example, get a good deal of game, but they are in most cases very bad shots. Once, while going up the Clear Fork of the Powder, in northern Wyoming, one of my men, an excellent hunter, and myself rode into a large camp of Cheyennes, and after a while started a shooting-match with some of them. We had several trials of skill with the rifle, and, a good deal to my astonishment, I found that most of the Indians (quite successful hunters, to judge by the quantity of smoked venison lying round) were very bad shots, indeed. None of them came anywhere near the hunter who was with me; nor, indeed, to myself. An Indian gets his game by his patience, his stealth, and his tireless perseverance; and a white, to be really successful in still-hunting, must learn to copy some of the Indian's traits.

While the game-butchers, the skin-hunters, and their like, work such brutal slaughter among the plains animals that these will soon be either totally extinct or so thinned out as to cease being prominent features of plains life, yet, on the other hand, the nature of the country debars them from following certain murderous and unsportsmanlike forms of hunting much in vogue

146

in other quarters of our land. There is no deep water into which a deer can be driven by hounds and then shot at arm's length from a boat, as is the fashion with some of the city sportsmen who infest the Adirondack forests during the hunting season; nor is the winter snow ever deep enough to form a crust over which a man can go on snow-shoes, and after running down a deer, which plunges as if in a quagmire, knock the poor worn-out brute on the head with an axe. Fire-hunting is never tried in the cattle country; it would be far more likely to result in the death of a steer or pony than in the death of a deer, if attempted on foot with a torch, as is done in some of the Southern States, while the streams are not suited to the floating or jack-ing with a lantern in the bow of the canoe, as practised in the Adirondacks. Floating and fire-hunting, though by no means to be classed among the nobler kinds of sport, yet have a certain fascination of their own, not so much for the sake of the actual hunting as for the novelty of being out in the wilderness at night; and the noiselessness absolutely necessary to insure success often enables the sportsman to catch curious glimpses of the night life of the different kinds of wild animals.

If it were not for the wolf poison, the plains country would be peculiarly fitted for hunting with hounds; and, if properly carried on, there is no manlier form of sport. It does not imply in the man who follows it the skill that distinguishes the successful still-hunter, but it has a dash and excitement all its own, if the hunter follows the hounds on horseback. But, as carried on in the Adirondacks and in the Eastern and Southern mountains generally, hounding deer is not worthy of much regard. There the hunter is stationed at a runway over which deer will probably pass, and has nothing to do but sit still for a number of weary hours and perhaps put a charge of buckshot into a deer running by but a few yards off. If a rifle instead of a shotgun is used, a certain amount of skill is necessary, for then it is hard to hit a deer running, no matter how close up; but even with this weapon all the sportsman has to do is to shoot well; he need not show knowledge of a single detail of hunting craft, nor need he have any trait of mind or body such as he must possess to follow most other kinds of the chase.

Deer-hunting on horseback is something widely different. Even if the hunters carry rifles and themselves kill the deer, using the dogs merely to drive it out of the brush, they must be bold and skilful horsemen, and must show good judgment in riding to cut off the quarry, so as to be able to get a shot at it. This is the common American method of hunting the deer in those places where it is followed with horse and hound; but it is also coursed with greyhounds in certain spots where the lay of the land permits this form of sport, and in many districts, even where ordinary hounds are used, the riders go unarmed and merely follow the pack till the deer is bayed and pulled down. All kinds of hunting on horseback—and most hunting on horseback is done with hounds—tend to bring out the best and manliest qualities in the men who follow them, and they should be encouraged in every way. Long after the rifleman, as well as the game he hunts, shall have vanished from the plains, the cattle country will afford fine sport in coursing hares; and both wolves and deer could be followed and killed with packs of properly trained hounds, and such sport would be even more exciting than still-hunting with the rifle. It is on the great plains lying west of the Missouri that riding to hounds will in the end receive its fullest development as a national pastime.

But at present, for the reasons already stated, it is almost unknown in the cattle country; and the ranchman who loves sport must try still-hunting—and by still-hunting is meant pretty much every kind of chase where a single man, unaided by a dog, and almost always on foot, outgenerals a deer and kills it with the rifle. To do this successfully, unless deer are very plenty and tame, implies a certain knowledge of the country, and a good knowledge of the habits of the game. The hunter must keep a sharp lookout for deer sign; for, though a man soon gets to have a general knowledge of the kind of places in which deer are likely to be, yet he will also find that they are either very capricious, or else that no man has more than a partial understanding of their tastes and likings; for many spots apparently just suited to them will be almost uninhabited, while in others they will be found where it would hardly occur to any one to suspect their presence. Any cause may temporarily drive deer out of a given locality. Still-hunting especially is sure to send many away, while rendering the others extremely wild and shy, and where deer have become used to being pursued in only one way, it is often an excellent plan to try some entirely different method.

A certain knowledge of how to track deer is very useful. To become a really skilful tracker is most difficult; and there are some kinds of ground—where, for instance, it is very hard and dry, or frozen solid—on which almost any man will be at fault. But any one with a little practice can learn to do a certain amount of tracking. On snow, of course, it is very easy; but on the other hand it is also peculiarly difficult to avoid being seen by the deer when the ground is white. After deer have been frightened once or twice, or have even merely been disturbed by man, they get the habit of keeping a watch back on their trail; and when snow has fallen, a man is such a conspicuous object deer see him a long way off and even the tamest become wild. A deer will often, before lying down, take a half-circle back to one side and make its bed a few yards from its trail, where it can, itself unseen, watch any person tracing it up. A man tracking in snow needs to pay very little heed to the footprints, which can be followed without effort, but requires to keep up the closest scrutiny over the ground ahead of him, and on either side of the trail.

In the early morning when there is a heavy dew the footprints will be as plain as possible in the grass, and can then be followed readily; and in any place where the ground is at all damp they will usually be plain enough to be made out without difficulty. When the ground is hard or dry the work is very much less easy, and soon becomes so difficult as not to be worth while following up. Indeed, at all times, even in the snow, tracks are chiefly of use to show the probable locality in which a deer may be found; and the still-hunter, instead of laboriously walking along a trail, will do far better merely to follow it until, from its freshness and direction, he feels confident that the deer is in some particular space of ground, and then hunt through it, guiding himself by his knowledge of the deer's habits and by the character of the land. Tracks are of most use in showing whether deer are plenty or scarce, whether they have been in the place recently or not. Generally, signs of deer are infinitely more plentiful than the animals themselves—although in regions where tracking is especially difficult deer are often jumped without any sign having been seen at all. Usually, however, the rule is the reverse, and as deer are likely to make any quantity of tracks the beginner is apt, judging purely from the sign, greatly to overestimate their number. Another mistake of the beginner is to look for the deer during the daytime in the places where their tracks were made in the morning, when their day beds will probably be a long distance off. In the night-time deer will lie down almost anywhere, but during the day they go some distance from their feeding or watering places, as already explained.

If deer are at all plenty—and if scarce only a master in the art can succeed at still-hunting—it is best not to try to follow the tracks at all, but merely to hunt carefully through any ground which from its looks seems likely to contain the animals. Of course the hunting must be done either against or across the wind, and the greatest care must be taken to avoid making a noise. Moccasins should be worn, and not a twig should be trodden on, nor should the dress be allowed to catch in a brush. Especial caution should be used in going over a ridge or crest; no man should ever let his whole body appear at once, but should first carefully peep over, not letting his rifle barrel come into view, and closely inspect every place in sight in which a deer could possibly stand or lie, always remembering that a deer is, when still, a most difficult animal to see, and that it will be completely hidden in cover which would apparently hardly hold a rabbit. The rifle should be carried habitually so that the sun will not glance upon it. Advantage must be taken, in walking, of all cover, so that the hunter will not be a conspicuous object at any distance. The heads of a series of brushy ravines should always be crossed; and a narrow, winding valley, with patches of bushes and young trees down through the middle, is always a likely place. Caution should never for a moment be forgotten, especially in the morning or evening, the times when a hunter will get nine-tenths of his shots; for it is just then, when moving and feeding, that deer are most watchful. One will never browse for more than a minute or two without raising its head and peering about for any possible foe, the great, sensitive ears thrown forward to catch the slightest sound. But while using such caution it is also well to remember that as much ground should be crossed as possible; other things being equal, the number of shots obtained will correspond to the amount of country covered. And of course a man should be on the hunting-ground—not starting for the hunting-ground—by the time there is enough light by which to shoot.

Deer are in season for hunting from August 1st to January 1st. August is really too early to get full enjoyment out of the sport. The bucks, though fat and good eating, are still in the velvet; and neither does nor fawns should be killed, as many of the latter are in the spotted coat. Besides, it is very hot in the middle of the day, though pleasant walking in the early morning and late evening, and with cool nights. December is apt to be too cold, although with many fine days. The true time for the chase of the blacktail is in the three fall months. Then the air is fresh and bracing, and a man feels as if he could walk or ride all day long without tiring. In the bright fall weather the country no longer keeps its ordinary look of parched desolation, and the landscape loses its sameness at the touch of the frost. Where everything before had been gray or dull green there are now patches of russet red and bright yellow. The clumps of ash, wild plum-trees, and rose-bushes in the heads and bottoms of the sloping valleys become spots of color that glow among the stretches of brown and withered grass; the young cottonwoods, growing on the points of land round which flow the rivers and streams, change to a delicate green or yellow on which the eye rests with pleasure after having so long seen only the dull drab of the prairies. Often there will be days of bitter cold, when a man who sleeps out in the open feels the need of warm furs; but still more often there will be days and days of sunny weather, not cold enough to bring discomfort, but yet so cold that the blood leaps briskly through a man's veins and makes him feel that to be out and walking over the hills is a pleasure in itself, even were he not in hopes of any moment seeing the sun glint on the horns and hide of some mighty buck as it rises to face the intruder. On days such as these, mere life is enjoyment; and on days such as these, the life of a hunter is at its pleasantest and best.

Many blacktail are sometimes killed in a day. I have never made big bags myself, for I rarely hunt except for a fine head or when we need meat, and, if it can be avoided, do not shoot at fawns or does; so the greatest number I have ever killed in a day was three. This was late one November, on an occasion when our larder was running low. My foreman and I, upon dis-covering this fact, determined to make a trip next day back in the broken country, away from the river, where blacktail were almost sure to be found.

We breakfasted hours before sunrise, and then mounted our horses and rode up the river-bottom. The bright prairie moon was at the full, and was sunk in the west till it hung like a globe of white fire over the long row of jagged bluffs that rose from across the river, while its beams brought into fantastic relief the peaks and crests of the buttes upon our left. The valley of the river itself was in partial darkness, and the stiff, twisted branches of the sage-brush seemed to take on uncanny shapes as they stood in the hollows. The cold was stinging, and we let our willing horses gallop with loose reins, their hoofs ringing on the frozen ground. After going up a mile or two along the course of the river we turned off to follow the bed of a large dry creek. At its mouth was a great space of ground much cut up by the hoofs of the cattle, which was in summer overflowed and almost a morass; but now the frost-bound earth was like wrinkled iron beneath the horses' feet. Behind us the westering moon sank down out of sight; and with no light but that of the stars, we let our horses tread their own way up the creek bottom. When we had gone a couple of miles from the river the sky in front of our faces took on a faint grayish tinge, the forerunner of dawn. Every now and then we passed by bunches of cattle, lying down or standing huddled together in the patches of brush or under the lee of some shelving bank or other windbreak; and as the eastern heavens grew brighter, a dark form suddenly appeared against the sky-line, on the crest of a bluff directly ahead of us. Another and another came up beside it. A glance told us that it was a troop of ponies, which stood motionless, like so many silhouettes, their outstretched necks and long tails vividly outlined against the light behind them. All in the valley was yet dark when we reached the place where the creek began to split up and branch out into the various arms and ravines from which it headed.

We galloped smartly over the divide into a set of coulées and valleys which ran into a different creek, and selected a grassy place where there was good feed to leave the horses. My companion picketed his; Manitou needed no picketing.

The tops of the hills were growing rosy, but the sun was not yet above the horizon when we started off, with our rifles on our shoulders, walking in cautious silence, for we were in good ground and might at any moment see a deer. Above us was a plateau of some size, breaking off sharply at the rim into a surrounding stretch of very rough and rugged country. It sent off low spurs with notched crests into the valleys round about, and its edges were indented with steep ravines and half-circular basins, their sides covered with clusters of gnarled and wind-beaten cedars, often gathered into groves of some size. The ground was so broken as to give excellent cover under which a man could approach game unseen; there were plenty of fresh signs of deer; and we were confident we should soon get a shot. Keeping at the bottom of the gullies, so as to be ourselves inconspicuous, we walked noiselessly on, cautiously examining every pocket or turn before we rounded the corner, and looking with special care along the edges of the patches of brush.

At last, just as the sun had risen, we came out by the mouth of a deep ravine or hollow, cut in the flank of the plateau, with steep, cedar-clad sides; and on the crest of a jutting spur, not more than thirty yards from where I stood, was a blacktail doe, half facing me. I was in the shadow, and for a moment she could not make me out, and stood motionless with her head turned toward me and her great ears thrown forward. Dropping on my knee, I held the rifle a little back of her shoulder—too far back, as it proved, as she stood quartering and not broadside to me. No fairer chance could ever fall to the lot of a hunter; but, to my intense chagrin, she bounded off at the report as if unhurt, disappearing instantly. My companion had now come up, and we ran up a rise of ground, and crouched down beside a great block of sandstone, in a position from which we overlooked the whole ravine or hollow. After some minutes of quiet watchfulness, we heard a twig snap—the air was so still we could hear anything— some rods up the ravine, but below us; and immediately afterward a buck stole out of the cedars. Both of us fired at once, and with a convulsive spring he rolled over backward, one bullet having gone through his neck, and the other—probably mine—having broken a hind leg. Immediately afterward, another buck broke from the upper edge of the cover, near the top of the plateau, and, though I took a hurried shot at him, bounded over the crest and was lost to sight.

We now determined to go down into the ravine and look for the doe, and as there was a good deal of snow in the bottom and under the trees, we knew we could soon tell if she were wounded. After a little search we found her track and, walking along it a few yards, came upon some drops and then a splash of blood. There being no need to hurry, we first dressed the dead buck —a fine, fat fellow, but with small misshapen horns— and then took up the trail of the wounded doe. Here, however, I again committed an error, and paid too much heed to the trail and too little to the country round about; and, while following it with my eyes down on the ground in a place where it was faint, the doe got up some distance ahead and to one side of me, and bounded off round a corner of the ravine. The bed where she had lain was not very bloody, but from the fact of her having stopped so soon, I was sure she was badly wounded. However, after she got out of the snow the ground was as hard as flint, and it was impossible to track her; the valley soon took a turn, and branched into a tangle of coulées and ravines. I deemed it probable that she would not go up the hill, but would run down the course of the main valley; but as it was so uncertain, we thought it would pay us best to look for a new deer.

Our luck, however, seemed—very deservedly—to have ended. We tramped on, as swiftly as was compatible with quiet, for hour after hour; beating through the valleys against the wind, and crossing the brushy heads of the ravines, sometimes close together and sometimes keeping about a hundred yards apart, according to the nature of the ground. When we had searched all through the country round the head of the creek, into which we had come down, we walked over to the next, and went over it with equal care and patience. The morning was now well advanced, and we had to change our method of hunting. It was no longer likely that we should find the deer feeding or in the open, and instead we looked for places where they might be expected to bed, following any trails that led into thick patches of brush or young trees, one of us then hunting through the patch while the other kept watch without. Doubtless we must have passed close to more than one deer, and doubtless others heard us and skulked off through the thick cover; but, although we saw plenty of signs, we saw neither hoof nor hair of living thing. It is under such circumstances that a still-hunter needs to show resolution, and to persevere until his luck turns—this being a euphemistic way of saying: until he ceases to commit the various blunders which alarm the deer and make them get out of the way. Plenty of good shots become disgusted if they do not see a deer early in the morning, and go home; still more, if they do not see one in two or three days. Others will go on hunting, but become careless, stumble and step on dried sticks, and let their eyes fall to the ground. It is a good test of a man's resolution to see if, at the end of a long and unsuccessful tramp after deer, he moves just as carefully and keeps just as sharp a lookout as he did at the beginning. If he does this, and exercises a little common sense—in still-hunting, as in everything else, common sense is the most necessary of qualities—he may be sure that his reward will come some day; and when it does come, he feels a gratification that only his fellow sportsmen can understand.

We lunched at the foot of a great clay butte, where there was a bed of snow. Fall or winter hunting in the Bad Lands has one great advantage; the hunter is not annoyed by thirst, as he is almost sure to be if walking for long hours under the blazing summer sun. If he gets very thirsty, a mouthful or two of snow from some hollow will moisten his lips and throat; and anyhow, thirstiness is largely a mere matter of habit. For lunch, the best thing a hunter can carry is dried or smoked venison, with not too much salt in it. It is much better than bread, and not nearly so dry; and it is easier to carry, as a couple of pieces can be thrust into the bosom of the hunting-shirt or the pocket, or in fact anywhere; and for keeping up a man's strength there is nothing that comes up to it.

After lunch we hunted until the shadows began to lengthen out, when we went back to our horses. The buck was packed behind good old Manitou, who can carry any amount of weight at a smart pace, and does not care at all if a strap breaks and he finds his load dangling about his feet, an event that reduces most horses to a state of frantic terror. As soon as loaded, we rode down the valley into which the doe had disappeared in the morning, one taking each side and looking into every possible lurking-place. The odds were all against our finding any trace of her; but a hunter soon learns that he must take advantage of every chance, however slight. This time we were rewarded for our care; for after riding about a mile our attention was attracted by a white patch in a clump of low briers. On getting off and looking in, it proved to be the white rump of the doe, which lay stretched out inside, stark and stiff. The ball had gone in too far aft and had come out on the opposite side near her hip, making a mortal wound, but one which allowed her to run over a mile before dying. It was little more than an accident that we in the end got her; and my so nearly missing at such short range was due purely to carelessness and bad judgment. I had killed too many deer to be at all nervous over them, and was as cool with a buck as with a rabbit; but as she was so close I made the common mistake of being too much in a hurry, and did not wait to see that she was standing quartering to me, and that, consequently, I should aim at the point of the shoulder. As a result, the deer was nearly lost.

Neither of my shots had so far done me much credit; but, at any rate, I had learned where the error lay, and this is going a long way toward correcting it. I kept wishing that I could get another chance to see if I had not profited by my lessons; and before we reached home my wish was gratified. We were loping down a grassy valley, dotted with clumps of brush, the wind blowing strong in our faces, and deadening the noise made by the hoofs on the grass. As we passed by a piece of broken ground a yearling blacktail buck jumped into view and cantered away. I was off Manitou's back in an instant. The buck was moving slowly, and was evidently soon going to stop and look around, so I dropped on one knee, with my rifle half raised, and waited. When about sixty yards off he halted and turned sideways to me, offering a beautiful broadside shot. I aimed at the spot just behind the shoulder and felt I had him. At the report he went off, but with short, weak bounds, and I knew he would not go far; nor did he, but stopped short, swayed unsteadily about, and went over on his side, dead, the bullet clean through his body.

Each of us already had a deer behind his saddle, so we could not take the last buck along with us. Accordingly, we dressed him, and hung him up by the heels to a branch of a tree, piling the brush around as if building a slight pen or trap, to keep off the coyotes; who, anyhow, are not apt to harm game that is hanging up, their caution seeming to make them fear that it will not be safe to do so. In such cold weather a deer hung up in this way will keep an indefinite length of time; and the carcass was all right when, a week or two afterward, we sent out the buckboard to bring it back.

A stout buckboard is very useful on a ranch, where men are continually taking short trips on which they do not wish to be encumbered by the heavy ranch wagon. Pack-ponies are always a nuisance, though of course an inevitable one in making journeys through mountains or forests. But on the plains a buckboard is far more handy. The blankets and provisions can be loaded upon it, and it can then be given a definite course to travel or point to reach; and meanwhile the hunters, without having their horses tired by carrying heavy packs, can strike off and hunt wherever they wish. There is little or no difficulty in going over the prairie, but it needs a skilful plainsman, as well as a good teamster, to take a wagon through the Bad Lands. There are but two courses to follow. One is to go along the bottoms of the valleys; the other is to go along the tops of the divides. The latter is generally the best; for each valley usually has at its bottom a deep winding ditch with perpendicular banks, which wanders first to one side and then to the other, and has to be crossed again and again, while a little way from it begin the gullies and gulches which come down from the side hills. It is no easy matter to tell which is the main divide, as it curves and twists about, and is all the time splitting up into lesser ones, which merely separate two branches of the same creek. If the teamster does not know the lay of the land he will be likely to find himself in a *cul-de-sac*, from which he can only escape by going back a mile or two and striking out afresh. In very difficult country the horsemen must be on hand to help the team pull up the steep places. Many horses that will not pull a pound in harness will haul for all there is in them from the saddle; Manitou is a case in point. Often obstacles will be encountered across which it is simply impossible for any team to drag a loaded or even an empty wagon. Such are steep canyons, or muddy-bottomed streams with sheer banks, especially if the latter have rotten edges. The horses must then be crossed first and the wagon dragged over afterward by the aid of long ropes. Often it may be needful to build a kind of rude bridge or causeway on which to get the animals over; and if the canyon is very deep the wagon may have to be taken in pieces, let down one side and hauled up the other. An immense amount of labor may be required to get over a very trifling distance. Pack-animals, however, can go almost anywhere that a man can.

Although still-hunting on foot, as described above, is on the whole the best way to get deer, yet there are many places where, from the nature of the land, the sport can be followed quite as well on horseback, than which there is no more pleasant kind of hunting. The best shot I ever made in my life—a shot into which, however, I am afraid the element of chance entered much more largely than the element of skill—was made while hunting blacktail on horseback.

We were at that time making quite a long trip with the wagon, and were going up the fork of a plains river in western Montana. As we were out of food, those two of our number who usually undertook to keep the camp supplied with game determined to make a hunt off back of the river after blacktail; for though there were some whitetail in the more densely timbered river-bottoms, we had been unable to get any. It was arranged that the wagon should go on a few miles, and then halt for the night, as it was already the middle of the afternoon when we started out. The country resembled in character other parts of the cattle plains, but it was absolutely bare of trees except along the bed of the river. The rolling hills sloped steeply off into long valleys and deep ravines. They were sparsely covered with coarse grass, and also with an irregular growth of tall sage-brush, which in some places gathered into dense thickets. A beginner would have thought the country entirely too barren of cover to hold deer, but a very little experience teaches one that deer will be found in thickets of such short and sparse growth that it seems as if they could hide nothing; and, what is more, that they will often skulk round in such thickets without being discovered. And a blacktail is a bold, free animal, liking to go out in comparatively open country, where he must trust to his own powers, and not to any concealment, to protect him from danger.

Where the hilly country joined the alluvial river-bottom, it broke short off into steep bluffs, up which none but a Western pony could have climbed. It is really wonderful to see what places a pony can get over and the indifference with which it regards tumbles. In getting up from the bottom we went into a washout, and then led our ponies along a clay ledge, from which we turned off and went straight up a very steep sandy bluff. My companion was ahead; just as he turned off the ledge, and as I was right underneath him, his horse, in plunging to try to get up the sand bluff, overbalanced itself, and, after standing erect on its hind legs for a second, came over backward. The second's pause while it stood bolt upright gave me time to make a frantic leap out of the way with my pony, which scrambled after me, and we clung with hands and hoofs to the side of the bank, while the other horse took two as complete somersaults as I ever saw, and landed with a crash at the bottom of the washout, feet uppermost. I thought it was done for, but not a bit. After a moment or two it struggled to its legs, shook itself, and looked round in rather a shame-faced way, apparently not in the least the worse for the fall. We now got my pony up to the top by vig-

orous pulling, and then went down for the other, which
at first strongly objected to making another trial, but,
after much coaxing and a good deal of abuse, took a
start and went up without trouble.

For some time after reaching the top of the bluffs we
rode along without seeing anything. When it was possible, we kept one on each side of a creek, avoiding the
tops of the ridges, because while on them a horseman
can be seen at a very long distance, and going with particular caution whenever we went round a spur or came
up over a crest. The country stretched away like an
endless, billowy sea of dull-brown soil and barren sage-
brush, the valleys making long parallel furrows, and
everything having a look of dreary sameness. At
length, as we came out on a rounded ridge, three blacktail bucks started up from a lot of sage-brush some two
hundred yards away and below us, and made off downhill. It was a very long shot, especially to try running,
but, as game seemed scarce and cartridges were plenty,
I leaped off the horse, and, kneeling, fired. The bullet
went low, striking in a line at the feet of the hindmost.
I held very high next time, making a wild shot above
and ahead of them, which had the effect of turning
them, and they went off round a shoulder of a bluff, being by this time down in the valley. Having plenty of
time, I elevated the sights (a thing I hardly ever do) to
four hundred yards and waited for their reappearance.
Meanwhile, they had evidently gotten over their fright,
for pretty soon one walked out from the other side of
the bluff, and came to a standstill, broadside toward
me. He was too far off for me to see his horns. As I
was raising the rifle another stepped out and began to
walk toward the first. I thought I might as well have
as much of a target as possible to shoot at, and waited

164

for the second buck to come out farther, which he did immediately and stood still just alongside of the first. I aimed above his shoulders and pulled the trigger. Over went the two bucks! And when I rushed down to where they lay I found I had pulled a little to one side, and the bullet had broken the backs of both. While my companion was dressing them I went back and paced off the distance. It was just four hundred and thirty-one long paces; over four hundred yards. Both were large bucks and very fat, with the velvet hanging in shreds from their antlers, for it was late in August. The day was waning and we had a long ride back to the wagon, each with a buck behind his saddle. When we came back to the river-valley it was pitch dark, and it was rather ticklish work for our heavily laden horses to pick their way down the steep bluffs and over the rapid streams; nor were we sorry when we saw ahead under a bluff the gleam of the camp-fire, as it was reflected back from the canvas-topped prairie-schooner that for the time being represented home to us.

This was much the best shot I ever made; and it is just such a shot as any one will occasionally make if he takes a good many chances and fires often at ranges where the odds are greatly against his hitting. I suppose I had fired a dozen times at animals four or five hundred yards off, and now, by the doctrine of chances, I happened to hit; but I would have been very foolish if I had thought for a moment that I had learned how to hit at over four hundred yards. I have yet to see the hunter who can hit with any regularity at that distance, when he has to judge it for himself; though I have seen plenty who could make such a long-range hit now and then. And I have noticed that such a hunter, in talking over his experience, was certain soon to forget the numerous misses he made, and to say, and even actually to think, that his occasional hits represented his average shooting.

One of the finest blacktail bucks I ever shot was killed while lying out in a rather unusual place. I was hunting mountain-sheep, in a stretch of very high and broken country, and about midday crept cautiously up to the edge of a great gorge, whose sheer walls went straight down several hundred feet. Peeping over the brink of the chasm, I saw a buck, lying out on a ledge so narrow as to barely hold him, right on the face of the cliff wall opposite, some distance below, and about seventy yards diagonally across from me. He lay with his legs half stretched out, and his head turned so as to give me an exact centre-shot at his forehead, the bullet going in between his eyes, so that his legs hardly so much as twitched when he received it. It was toilsome and almost dangerous work climbing out to where he lay; I have never known any other individual, even of this bold and adventurous species of deer, to take its noonday siesta in a place so barren of all cover and so difficult of access even to the most surefooted climber. This buck was as fat as a prize sheep, and heavier than any other I have ever killed; while his antlers also were, with two exceptions, the best I ever got.

CHAPTER VI

A TRIP ON THE PRAIRIE

No antelope are found, except rarely, immediately round my ranch-house, where the ground is much too broken to suit them; but on the great prairies, ten or fifteen miles off, they are plentiful, though far from as abundant as they were a few years ago when the cattle were first driven into the land. By plainsmen they are called either pronghorn or antelope, but are most often known by the latter and much less descriptive title. Where they are found they are always very conspicuous figures in the landscape; for, far from attempting to conceal itself, an antelope really seems anxious to take up a prominent position, caring only to be able itself to see its foes. It is the smallest in size of the plains game, even smaller than a whitetail deer; and its hide is valueless being thin and porous, and making very poor buckskin. In its whole appearance and structure it is a most singular creature. Unlike all other hollow-horned animals, it sheds its horns annually, exactly as the deer shed their solid antlers; but the shedding process in the pronghorn occupies but a very few days—so short a time, indeed, that many hunters stoutly deny that it takes place at all. The hair is of a remarkable texture, very long, coarse, and brittle; in the spring it comes off in handfuls. In strong contrast to the reddish yellow of the other parts of the body, the rump is pure white, and when alarmed or irritated every hair in the white patch bristles up on end, greatly increasing the apparent area of the color.

167

The flesh, unlike that of any other plains animal, is equally good all through the year. In the fall it is hardly so juicy as deer venison, but in the spring, when no other kind of game is worth eating, it is perfectly good; and at that time of the year, if we have to get fresh meat, we would rather kill antelope than anything else; and as the bucks are always to be instantly distinguished from the does by their large horns, we confine ourselves to them, and so work no harm to the species.

The antelope is a queer-looking rather than a beautiful animal. The curious pronged horns, great bulging eyes, and strange bridle-like marks and bands on the face and throat are more striking, but less handsome, than the delicate head and branching antlers of a deer; and it entirely lacks the latter animal's grace of movement. In its form and look, when standing still, it is rather angular and goat-like, and its movements merely have the charm that comes from lightness, speed, and agility. Its gait is singularly regular and even, without any of the bounding, rolling movement of a deer; and it is, consequently, very easy to hit running, compared with other kinds of game.

Antelope possess a most morbid curiosity. The appearance of anything out of the way or to which they are not accustomed, often seems to drive them nearly beside themselves with mingled fright and desire to know what it is, a combination of feelings that throws them into a perfect panic during whose continuance they will at times seem utterly unable to take care of themselves. In very remote, wild places, to which no white man often penetrates, the appearance of a white-topped wagon will be enough to excite this feeling in the pronghorn, and in such cases it is not unusual for

where antelope are most plentiful during the hot months and never see one; but if he does come across any they will be apt to be in great numbers, most probably along the edge of the Bad Lands, where the ground is rolling rather than broken, but where there is some shelter from the furious winter gales. Often they will even come down to the river-bottom or find their way up to some plateau. They now always hang closely about the places they have chosen for their winter haunts, and seem very reluctant to leave them. They go in dense herds, and when starved and weak with cold are less shy; and can often be killed in great numbers by any one who has found out where they are— though a true sportsman will not molest them at this season.

Sometimes a small number of individuals will at this time get separated from the main herd, and take up their abode in some place by themselves; and when they have once done so it is almost impossible to drive them away. Last winter a solitary pronghorn strayed into the river-bottom at the mouth of a wide creek-valley, half a mile from my ranch, and stayed there for three months, keeping with the cattle, and always being found within a mile of the same spot. A little band at the same time established itself on a large plateau, about five miles long by two miles wide, some distance up the river above me, and afforded fine sport to a couple of ranchmen who lived not far from its base. The antelope, twenty or thirty in number, would not leave the plateau, which lies in the midst of broken ground; for it is a peculiarity of these animals, which will be spoken of further on, that they will try to keep in the open ground at any cost or hazard. The two ranchmen agreed never to shoot at the antelope on foot, but only to try to kill them from horseback, either with their revolvers or their Winchesters. They thus hunted them for the sake of the sport purely; and certainly they got plenty of fun out of them. Very few horses indeed are as fast as a pronghorn; and these few did not include any owned by either of my two friends. But the antelope were always being obliged to break back from the edge of the plateau, and so were forced constantly to offer opportunities for cutting them off; and these opportunities were still further increased by the two hunters separating. One of them would go to the upper end of the plateau and start the band, riding after them at full speed. They would distance him, but would be checked in their career by coming to the brink of the cliff; then they would turn at an angle and give their pursuer a chance to cut them off; and if they kept straight up the middle the other hunter would head them. When a favorable moment came the hunters would dash in as close as possible and empty their revolvers or repeaters into the herd; but it is astonishing how hard it is, when riding a horse at full speed, to hit any object, unless it is directly under the muzzle of the weapon. The number of cartridges spent compared to the number of pronghorn killed was enormous; but the fun and excitement of the chase were the main objects with my friends to whom the actual killing of the game was of entirely secondary importance. They went out after them about a dozen times during the winter, and killed in all ten or fifteen pronghorns.

A pronghorn is by far the fleetest animal on the plains; one can outrun and outlast a deer with the greatest ease. Very swift greyhounds can overtake them, if hunted in leashes or couples; but only a remarkably good dog can run one down single-handed.

Besides, pronghorn are most plucky little creatures, and will make a most resolute fight against a dog or wolf, striking with their forefeet and punching with their not very formidable horns, and are so quick and wiry as to be really rather hard to master.

Antelope have the greatest objection to going on anything but open ground, and seem to be absolutely unable to make a high jump. If a band is caught feeding in the bottom of a valley leading into a plain they invariably make a rush to the mouth, even if the foe is stationed there, and will run heedlessly by him, no matter how narrow the mouth is, rather than not try to reach the open country. It is almost impossible to force them into even a small patch of brush, and they will face almost certain death rather than try to leap a really very trifling obstacle. If caught in a glade surrounded by a slight growth of brushwood, they make no effort whatever to get through or over this growth, but dash frantically out through the way by which they got in. Often the deer, especially the blacktail, will wander out on the edge of the plain frequented by antelope; and it is curious to see the two animals separate the second there is an alarm, the deer making for the broken country, while the antelope scud for the level plains. Once two of my men nearly caught a couple of antelope in their hands. They were out driving in the buckboard, and saw two antelope, a long distance ahead, enter the mouth of a washout (a canyon *in petto*); they had strayed away from the prairie to the river-bottom, and were evidently feeling lost. My two men did not think much of the matter, but when opposite the mouth of the washout, which was only thirty feet or so wide, they saw the two antelopes starting to come out, having found that it was a blind passage, with no outlet at the other end. Both men jumped out of the buckboard and ran to the entrance; the two antelope dashed frantically to and fro inside the washout. The sides were steep, but a deer would have scaled them at once; yet the antelope seemed utterly unable to do this, and finally broke out past the two men and got away. They came so close that the men were able to touch each of them, but their movements were too quick to permit of their being caught.

However, though unable to leap any height, an antelope can skim across a level jump like a bird, and will go over watercourses and washouts that very few horses indeed will face. A mountain-sheep, on the other hand, is a marvellous vertical leaper; the blacktail deer comes next; the whitetail is pretty good, and the elk is at any rate better than the antelope; but when it comes to horizontal jumping the latter can beat them all.

In May or early June the doe brings forth her fawns, usually two in number, for she is very prolific. She makes her bed in some valley or hollow, and keeps with the rest of the band, only returning to the fawns to feed them. They lie out in the grass or under some slight bush, but are marvellously hard to find. By instinct they at once know how to crouch down so as to be as inconspicuous as possible. Once we scared away a female pronghorn from an apparently perfectly level hillside; and in riding along passed over the spot she had left and came upon two little fawns that could have been but a few hours old. They lay flat in the grass, with their legs doubled under them and their necks and heads stretched out on the ground. When we took them up and handled them, they soon got used to us and moved awkwardly around, but at any sudden noise

174

or motion they would immediately squat flat down again. But at a very early age the fawns learn how to shift for themselves, and can then run almost as fast as their parents, even when no larger than a jack-rabbit. Once, while we were haying, a couple of my cowboys spent half an hour in trying to run down and capture a little fawn, but they were unable to catch it, it ran so fast and ducked about so quickly. Antelope fawns are very easily tamed and make most amusing pets. We have had two or three, but have never succeeded in rearing any of them; but some of the adjoining ranchmen have been more fortunate. They are not nearly so pretty as deer fawns, having long, gangling legs and angular bodies, but they are much more familiar and interesting. One of my neighbors has three live pronghorns, as well as two little spotted whitetail deer. The deer fawns are always skulking about, and are by no means such bold, inquisitive little creatures as the small antelope are. The latter have a nurse in the shape of a fat old ewe; and it is funny to see her, when alarmed, running off at a waddling gait, while her ungainly little foster-children skip round and round her, cutting the most extraordinary antics. There are a couple of very large dogs, mastiffs, on the place, whose natural solemnity is completely disconcerted by the importunities and fearlessness of the little antelope fawns. Where one goes the other two always follow, and so one of the mastiffs, while solemnly blinking in the sun, will suddenly find himself charged at full speed by the three queer little creatures, who will often fairly butt up against him. The uneasy look of the dog, and his efforts to get out of the way without compromising his dignity, are really very comical.

Young fawns seem to give out no scent, and thus

many of them escape from the numerous carnivorous beasts that are ever prowling about at night over the prairie, and which, during the spring months, are always fat from feeding on the bodies of the innocents they have murdered. If discovered by a fox or coyote during its first few days of existence a little fawn has no chance of life, although the mother, if present, will fight desperately for it; but after it has acquired the use of its legs it has no more to fear than have any of the older ones.

Sometimes the fawns fall victims to the great golden eagle. This grand bird, the war-eagle of the Sioux, is not very common in the Bad Lands, but is sometimes still seen with us; and, as everywhere else, its mere presence adds a certain grandeur to its lonely haunts. Two or three years ago a nest was found by one of my men on the face of an almost inaccessible cliff, and a young bird was taken out from it and reared in a roughly extemporized cage. Wherever the eagle exists it holds undisputed sway over everything whose size does not protect it from the great bird's beak and talons; not only does it feed on hares, grouse, and ducks, but it will also attack the young fawns of the deer and antelope. Still, the eagle is but an occasional foe, and, aside from man, the only formidable enemies the antelope has to fear are the wolves and coyotes. These are very destructive to the young, and are always lounging about the band to pick up any wounded straggler; in winter, when the ground is slippery and the antelope numbed and weak, they will often commit great havoc even among those that are grown up.

The voice of the antelope is not at all like that of the deer. Instead of bleating it utters a quick, harsh noise, a kind of bark; a little like the sound "kau," sharply and clearly repeated. It can be heard a long distance off; and is usually uttered when the animal is a little startled or surprised by the presence of something it does not understand.

The pronghorn cannot go without water any longer than a deer can, and will go great distances to get it; for space is nothing to a traveller with such speed and such last. No matter how dry and barren may be the desert in which antelope are found, it may be taken for granted that they are always within reaching distance of some spring or pool of water, and that they visit it once a day. Once or twice I have camped out by some pool, which was the only one for miles around, and in every such case have been surprised at night by the visits of the antelope, who, on finding that their drinking-place was tenanted, would hover round at a short distance, returning again and again and continually uttering the barking "kau, kau," until they became convinced that there was no hope of their getting in, when they would set off at a run for some other place.

Pronghorn perhaps prefer the rolling prairies of short grass as their home, but seem to do almost equally well on the desolate and monotonous wastes where the sage-brush and prickly-pear and a few blades of coarse grass are the only signs of plant life to be seen. In such places, the pronghorn, the sage-cock, the rattlesnake, and the horned frog alone are able to make out a livelihood.

The horned frog is not a frog at all, but a lizard—a queer, stumpy little fellow with spikes all over the top of its head and back, and given to moving in the most leisurely manner imaginable. Nothing will make it hurry. If taken home it becomes a very tame and quaint but also very uninteresting little pet.

Rattlesnakes are only too plentiful everywhere; along the river-bottoms, in the broken, hilly ground, and on the prairies and the great desert wastes alike. Every cowboy kills dozens each season. To a man wearing top-boots there is little or no danger while he is merely walking about, for the fangs cannot go through the leather, and the snake does not strike as high as the knee. Indeed, the rattlesnake is not nearly as dangerous as are most poisonous serpents, for it always gives fair warning before striking, and is both sluggish and timid. If it can, it will get out of the way, and only coils up in its attitude of defense when it believes that it is actually menaced. It is, of course, however, both a dangerous and a disagreeable neighbor, and one of its annoying traits is the fondness it displays for crawling into a hut or taking refuge among the blankets left out on the ground. Except in such cases, men are rarely in danger from it, unless they happen to be stooping over, as was the case with one of my cowboys who had leaned over to pick up a log, and was almost bitten by a snake which was underneath it; or unless the snake is encountered while stalking an animal. Once I was creeping up to an antelope under cover of some very low sage-brush—so low that I had to lie flat on my face and push myself along with my hands and feet. While cautiously moving on in this way I was electrified by hearing almost by my ears the well-known ominous "whir-r-r" of a rattlesnake, and on hastily glancing up there was the reptile, not ten feet away from me, all coiled up and waiting. I backed off and crawled to one side, the rattler turning its head round to keep watch over my movements; when the stalk was over (the antelope took alarm and ran off before I was within rifle-shot) I came back, hunted up the snake, and killed it. Although I have known of several men being bitten, I know of but one case where the bite caused the death of a human being. This was a girl who had been out milking, and was returning, in bare feet; the snake struck her just above the ankle, and in her fright she fell and was struck again in the neck. The double wound was too much for her, and the poison killed her in the course of a couple of hours.

Occasionally one meets a rattlesnake whose rattle has been lost or injured, and such a one is always dangerous, because it strikes without warning. I once nearly lost a horse by the bite of one of these snakes without rattles. I was riding along a path when my horse gave a tremendous start and jump; looking back, I saw that it had been struck by a rattlesnake with an injured tail, which had been lying hid in a bunch of grass, directly beside the path. Luckily, it had merely hit the hard hoof, breaking one of its fangs.

Horses differ very much in their conduct toward snakes. Some show great fright at sight of them or on hearing their rattles, plunging and rearing and refusing to go anywhere near the spot; while others have no fear of them at all, being really perfectly stupid about them. Manitou does not lose his wits at all over them, but at the same time takes very good care not to come within striking distance.

Ranchmen often suffer some loss among their stock owing to snake-bites, both horned cattle and horses, in grazing, frequently coming on snakes and having their noses or cheeks bitten. Generally these wounds are not fatal, though very uncomfortable; it is not uncommon to see a woebegone-looking mule with its head double the natural size, in consequence of having incautiously browsed over a snake. A neighbor lost a weak pony in this way, and one of our best steers also perished from the same cause. But in the latter case the animal, like the poor girl spoken of above, had received two wounds with the poison fangs; apparently it had, while grazing with its head down, been first struck in the nose and been again struck in the fore leg as it started away.

Of all kinds of hunting, the chase of the antelope is pre-eminently that requiring skill in the use of the rifle at long range. The distance at which shots have to be taken in antelope-hunting is at least double the ordinary distance at which deer are fired at. In pursuing most other kinds of game, a hunter who is not a good shot may still do excellent work; but in pronghorn-hunting, no man can make even a fairly good record unless he is a skilful marksman. I have myself done but little hunting after antelopes, and have not, as a rule, been very successful in the pursuit.

Ordinary hounds are rarely, or never, used to chase this game; but coursing it with greyhounds is as manly and exhilarating a form of sport as can be imagined— a much better way of hunting it than is shooting it with the rifle, which latter, though needing more skill in the actual use of the weapon, is in every other respect greatly inferior as a sport to still-hunting the blacktail or bighorn.

I never but once took a trip of any length with antelope-hunting for its chief object. This was one June, when all the men were away on the round-up. As is usual during the busy half of the ranchman's year, the spring and summer, when men have no time to hunt and game is out of condition, we had been living on salt pork, beans, potatoes, and bread; and I had hardly had a rifle in my hand for months; so, finding I had a

few days to spare, I thought I should take a short trip
on the prairie, in the beautiful June weather, and get a
little sport and a little fresh meat out of the bands of
pronghorn bucks which I was sure to encounter. Intending to be gone but a couple of days, it was not necessary to take many articles. Behind my saddle I
carried a blanket for bedding, and an oilskin coat to
ward off the wet; a large metal cup with the handle
riveted, not soldered, on, so that water could be boiled
in it; a little tea and salt, and some biscuits; and a small
water-proof bag containing my half-dozen personal necessaries—not forgetting a book. The whole formed a
small, light pack, very little encumbrance to stout old
Manitou. In June, fair weather can generally be
counted on in the dry plains country.

I started in the very earliest morning, when the intense brilliancy of the stars had just begun to pale before the first streak of dawn. By the time I left the
river-bottom and struck off up the valley of a winding
creek, which led through the Bad Lands, the eastern
sky was growing rosy; and soon the buttes and cliffs
were lit up by the level rays of the cloudless summer
sun. The air was fresh and sweet, and odorous with
the sweet scents of the springtime that was but barely
passed; the dew lay heavy, in glittering drops, on the
leaves and the blades of grass, whose vivid green, at
this season, for a short time brightens the desolate and
sterile-looking wastes of the lonely Western plains.
The rose-bushes were all in bloom, and their pink blos-
soms clustered in every point and bend of the stream;
and the sweet, sad songs of the hermit-thrushes rose
from the thickets, while the meadow-larks perched
boldly in sight as they uttered their louder and more
cheerful music. The round-up had passed by our

ranch, and all the cattle with our brands—the Maltese cross and cut dewlap, or the elk-horn and triangle—had been turned loose; they had not yet worked away from the river, and I rode by long strings of them, walking in single file off to the hills, or standing in groups to look at me as I passed.

Leaving the creek, I struck off among a region of scoria buttes, the ground rising into rounded hills, through whose grassy covering the red volcanic rock showed in places, while boulder-like fragments of it were scattered all through the valleys between. There were a few clumps of bushes here and there, and near one of them were two magpies, who lit on an old buffalo skull, bleached white by sun and snow. Magpies are birds that catch the eye at once from their bold black-and-white plumage and long tails; and they are very saucy and at the same time very cunning and shy. In spring we do not often see them; but in the late fall and winter they will come close round the huts and outbuildings, on the lookout for anything to eat. If a deer is hung up and they can get at it they will pick it to pieces with their sharp bills; and their carnivorous tastes and their habit of coming round hunters' camps after the game that is left out call to mind their kinsman, the whiskey-jack, or moose-bird, of the Northern forests.

After passing the last line of low, rounded scoria buttes, the horse stepped out on the border of the great, seemingly endless stretches of rolling or nearly level prairie, over which I had planned to travel and hunt for the next two or three days. At intervals of ten or a dozen miles this prairie was crossed by dry creeks, with, in places in their beds, pools or springs of water, and alongside a spindling growth of trees and bushes;

and my intention was to hunt across these creeks, and camp by some water-hole in one of them at night.

I rode over the land in a general southerly course, bending to the right or left according to the nature of the ground and the likelihood of finding game. Most of the time the horse kept on a steady single-foot, but this was varied by a sharp lope every now and then, to ease the muscles of both steed and rider. The sun was well up, and its beams beat fiercely down on our heads from out of the cloudless sky; for at this season, though the nights and the early morning and late evening are cool and pleasant, the hours around noon are very hot. My glass was slung alongside the saddle, and from every one of the scattered hillocks the country was scanned carefully far and near; and the greatest caution was used in riding up over any divide, to be sure that no game on the opposite side was scared by the sudden appearance of my horse or myself.

Nowhere, not even at sea, does a man feel more lonely than when riding over the far-reaching, seemingly never-ending plains; and after a man has lived a little while on or near them, their very vastness and loneliness and their melancholy monotony have a strong fascination for him. The landscape seems always the same, and after the traveller has plodded on for miles and miles he gets to feel as if the distance was indeed boundless. As far as the eye can see there is no break; either the prairie stretches out into perfectly level flats, or else there are gentle, rolling slopes, whose crests mark the divides between the drainage systems of the different creeks; and when one of these is ascended, immediately another precisely like it takes its place in the distance, and so roll succeeds roll in a succession as interminable as that of the waves of the ocean. Nowhere else does one seem so far off from all mankind; the plains stretch out in deathlike and measureless expanse, and as he journeys over them they will for many miles be lacking in all signs of life. Although he can see so far, yet all objects on the outermost verge of the horizon, even though within the ken of his vision, look unreal and strange; for there is no shade to take away from the bright glare, and at a little distance things seem to shimmer and dance in the hot rays of the sun. The ground is scorched to a dull brown, and against its monotonous expanse any objects stand out with a prominence that makes it difficult to judge of the distance at which they are. A mile off one can see, through the strange shimmering haze, the shadowy white outlines of something which looms vaguely up till it looks as large as the canvas top of a prairie wagon; but as the horseman comes nearer it shrinks and dwindles and takes clearer form, until at last it changes into the ghastly staring skull of some mighty buffalo, long dead and gone to join the rest of his vanished race.

When the grassy prairies are left and the traveller enters a region of alkali desert and sage-brush, the look of the country becomes even more grim and forbidding. In places the alkali forms a white frost on the ground that glances in the sunlight like the surface of a frozen lake; the dusty little sage-brush, stunted and dried up, sprawls over the parched ground, from which it can hardly extract the small amount of nourishment necessary for even its wizened life; the spiny cactus alone seems to be really in its true home. Yet even in such places antelope will be found, as alert and as abounding with vivacious life as elsewhere. Owing to the magnifying and distorting power of the clear, dry plains air,

184

every object, no matter what its shape or color or apparent distance, needs the closest examination. A magpie sitting on a white skull, or a couple of ravens, will look, a quarter of a mile off, like some curious beast; and time and again a raw hunter will try to stalk a lump of clay or a burnt stick; and after being once or twice disappointed he is apt to rush to the other extreme, and conclude too hastily that a given object is not an antelope, when it very possibly is.

During the morning I came in sight of several small bands or pairs of antelope. Most of them saw me as soon as or before I saw them, and after watching me with intense curiosity as long as I was in sight and at a distance, made off at once as soon as I went into a hollow or appeared to be approaching too near. Twice, in scanning the country narrowly with the glasses, from behind a sheltering divide, bands of pronghorn were seen that had not discovered me. In each case the horse was at once left to graze, while I started off after the game nearly a mile distant. For the first half-mile I could walk upright or go along half stooping; then, as the distance grew less, I had to crawl on all fours and keep behind any little broken bank, or take advantage of a small, dry watercourse, and toward the end work my way flat on my face, wriggling like a serpent, using every stunted sage-brush or patch of cactus as a cover, bareheaded under the blazing sun. In each case, after nearly an hour's irksome, thirsty work, the stalk failed. One band simply ran off without a second's warning, alarmed at some awkward movement on my part and without giving a chance for a shot. In the other instance, while still at very long and uncertain range, I heard the sharp barking alarm-note of one of the pronghorn, the whole band instantly raising their heads and gazing intently at their would-be destroyer. They were a very long way off; but, seeing it was hopeless to try to get nearer, I rested my rifle over a little mound of earth and fired. The dust came up in a puff to one side of the nearest antelope; the whole band took a few jumps and turned again; the second shot struck at their feet, and they went off like so many race-horses, being missed again as they ran. I sat up by a sage-brush, thinking they would, of course, not come back, when to my surprise I saw them wheel round with the precision of a cavalry squadron, all in line and fronting me, the white and brown markings on their heads and throats showing like the facings on soldiers' uniforms; and then back they came charging up till again within long range, when they wheeled their line as if on a pivot and once more made off, this time for good, not heeding an ineffectual fusillade from the Winchester. Antelope often go through a series of regular evolutions, like so many trained horsemen, wheeling, turning, halting, and running as if under command; and their coming back to again run the (as it proved, very harmless) gantlet of my fire was due either to curiosity or to one of those panicky freaks which occasionally seize those ordinarily wary animals and cause them to run into danger easily avoided by creatures commonly much more readily approached than they are. I had fired half a dozen shots without effect; but while no one ever gets over his feeling of self-indignation at missing an easy shot at close quarters, any one who hunts antelope and is not of a disposition so timid as never to take chances, soon learns that he has to expect to expend a good deal of powder and lead before bagging his game.

By midday I reached a dry creek and followed up

its course for a mile or so, till a small spot of green in the side of a bank showed the presence of water, a little pool of which lay underneath. The ground was so rotten that it was with difficulty I could get Manitou down to where he could drink; but at last both of us satisfied our thirst, and he was turned loose to graze, with his saddle off, so as to cool his back, and I, after eating a biscuit, lay on my face on the ground—there was no shade of any sort near—and dozed until a couple of hours' rest and feed had put the horse in good trim for the afternoon ride. When it came to crossing over the dry creek on whose bank we had rested, we almost went down in a quicksand, and it was only by frantic struggles and flounderings that we managed to get over.

On account of these quicksands and mud-holes, crossing the creeks on the prairie is often very disagreeable work. Even when apparently perfectly dry, the bottom may have merely a thin crust of hard mud and underneath a fathomless bed of slime. If the grass appears wet and with here and there a few tussocks of taller blades in it, it is well to avoid it. Often a man may have to go along a creek nearly a mile before he can find a safe crossing, or else run the risk of seeing his horse mired hard and fast. When a horse is once in a mud-hole it will perhaps so exhaust itself by its first desperate and fruitless struggle that it is almost impossible to get it out. Its bridle and saddle have to be taken off; if another horse is along, the lariat is drawn from the pommel of the latter's saddle to the neck of the one that is in, and it is hauled out by main force. Otherwise, a man may have to work half a day fixing the horse's legs in the right position, and then taking it by the forelock and endeavoring to get it to

187

make a plunge, each plunge bringing it perhaps a few inches nearer the firm ground. Quicksands are even more dangerous than these mud-holes, as, if at all deep, a creature that cannot get out immediately is sure to be speedily engulfed. Many parts of the Little Missouri are impassable on account of these quicksands. Always in crossing unknown ground that looks dangerous it is best to feel your way very cautiously along and, if possible, to find out some cattle trail or even game trail which can be followed.

For some time after leaving the creek nothing was seen; until, on coming over the crest of the next great divide, I came in sight of a band of six or eight pronghorn about a quarter of a mile off to my right hand. There was a slight breeze from the southeast, which blew diagonally across my path toward the antelope. The latter, after staring at me a minute, as I rode slowly on, suddenly started at full speed to run directly up wind, and therefore in a direction that would cut the line of my course less than half a mile ahead of where I was. Knowing that when antelope begin running in a straight line they are very hard to turn, and seeing that they would have to run a longer distance than my horse would to intercept them, I clapped spurs into Manitou, and the game old fellow, a very fleet runner, stretched himself down to the ground and seemed to go almost as fast as the quarry. As I had expected, the latter, when they saw me running, merely straightened themselves out and went on, possibly even faster than before, without changing the line of their flight, keeping right up wind. Both horse and antelope fairly flew over the ground, their courses being at an angle that would certainly bring them together. Two of the antelope led, by some fifty yards or so, the others, who were all bunched together. Nearer and nearer we came, Manitou, in spite of carrying myself and the pack behind the saddle, gamely holding his own, while the antelope, with outstretched necks, went at an even, regular gait that offered a strong contrast to the springing bounds with which a deer runs. At last the two leading animals crossed the line of my flight ahead of me; when I pulled short up, leaped from Manitou's back, and blazed into the band as they went by not forty yards off, aiming well ahead of a fine buck who was on the side nearest me. An antelope's gait is so even that it offers a good running mark; and as the smoke blew off I saw the buck roll over like a rabbit, with both shoulders broken. I then emptied the Winchester at the rest of the band, breaking one hind leg of a young buck. Hastily cutting the throat of, and opening, the dead buck, I again mounted and started off after the wounded one. But, though only on three legs, it went astonishingly fast, having had a good start; and after following it over a mile I gave up the pursuit, though I had gained a good deal; for the heat was very great, and I did not deem it well to tire the horse at the beginning of the trip. Returning to the carcass, I cut off the hams and strung them beside the saddle; an antelope is so spare that there is very little more meat on the body.

This trick of running in a straight line is another of the antelope's peculiar characteristics which frequently lead it into danger. Although with so much sharper eyes than a deer, antelope are in many ways far stupider animals, more like sheep, and they especially resemble the latter in their habit of following a leader, and in their foolish obstinacy in keeping to a course they have once adopted. If a horseman starts to head off a deer the latter will always turn long before he has come within range, but quite often an antelope will merely increase his speed and try to pass ahead of his foe. Almost always, however, one, if alone, will keep out of gunshot, owing to the speed at which he goes, but if there are several in a band which is well strung out, the leader only cares for his own safety and passes well ahead himself. The others follow like sheep, without turning in the least from the line the first followed, and thus may pass within close range. If the leader bounds into the air, those following will often go through exactly the same motions; and if he turns, the others are very apt to, each in succession, run up and turn in the same place, unless the whole band are manœuvring together, like a squadron of cavalry under orders, as has already been spoken of.

After securing the buck's hams and head (the latter for the sake of the horns, which were unusually long and fine), I pushed rapidly on without stopping to hunt, to reach some large creek which should contain both wood and water, for even in summer a fire adds greatly to the comfort and cosiness of a night camp. When the sun had nearly set I went over a divide and came in sight of a creek fulfilling the required conditions. It wound its way through a valley of rich bottom-land, cottonwood-trees of no great height or size growing in thick groves along its banks, while its bed contained many deep pools of water, some of it fresh and good. I rode into a great bend, with a grove of trees on its right and containing excellent feed. Manitou was loosed, with the lariat round his neck, to feed where he wished until I went to bed, when he was to be taken to a place where the grass was thick and succulent, and tethered out for the night. There was any amount of wood with which a fire was started for cheerfulness, and some of the coals were soon raked off apart to cook over. The horse-blanket was spread on the ground, with the oilskin over it as a bed, underneath a spreading cottonwood-tree, while the regular blanket served as covering. The metal cup was soon filled with water and simmering over the coals to make tea, while an antelope steak was roasting on a forked stick. It is wonderful how cosey a camp, in clear weather, becomes if there is a good fire and enough to eat, and how sound the sleep is afterward in the cool air, with the brilliant stars glimmering through the branches overhead. In the country where I was there was absolutely no danger from Indian horse-thieves, and practically none from white ones, for I felt pretty sure no one was anywhere within a good many miles of me, and none could have seen me come into the valley. Besides, in the cattle country stealing horses is a hazardous profession, as any man who is found engaged in it is at once, and very properly, strung up to the nearest tree, or shot if no trees are handy; so very few people follow it, at least for any length of time, and a man's horses are generally safe.

Near where we had halted for the night camp was a large prairie-dog town. Prairie-dogs are abundant all over the cattle country; they are in shape like little woodchucks, and are the most noisy and inquisitive animals imaginable. They are never found singly, but always in towns of several hundred inhabitants; and these towns are found in all kinds of places where the country is flat and treeless. Sometimes they will be placed on the bottoms of the creeks or rivers, and again far out on the prairie or among the Bad Lands, a long distance from any water. Indeed, so dry are some of the localities in which they exist that it is a marvel how they can live at all; yet they seem invariably plump and in good condition. They are exceedingly destructive to grass, eating away everything round their burrows, and thus each town is always extending at the borders, while the holes in the middle are deserted; in many districts they have become a perfect bane to the cattlemen, for the incoming of man has been the means of causing a great falling off in the ranks of their four-footed foes, and this main check to their increase being gone, they multiply at a rate that threatens to make them a serious pest in the future. They are among the few plains animals that are benefited instead of being injured by the presence of man; and it is most difficult to exterminate them or to keep their number in any way under, as they are prolific to a most extraordinary degree; and the quantity of good feed they destroy is very great, and as they eat up the roots of the grass it is a long time before it grows again. Already in many districts the stockmen are seriously considering the best way in which to take steps against them. Prairie-dogs, wherever they exist, are sure to attract attention, all the more so because, unlike most other rodents, they are diurnal and not nocturnal, offering therein a curious case of parallelism to their fellow denizen of the dry plains, the antelope, which is also a creature loving to be up and stirring in the bright daylight, unlike its relatives, the dusk-loving deer. They are very noisy, their shrill yelping resounding on all sides whenever a man rides through a town. None go far from their homes, always keeping close enough to be able to skulk into them at once; and as soon as a foe appears they take refuge on the hillocks beside their burrows, yelping continuously, and accompany-

192

ing each yelp by a spasmodic jerking of the tail and body. When the man comes a little nearer they disappear inside and then thrust their heads out, for they are most inquisitive. Their burrows form one of the chief dangers to riding at full speed over the plains country; hardly any man can do much riding on the prairie for more than a year or two without coming to grief on more than one occasion by his horse putting his foot in a prairie-dog hole. A badger hole is even worse. When a horse gets his foot in such a hole, while going at full speed, he turns a complete somersault and is lucky if he escape without a broken leg, while I have time and again known the rider to be severely injured. There are other smaller animals whose burrows sometimes cause a horseman to receive a sharp tumble. These are the pocket-gophers, queer creatures, shaped like moles and having the same subterranean habits, but with teeth like a rat's and great pouches on the outside of their jaws—whose long, rambling tunnels cover the ground in certain places, though the animals themselves are very rarely seen; and the little striped gophers and gray gophers, entirely different animals, more like ground-squirrels. But the prairie-dog is always the main source of danger to the horseman, as well as of mischief to the cattle-herder.

Around the prairie-dog towns it is always well to keep a lookout for the smaller carnivora, especially coyotes and badgers, as they are very fond of such neighborhoods, and almost always it is also a favorite resort for the larger kinds of hawks, which are so numerous throughout the cattle country. Rattlesnakes are quite plenty, living in the deserted holes, and the latter are also the homes of the little burrowing owls, which will often be seen standing at the opening, ready

193

to run in as quickly as any of the prairie-dogs if danger threatens. They have a funny habit of gravely bowing or posturing at the passer-by, and stand up very erect on their legs. With the exception of this species, owls are rare in the cattle country.

A prairie-dog is rather a difficult animal to get, as it stands so close to its burrow that a spasmodic kick, even if at the last gasp, sends the body inside, where it cannot be recovered. The cowboys are always practising at them with their revolvers, and, as they are pretty good shots, mortally wound a good many, but unless the force of the blow fairly knocks the prairie-dog away from the mouth of the burrow, it almost always manages to escape inside. But a good shot with the rifle can kill any number by lying down quietly and waiting a few minutes until the dogs get a little distance from the mouths of their homes.

Badgers are more commonly found around prairie-dog towns than anywhere else; and they get their chief food by digging up the prairie-dogs and gophers with their strong forearms and long, stout claws. They are not often found wandering away from their homes in the daytime, but if so caught are easily run down and killed. A badger is a most desperate fighter, and an overmatch for a coyote, his hide being very thick and his form so squat and strong that it is hard to break his back or legs, while his sharp teeth grip like a steel trap. A very few seconds allow him to dig a hole in the ground, into which he can back all except his head; and when placed thus, with his rear and flanks protected, he can beat off a dog many times his own size. A young badger one night came up round the ranch-house, and began gnawing at some bones that had been left near the door. Hearing the noise

194

one of my men took a lantern and went outside. The glare of the light seemed to make the badger stupid, for after looking at the lantern a few moments, it coolly turned and went on eating the scraps of flesh on the bones, and was knocked on the head without attempting to escape.

To come back to my trip. Early in the morning I was awakened by the shrill yelping of the prairie-dogs, whose town was near me. The sun had not risen, and the air had the peculiar chill it always takes on toward morning, while little wreaths of light mist rose from the pools. Getting up and loosing Manitou to let him feed round where he wished and slake his thirst, I took the rifle, strolled up the creek-valley a short distance, and turned off out on the prairie. Nothing was in sight in the way of game; but overhead a skylark was singing, soaring up above me so high that I could not make out his form in the gray morning light. I listened for some time, and the music never ceased for a moment, coming down clear, sweet, and tender from the air above. Soon the strains of another answered from a little distance off, and the two kept soaring and singing as long as I stayed to listen; and when I walked away I could still hear their notes behind me. In some ways the skylark is the sweetest singer we have; only certain of the thrushes rival it, but though the songs of the latter have perhaps even more melody, they are far from being as uninterrupted and well sustained, being rather a succession of broken bursts of music.

The sun was just appearing when I walked back to the creek bottom. Coming slowly out of a patch of brushwood was a doe, going down to drink—her great, sensitive ears thrown forward as she peered anxiously and timidly round. She was very watchful, lifting her head and gazing about between every few mouthfuls. When she had drunk her fill she snatched a hasty mouthful or two of the wet grass, and then cantered back to the edge of the brush, when a little spotted fawn came out and joined her. The two stood together for a few moments, and then walked off into the cover. The little pond at which they had drunk was within fifty yards of my night bed; and it had other tenants in the shape of a mallard duck, with a brood of little ducklings, balls of fuzzy yellow down, that bobbed off into the reeds like little corks as I walked by.

Breaking camp is a simple operation for one man; and but a few minutes after breakfast Manitou and I were off, the embers of the fire having been extinguished with the care that comes to be almost second nature with the cattleman, one of whose chief dreads is the prairie fire that sometimes robs his stock of such an immense amount of feed. Very little game was seen during the morning, as I rode in an almost straight line over the hot, parched plains, the ground cracked and seamed by the heat, and the dull-brown blades bending over as if the sun was too much even for them. The sweat drenched the horse even when we were walking; and long before noon we halted for rest by a bitter alkaline pool with border so steep and rotten that I had to bring water up to the horse in my hat—having taken some along in a canteen for my own use. But there was a steep bank near, overgrown with young trees, and thus giving good shade; and it was this that induced me to stop. When leaving this halting-place, I spied three figures in the distance, loping toward me; they turned out to be cowboys, who had been out a couple of days looking up a band of strayed ponies,

and, as they had exhausted their supply of food, I gave
them the antelope hams, trusting to shoot another for
my own use.

Nor was I disappointed. After leaving the cowboys
I headed the horse toward the more rolling country
where the prairies begin to break off into the edges of
the Bad Lands. Several bands of antelope were seen,
and I tried one unsuccessful stalk, not being able to
come within rifle-range; but toward evening, when
only about a mile from a wooded creek on whose banks
I intended to sleep, I came across a solitary buck, just
as I was topping the ridge of the last divide. As I was
keeping a sharp lookout at the time, I reined in the
horse the instant the head of the antelope came in
sight, and jumping off crept up till I could see his
whole body, when I dropped on my knee and took
steady aim. He was a long way off (three hundred
yards by actual pacing), and not having made out exactly what we were he stood still, looking intently in
our direction and broadside to us. I held well over his
shoulder, and at the report he dropped like a shot, the
ball having broken his neck. It was a very good shot;
the best I ever made at antelope, of which game, as
already said, I have killed but very few individuals.
Taking the hams and saddle, I rode on down to the
creek and again went into camp among timber. Thus
on this trip I was never successful in outwitting antelope on the several occasions when I pitted my craft
and skill against their wariness and keen senses, always
either failing to get within range or else missing them;
but nevertheless I got two by taking advantage of the
stupidity and curiosity which they occasionally show.

The middle part of the days having proved so very
hot, and as my store of biscuits was nearly gone, and

as I knew, moreover, that the antelope meat would not keep over twenty-four hours, I decided to push back home next day; and, accordingly, I broke camp at the first streak of dawn, and took Manitou back to the ranch at a smart lope.

A solitary trip such as this was, through a comparatively wild region in which game is still plentiful, always has great attraction for any man who cares for sport and for nature and who is able to be his own companion, but the pleasure after all depends a good deal on the weather. To be sure, after a little experience in roughing it, the hardships seem a good deal less formidable than they formerly did, and a man becomes able to roll up in a wet blanket and sleep all night in a pelting rain without hurting himself—though he will shiver a good deal, and feel pretty numb and stiff in those chill and dreary hours just before dawn. But when a man's clothes and bedding and rifle are all wet, no matter how philosophically he may bear it, it may be taken for granted that he does not enjoy it. So fair weather is a very vital and important element among those that go to make up the pleasure and success of such a trip. Luckily, fair weather can be counted on with a good deal of certainty in late spring and throughout most of the summer and fall on the Northern cattle plains. The storms that do take place, though very violent, do not last long.

Every now and then, however, there will be in the fall a three days' storm in which it is almost impossible to travel, and then the best thing to be done is to lie up under any shelter that is at hand until it blows over. I remember one such camp which was made in the midst of the most singular and picturesque surroundings. It was toward the end of a long wagon trip that we had been taking, and all of the horses were tired by incessant work. We had come through country which was entirely new to us, passing nearly all day in a low, flat prairie through which flowed a stream that we supposed to be either the Box Alder or the Little Beaver. In leaving this we had struck some heavy sand-hills, and while pulling the loaded wagon up them one of the team played out completely, and we had to take her out and put in one of the spare saddle-ponies, a tough little fellow. Night came on fast, and the sun was just setting when we crossed the final ridge and came in sight of as singular a bit of country as I have ever seen. The cowboys, as we afterward found, had christened the place " Medicine Buttes." In plains dialect, I may explain, " Medicine " has been adopted from the Indians, among whom it means anything supernatural or very unusual. It is used in the sense of " magic," or " out of the common."

Over an irregular tract of gently rolling sandy hills, perhaps about three-quarters of a mile square, were scattered several hundred detached and isolated buttes or cliffs of sandstone, each butte from fifteen to fifty feet high, and from thirty to a couple of hundred feet across. Some of them rose as sharp peaks or ridges, or as connected chains, but much the greater number had flat tops like little table-lands. The sides were perfectly perpendicular, and were cut and channelled by the weather into most extraordinary forms: caves, columns, battlements, spires, and flying buttresses were mingled in the strangest confusion. Many of the caves were worn clear through the buttes, and they were at every height in the sides, while ledges ran across the faces, and shoulders and columns jutted out from the corners. On the tops and at the bases of most of the cliffs grew pine-trees, some of considerable height, and the sand gave everything a clean, white look.

Altogether, it was as fantastically beautiful a place as I have ever seen; it seemed impossible that the hand of man should not have had something to do with its formation. There was a spring of clear cold water a few hundred yards off, with good feed for the horses round it; and we made our camp at the foot of one of the largest buttes, building a roaring pine-log fire in an angle in the face of the cliff, while our beds were under the pine-trees. It was the time of the full moon, and the early part of the night was clear. The flame of the fire leaped up the side of the cliff, the red light bringing out into lurid and ghastly relief the bold corners and strange-looking escarpments of the rock, while against it the stiff limbs of the pines stood out like rigid bars of iron. Walking off out of sight of the circle of fire-light, among the tall crags, the place seemed almost as unreal as if we had been in fairyland. The flood of clear moonlight turned the white faces of the cliffs and the grounds between them into shining silver, against which the pines showed dark and sombre, while the intensely black shadows of the buttes took on forms that were grimly fantastic. Every cave or cranny in the crags looked so black that it seemed almost to be thrown out from the surface, and when the branches of the trees moved, the bright moonlight danced on the ground as if it were a sheet of molten metal. Neither in shape nor in color did our surroundings seem to belong to the dull gray world through which we had been travelling all day.

But by next morning everything had changed. A furious gale of wind was blowing, and we were shrouded in a dense, drizzling mist, through which at times the rain drove in level sheets. Now and then the fog would blow away, and then would come on thicker than ever, and when it began to clear off a steady rain took its place, and the wind increased to a regular hurricane. With its canvas top on, the wagon would certainly have been blown over if on open ground, and it was impossible to start or keep a fire except under the sheltered lee of the cliff. Moreover, the wind kept shifting, and we had to shift too as fast as ever it started to blow from a new quarter; and thus in the course of the twenty-four hours we made a complete circle of the cliff at whose base we were. Our blankets got wet during the night; and they got no drier during the day; and the second night as we slept on them they got steadily damper. Our provisions were pretty nearly out, and so, with little to eat and less to do, wet and uncomfortable, we cowered over the sputtering fire, and whiled the long day away as best we might with our own thoughts; fortunately, we had all learned that no matter how bad things are, grumbling and bad temper can always be depended upon to make them worse, and so bore our ill fortune, if not with stoical indifference, at least in perfect quiet. Next day the storm still continued, but the fog was gone and the wind somewhat easier; we spent the whole day looking up the horses, which had drifted a long distance before the storm; nor was it till the morning of the third day that we left our beautiful but, as events had made it, uncomfortable camping-ground.

In midsummer the storms are rarely of long duration, but are very severe while they last. I remember well one day when I was caught in such a storm. I had gone some twenty-five miles from the ranch to see the round-up, which had reached what is known as the Oxbow of the Little Missouri, where the river makes a great loop round a flat, grassy bottom, on which the cattle herd was gathered. I stayed, seeing the cattle cut out and the calves branded, until after dinner; for it was at the time of the year when the days were longest.

At last the work was ended, and I started home in the twilight. The horse splashed across the shallow ford, and then spent half an hour in climbing up through the rugged side hills, till we reached the top of the first great plateau that had to be crossed. As soon as I got on it I put in the spurs and started off at a gallop. In the dusk the brown, level land stretched out in formless expanse ahead of me, unrelieved, except by the bleached white of a buffalo's skull, whose outlines glimmered indistinctly to one side of the course I was riding. On my left the sun had set behind a row of jagged buttes, that loomed up in sharp relief against the western sky; above them it had left a bar of yellow light, which only made more intense the darkness of the surrounding heavens. In the quarter toward which I was heading there had gathered a lowering mass of black storm-clouds, lit up by the incessant play of the lightning. The wind had totally died away, and the deathlike stillness was only broken by the continuous, measured beat of the horse's hoofs as he galloped over the plain, and at times the muttered roll of the distant thunder.

Without slacking pace, I crossed the plateau, and as I came to the other edge the storm burst in sheets and torrents of water. In five minutes I was drenched through, and to guide myself had to take advantage of the continual flashes of lightning; and I was right glad, half an hour afterward, to stop and take shelter in the log hut of a couple of cowboys, where I could get dry and warm.

CHAPTER VII

A TRIP AFTER MOUNTAIN-SHEEP

LATE one fall a spell of bitter weather set in, and lasted on through the early part of the winter. For many days together the cold was fierce in its intensity; and the wheels of the ranch wagon, when we drove out for a load of fire-wood, creaked and sang as they ground through the powdery snow that lay light on the ground. At night in the clear sky the stars seemed to snap and glitter; and for weeks of cloudless white weather the sun shone down on a land from which his beams glanced and glistened as if it had been the surface of a mirror, till the glare hurt the eyes that looked upon it. In the still nights we could hear the trees crack and jar from the strain of the biting frost; and in its winding bed the river lay fixed like a huge bent bar of blue steel.

We had been told that a small band of bighorn was hanging around some very steep and broken country about twenty-five miles from the ranch-house. I had been out after them once alone, but had failed to find even their tracks, and had made up my mind that in order to hunt them it would be necessary to make a three or four days' trip, taking along the buckboard with our bedding and eatables. The trip had been delayed owing to two of my men, who had been sent out to buy ponies, coming in with a bunch of fifty, for the most part hardly broken. Some of them were meant for the use of the lower ranch, and the men from the latter had come up to get them. At night the ponies were let loose, and each day were gathered into the horse corral and broken as well as we could break them in such weather. It was my intention not to start on the hunt until the ponies were separated into the two bands and the men from the lower ranch (the Elkhorn) had gone off with theirs. Then one of the cowboys was to take the buckboard up to a deserted hunter's hut, which lay on a great bend of the river near by the ground over which the bighorn were said to wander, while my foreman, Merrifield, and myself would take saddle-horses and each day ride to the country through which we intended to hunt, returning at night to the buckboard and hut. But we started a little sooner than we intended, owing to a funny mistake made by one of the cowboys.

The sun did not rise until nearly eight, but each morning we breakfasted at five, and the men were then sent out on the horses which had been kept in overnight, to find and drive home the pony band; of course they started in perfect darkness, except for the starlight. On the last day of our proposed stay the men had come in with the ponies before sunrise; and, leaving the latter in the corral, they entered the house and crowded round the fire, stamping and beating their numbed hands together. In the midst of the confusion word was brought by one of the cowboys that while hunting for the horses he had seen two bears go down into a washout; and he told us that he could bring us right to the place where he had seen them, for as soon as he left it he had come in at speed on his swift, iron-gray horse—a vicious, clean-limbed devil, with muscles like bundles of tense wire; the cold had made the brute savage, and it had been punished with the cruel curb-bit until long, bloody icicles hung from its lips.

A TRIP AFTER MOUNTAIN-SHEEP

At once Merrifield and I mounted in hot haste and rode off with the bringer of good tidings, leaving hasty instructions where we were to be joined by the buckboard. The sun was still just below the horizon as we started, wrapped warmly in our fur coats and with our caps drawn down over our ears to keep out the cold. The cattle were standing in the thickets and sheltered ravines, huddled together with their heads down, the frost lying on their backs and the icicles hanging from their muzzles; they stared at us as we rode along, but were too cold to move a hair's breadth out of our way; indeed, it is a marvel how they survive the winter at all. Our course at first lay up a long valley, cut up by cattle trails; then we came out, just as the sun had risen, upon the rounded, gently sloping highlands, thickly clad with the short, nutritious grass, which curls on the stalk into good hay and on which the cattle feed during the winter. We galloped rapidly over the hills, our blood gradually warming up from the motion, and soon came to the long washout, cutting down like a miniature canyon for a space of two or three miles through the bottom of a valley, into which the cowboy said he had seen the bears go. One of us took one side and one the other, and we rode along up wind, but neither the bears nor any traces of them could we see; at last, half a mile ahead of us, two dark objects suddenly emerged from the washout, and came out on the plain. For a second we thought they were the quarry; then we saw that they were merely a couple of dark-colored ponies. The cowboy's chapfallen face was a study; he had seen, in the dim light, the two ponies going down with their heads held near the ground, and had mistaken them for bears (by no means the unnatural mistake that it seems; I have known an experi-

enced hunter fire twice at a black calf in the late evening, thinking it was a bear). He knew only too well
the merciless chaff to which he would be henceforth
exposed, and a foretaste of which he at once received
from my companion. The ponies had strayed from
the main herd, and the cowboy was sent to drive them
to the home corral, while Merrifield and myself continued our hunt.

We had all day before us, and but twenty miles or
so to cover before reaching the hut where the buckboard was to meet us; but the course we intended to
take was through country so rough that no Eastern
horse could cross it, and even the hardy Western hunting-ponies, who climb like goats, would have difficulty
in keeping their feet. Our route lay through the
heart of the Bad Lands, but of course the country was
not equally rough in all parts. There were tracts of
varying size, each covered with a tangled mass of
chains and peaks, the buttes in places reaching a height
that would in the East entitle them to be called mountains. Every such tract was riven in all directions by
deep chasms and narrow ravines, whose sides sometimes
rolled off in gentle slopes, but far more often rose as
sheer cliffs, with narrow ledges along their fronts. A
sparse growth of grass covered certain portions of these
lands, and on some of the steep hillsides, or in the canyons, were scanty groves of coniferous evergreens, so
stunted by the thin soil and bleak weather that many
of them were bushes rather than trees. Most of the
peaks and ridges and many of the valleys were entirely
bare of vegetation, and these had been cut by wind
and water into the strangest and most fantastic shapes.
Indeed, it is difficult, in looking at such formations, to
get rid of the feeling that their curiously twisted and

contorted forms are due to some vast volcanic upheavals or other subterranean forces; yet they are merely caused by the action of the various weathering forces of the dry climate on the different strata of sandstones, clays, and marls. Isolated columns shoot up into the air, bearing on their summits flat rocks like tables; square buttes tower high above surrounding depressions, which are so cut up by twisting gullies and low ridges as to be almost impassable; shelving masses of sandstone jut out over the sides of the cliffs; some of the ridges, with perfectly perpendicular sides, are so worn away that they stand up like gigantic knife-blades; and gulches, washouts, and canyons dig out the sides of each butte, while between them are thrust out long spurs, with sharp, ragged tops. All such patches of barren, broken ground, where the feed seems too scant to support any large animal, are the favorite haunts of the bighorn, though it also wanders far into the somewhat gentler and more fertile, but still very rugged, domain of the blacktail deer.

Between all such masses of rough country lay wide, grassy plateaus or long stretches of bare plain, covered with pebbly shingle. We loped across all these open places; and when we came to a reach of broken country would leave our horses and hunt through it on foot. Except where the wind had blown it off, there was a thin coat of snow over everything, and the icy edges and sides of the cliffs gave only slippery and uncertain foothold, so as to render the climbing doubly toilsome. Hunting the bighorn is at all times the hardest and most difficult kind of sport, and is equally trying to both wind and muscle; and for that very reason the bighorn ranks highest among all the species of game that are killed by still-hunting, and its chase constitutes the noblest form of sport with the rifle, always excepting, of course, those kinds of hunting where the quarry is itself dangerous to attack. Climbing kept us warm in spite of the bitter weather; we wore our fur coats and chaps only while on horseback, leaving them where we left the horses, and doing our still-hunting in buckskin shirts, fur caps, and stout shoes.

Bighorn, more commonly known as mountain-sheep, are extremely wary and cautious animals, and are plentiful in but few places. This is rather surprising, for they seem to be fairly prolific (although not as much so as deer and antelope), and comparatively few are killed by the hunters; indeed, many less are shot than of any other kind of Western game, in proportion to their numbers. They hold out in a place long after the elk and buffalo have been exterminated, and for many years after both of these have become things of the past the bighorn will still exist to afford sport to the man who is a hardy mountaineer and skilful with the rifle. For it is the only kind of game on whose haunts cattle do not trespass. Good buffalo or elk pasture is sure to be also good pasture for steers and cows; and in summer the herds of the ranchman wander far into the prairies of the antelope, while in winter their chosen and favorite resorts are those of which the blacktail is equally fond. Thus, the cattlemen are almost as much foes of these kinds of game as are the hunters, but neither cattle nor cowboys penetrate into the sterile and rocky wastes where the bighorn is found. And it is too wary game, and the labor of following it is too great, for it ever to be much persecuted by the skin or market hunters.

In size the bighorn comes next to buffalo and elk, averaging larger than the blacktail deer, while an old ram will sometimes be almost as heavy as a small cow elk. In his movements he is not light and graceful like the pronghorn and other antelopes, his marvellous agility seeming rather to proceed from sturdy strength and wonderful command over iron sinews and muscles. The huge horns are carried proudly erect by the massive neck; every motion of the body is made with perfect poise, and there seems to be no ground so difficult that the bighorn cannot cross it. There is probably no animal in the world his superior in climbing, and his only equals are the other species of mountain-sheep and the ibexes. No matter how sheer the cliff, if there are ever so tiny cracks or breaks in the surface, the bighorn will bound up or down it with wonderful ease and seeming absence of effort. The perpendicular bounds it can make are truly startling—in strong contrast with its distant relative, the pronghorn, which can leap almost any level jump but seems unable to clear the smallest height. In descending a sheer wall of rock the bighorn holds all four feet together and goes down in long jumps, bounding off the surface almost like a rubber ball every time he strikes it. The way that one will vanish over the roughest and most broken ground is a perpetual surprise to any one who has hunted them; and the ewes are quite as skilful as the rams, while even the very young lambs seem almost as well able to climb, and certainly follow wherever their elders lead. Time and again one will rush over a cliff to what appears certain death, and will gallop away from the bottom unharmed. Their perfect self-confidence seems to be justified, however, for they never slip or make a misstep, even in the narrowest ledges when covered with ice and snow. And all their marvellous jumping and climbing is done with an apparent ease that renders it the more wonderful. Rapid though the movements of one are, they are made without any of the nervous hurry so characteristic of the antelopes and smaller deer; the onlooker is really as much impressed with the animal's sinewy power and self-command as with his agility. His strength and his self-reliance seem to fit him above all other kinds of game to battle with the elements and with his brute foes; he does not care to have the rough ways of his life made smooth; were his choice free, his abode would still be the vast and lonely wilderness in which he is found. To him the barren wastes of the Bad Lands offer a most attractive home; yet to other living creatures they are at all times as grimly desolate and forbidding as any spot on earth can be; at all seasons they seem hostile to every form of life. In the raging heat of summer the dry earth cracks and crumbles, and the sultry, lifeless air sways and trembles as if above a furnace. Through the high, clear atmosphere, the intense sunlight casts unnaturally deep shadows; and where there are no shadows, brings out in glaring relief the weird, fantastic shapes and bizarre coloring of the buttes. In winter, snow and ice coat the thin crests and sharp sides of the cliffs, and increase their look of savage wildness; the cold turns the ground into ringing iron; and the icy blasts sweep through the clefts and over the ridges with an angry fury even more terrible than is the intense, deathlike, silent heat of midsummer. But the mountain ram is alike proudly indifferent to the hottest summer sun and to the wildest winter storm.

The lambs are brought forth late in May or early in June. Like the antelope, the dam soon leads her kids to join the herd, which may range in size from a dozen to four or five times as many individuals, generally approaching nearer the former number. The ewes, lambs, and yearling or two-year-old rams go together. The young but full-grown rams keep in small parties of three or four, while the old fellows, with monstrous heads, keep by themselves, except when they join the ewes in the rutting season. At this time they wage savage war with each other. The horns of the old rams are always battered and scarred from these butting contests—which appearance, by the way, has given rise to the ridiculous idea that they were in the habit of jumping over precipices and landing on their heads.

Occasionally the bighorn come down into the valleys or along the grassy slopes to feed, but this is not often, and in such cases every member of the band is always keeping the sharpest lookout, and at the slightest alarm they beat a retreat to their broken fastnesses. At night-time or in the early morning they come down to drink at the small pools or springs, but move off the instant they have satisfied their thirst. As a rule, they spend their time among the rocks and rough ground, and it is in these places that they must be hunted. They cover a good deal of ground when feeding, for the feed is scanty in their haunts, and they walk quite rapidly along the ledges or peaks, by preference high up, as they graze or browse. When through feeding they always choose as a resting-place some point from which they can command a view over all the surrounding territory. An old ram is peculiarly wary. The crest of a ridge or the top of a peak is a favorite resting-bed; but even more often they choose some ledge, high up, but just below the crest, or lie on a shelf of rock that juts out from where a ridge ends, and thus enables them to view the country on three sides of them. In color they harmonize curiously with the grayish or yellowish brown of the ground on which they are found, and it is often very difficult to make them out when lying motionless on a ledge of rock. Time and again they will be mistaken for boulders, and, on the other hand, I have more than once stalked up to masses of sandstone that I have mistaken for sheep.

When lying down, the bighorn can thus scan everything below it; and both while feeding and resting it invariably keeps the sharpest possible lookout for all danger from beneath, and this trait makes it needful for the hunter always to keep on the highest ground and try to come on it from above. For protection against danger it relies on ears, eyes, and nose alike. The slightest sound startles it and puts it on its guard, while if it sees or smells anything which it deems may bode danger it is off like a flash. It is as wary and quick-sighted as the antelope, and its senses are as keen as are those of the elk, while it is not afflicted by the occasional stupidity nor heedless recklessness of these two animals, nor by the intense curiosity of the blacktail, and it has all the whitetail's sound common sense, coupled with a much shyer nature and much sharper faculties, so that it is more difficult to kill than are any of these creatures. And the climbing is rendered all the more tiresome by the traits above spoken of, which make it necessary for the hunter to keep above it. The first thing to do is to clamber up to the top of a ridge, and after that to keep on the highest crests.

At all times, and with all game, the still-hunter should be quiet and should observe caution, but when after mountain-sheep he must be absolutely noiseless and must not neglect a single chance. He must be careful not to step on a loose stone or to start any crumbling earth; he must always hunt up or across wind, and he must take advantage of every crag or boulder to shelter himself from the gaze of his watchful quarry. While keeping up as high as possible, he should not go on the very summit, as that brings him out in too sharp relief against the sky. And all the while he will be crossing land where he will need to pay good heed to his own footing or else run the risk of breaking his neck.

As far as lay in us, on our first day's hunt we paid proper heed to all the rules of hunting craft, but without success. Up the slippery, ice-covered buttes we clambered, clinging to the rocks, and slowly working our way across the faces of the cliffs, or cautiously creeping along the narrow ledges, peering over every crest long and carefully, and from the peaks scanning the ground all about with the field-glasses. But we saw no sheep, and but little sign of them. Still we did see some sign, and lost a shot, either through bad luck or bad management. This was while going through a cluster of broken buttes, whose peaks rose up like sharp cones. On reaching the top of one at the leeward end, we worked cautiously up the side, seeing nothing, to the other end, and then down along the middle. When about half-way back we came across the fresh foot-prints of a ewe or yearling ram in a little patch of snow. On tracing them back we found that it had been lying down on the other side of a small bluff, within a hundred yards of where we had passed, and must have either got our wind or else have heard us make some noise. At any rate, it had gone off, and though we followed its tracks a little in the snow, they soon got on the bare, frozen ground and we lost them.

After that we saw nothing. The cold, as the day

wore on, seemed gradually to chill us through and through; our hands and feet became numb and our ears tingled under our fur caps. We hunted carefully through two or three masses of jagged buttes which seemed most likely places for the game we were after, taking a couple of hours to each place; and then, as the afternoon was beginning to wane, mounted our shivering horses for good, and pushed toward the bend of the river where we were to meet the buckboard. Our course lay across a succession of bleak, wind-swept plateaus, broken by deep and narrow pine-clad gorges. We galloped swiftly over the plateaus, where the footing was good and the going easy, for the gales had driven the feathery snow off the withered brown grass; but getting on and off these table-lands was often a real labor, their sides were so sheer. The horses plunged and scrambled after us as we led them up; while in descending they would sit back on their haunches and half walk, half slide down the steep inclines. Indeed, one or two of the latter were so very straight that the horses would not face them, and we had to turn them round and back them over the edge, and then all go down with a rush. At any rate, it warmed our blood to keep out of the way of the hoofs. On one of the plateaus I got a very long shot at a blacktail, which I missed.

Finally, we struck the head of a long, winding valley with a smooth bottom, and after cantering down it four or five miles, came to the river, just after the cold, pale-red sun had sunk behind the line of hills ahead of us. Our horses were sharp shod, and crossed the ice without difficulty; and in a grove of leafless cottonwoods on the opposite side, we found the hut for which we had been making, the cowboy already inside with the fire started. Throughout the night the temperature sank lower and lower, and it was impossible to keep the crazy old hut anywhere near freezing-point; the wind whistled through the chinks and crannies of the logs, and, after a short and by no means elaborate supper, we were glad to cower down with our great fur coats still on, under the pile of buffalo-robes and bearskins. My sleeping-bag came in very handily and kept me as warm as possible, in spite of the bitter frost.

We were up and had taken breakfast next morning by the time the first streak of dawn had dimmed the brilliancy of the stars, and immediately afterward strode off on foot, as we had been hampered by the horses on the day before. We walked briskly across the plain until, by the time it was light enough to see to shoot, we came to the foot of a great hill known as Middle Butte, a huge, isolated mass of rock, several miles in length, and with high sides, very steep toward the nearly level summit; it would be deemed a mountain of no inconsiderable size in the East. We hunted carefully through the outlying foot-hills and projecting spurs around its base, without result, finding but a few tracks, and those very old ones, and then toiled up to the top, which, though narrow in parts, in others widened out into plateaus half a mile square. Having made a complete circuit of the top, peering over the edge and closely examining the flanks of the butte with the field-glass, without having seen anything, we slid down the other side and took off through a streak of very rugged but low country. This day, though the weather had grown even colder, we did not feel it, for we walked all the while with a quick pace, and the climbing was very hard work. The shoulders and ledges of the cliffs had become round and slippery with the ice, and it was no easy task to move up and along them, clutching the gun in one hand, and grasping each little projection with the other. Climbing through the Bad Lands is just like any other kind of mountaineering, except that the precipices and chasms are much lower; but this really makes very little difference when the ground is frozen as solid as iron, for it would be almost as unpleasant to fall fifty feet as to fall two hundred, and the result to the person who tried it would be very much the same in each case.

Hunting for a day or two without finding game where the work is severe and toilsome is a good test of the sportsman's staying qualities; the man who at the end of the time is proceeding with as much caution and determination as at the beginning has got the right stuff in him. On this day I got rather tired, and committed one of the blunders of which no hunter ought ever to be guilty; that is, I fired at small game while on ground where I might expect large. We had seen two or three jack-rabbits scudding off like noiseless white shadows, and finally came upon some sharptail prairie-fowl in a hollow. One was quite near me, perched on a bush, and with its neck stretched up offered a beautiful mark; I could not resist it, so knelt and fired. At the report of the rifle (it was a miss, by the bye) a head suddenly appeared over a ridge some six hundred yards in front—too far off for us to make out what kind of animal it belonged to—looked fixedly at us, and then disappeared. We feared it might be a mountain-sheep, and that my unlucky shot had deprived us of the chance of a try at it; but on hurrying up to the place where it had been we were relieved to find that the tracks were only those of a blacktail. After this lesson we proceeded in silence, making a long circle through the roughest kind of country. When on the way back to camp, where the buttes rose highest and steepest, we came upon fresh tracks, but as it was then late in the afternoon, did not try to follow them that day. When near the hut I killed a sharptail for supper, making rather a neat shot, the bird being eighty yards off. The night was even colder than the preceding one, and all signs told us that we would soon have a change for the worse in the weather, which made me doubly anxious to get a sheep before the storm struck us. We determined that next morning we would take the horses and make a quick push for the chain of high buttes where we had seen the fresh tracks, and hunt them through with thorough care.

We started in the cold gray of the next morning and pricked rapidly off over the frozen plain, columns of white steam rising from the nostrils of the galloping horses. When we had reached the foot of the hills where we intended to hunt, and tethered the horses, the sun had already risen, but it was evident that the clear weather of a fortnight past was over. The air was thick and hazy, and away off in the northwest a towering mass of grayish-white clouds looked like a weather-breeder; everything boded a storm at no distant date. The country over which we now hunted was wilder and more mountainous than any we had yet struck. High, sharp peaks and ridges broke off abruptly into narrow gorges and deep ravines; they were bare of all but the scantiest vegetation, save on some of the sheltered sides where grew groves of dark pines, now laden down with feathery snow. The climbing was as hard as ever. At first we went straight up the side of the tallest peak, and then along the knife-like ridge which joined it with the next. The ice made the footing very

217

slippery as we stepped along the ledges or crawled round the jutting shoulders, and we had to look carefully for our footholds; while in the cold, thin air every quick burst we made up a steep hill caused us to pant for breath. We had gone but a little way before we saw fresh signs of the animals we were after, but it was some time before we came upon the quarry itself.

We left the high ground and, descending into a narrow chasm, walked along its bottom, which was but a couple of feet wide, while the sides rose up from it at an acute angle. After following this for a few hundred yards, we turned a sharp corner, and shortly afterward our eyes were caught by some grains of fresh earth lying on the snow in front of our feet. On the sides, some feet above our heads, were marks in the snow which a moment's glance showed us had been made by a couple of mountain-sheep that had come down one side of the gorge and had leaped across to the other, their sharp toes going through the thin snow and displacing the earth that had fallen to the bottom. The tracks had evidently been made just before we rounded the corner, and as we had been advancing noiselessly on the snow, with the wind in our favor, we knew that the animals could have no suspicion of our presence. They had gone up the cliff on our right, but as that on our left was much lower and continued for some distance parallel to the other, we concluded that by running along its top we would be most certain to get a good shot. Clambering instantly up the steep side, digging my hands and feet into the loose snow, and grasping at every little rock or frozen projection, I reached the top, and then ran forward along the ridge a few paces, crouching behind the masses of queerly shaped sandstone, and saw, about ninety yards off across the ravine, a couple of mountain rams. The one with the largest horns was broadside toward me, his sturdy, massive form outlined clearly against the sky as he stood on the crest of the ridge. I dropped on my knee, raising the rifle as I did so; for a second he did not quite make me out, turning his head half round to look. I held the sight fairly on the point just behind his shoulder and pulled the trigger. At the report he staggered and pitched forward, but recovered himself and crossed over the ridge out of sight. We jumped and slid down into the ravine again, and clambered up the opposite side as fast as our lungs and the slippery ice would let us; then taking the trail of the wounded ram we trotted along it. We had not far to go; for, as I expected, we found him lying on his side a couple of hundred yards beyond the ridge, his eyes already glazed in death. The bullet had gone in behind the shoulder and ranged clean through his body crosswise, going a little forward; no animal less tough than a mountain ram could have gone any distance at all with such a wound. He had most obligingly run round to a part of the hill where we could bring up one of the horses without very much difficulty. Accordingly, I brought up old Manitou, who can carry anything and has no fear, and the bighorn was soon strapped across his back. It was a fine ram, with perfectly shaped but not very large horns.

The other ram, two years old, with small horns, had bounded over the ridge before I could get a shot at him; we followed his trail for half a mile, but as he showed no signs of halting and we were anxious to get home, we then gave up the pursuit.

It was still early in the day, and we made up our minds to push back for the home ranch, as we did not wish to be caught out in a long storm. The lowering sky was already overcast by a mass of leaden-gray clouds; and it was evident that we had no time to lose. In a little over an hour we were back at the log camp, where the ram was shifted from Manitou's back to the buckboard. A very few minutes sufficed to pack up our bedding and provisions, and we started home. Merrifield and I rode on ahead, not sparing the horses; but before we got home the storm had burst, and a furious blizzard blew in our teeth as we galloped along the last mile of the river-bottom, before coming to the home ranch-house; and as we warmed our stiffened limbs before the log fire I congratulated myself upon the successful outcome of what I knew would be the last hunting trip I should take during that season.

The death of this ram was accomplished without calling for any very good shooting on our part. He was standing still, less than a hundred yards off, when the shot was fired; and we came across him so close merely by accident. Still, we fairly deserved our luck, for we had hunted with the most patient and painstaking care from dawn till nightfall for the better part of three days, spending most of the time in climbing at a smart rate of speed up sheer cliffs and over rough and slippery ground. Still-hunting the bighorn is always a toilsome and laborious task, and the very bitter weather during which we had been out had not lessened the difficulty of the work, though in the cold it was much less exhausting than it would have been to have hunted across the same ground in summer. No other kind of hunting does as much to bring out the good qualities, both moral and physical, of the sportsmen who follow it. If a man keeps at it, it is bound to make him both hardy and resolute; to strengthen his muscles and fill out his lungs.

Mountain mutton is in the fall the most delicious eating furnished by any game animal. Nothing else compares with it for juiciness, tenderness, and flavor; but at all other times of the year it is tough, stringy, and worthless.

CHAPTER VIII

THE LORDLY BUFFALO

Gone forever are the mighty herds of the lordly buffalo. A few solitary individuals and small bands are still to be found scattered here and there in the wilder parts of the plains; and, though most of these will be very soon destroyed, others will for some years fight off their doom and lead a precarious existence either in remote and almost desert portions of the country near the Mexican frontier, or else in the wildest and most inaccessible fastnesses of the Rocky Mountains; but the great herds, that for the first three-quarters of this century formed the distinguishing and characteristic feature of the Western plains, have vanished forever.

It is only about a hundred years ago that the white man, in his march westward, first encroached upon the lands of the buffalo, for these animals had never penetrated in any number to the Appalachian chain of mountains. Indeed, it was after the beginning of the century before the inroads of the whites upon them grew at all serious. Then, though constantly driven westward, the diminution in their territory, if sure, was at least slow, although growing progressively more rapid. Less than a score of years ago the great herds, containing many millions of individuals, ranged over a vast expanse of country that stretched in an unbroken line from near Mexico to far into British America; in fact, over almost all the plains that are now known as the cattle region. But since that time their destruction has gone on with appalling rapidity and thoroughness; and the main factors in bringing it about have been the railroads, which carried hordes of hunters into the land and gave them means to transport their spoils to market. Not quite twenty years since, the range was broken in two, and the buffalo herds in the middle slaughtered or thrust aside; and thus there resulted two ranges, the northern and the southern. The latter was the larger but, being more open to the hunters, was the sooner to be depopulated; and the last of the great southern herds was destroyed in 1878, though scattered bands escaped and wandered into the desolate wastes to the southwest. Meanwhile, equally savage war was waged on the northern herds, and five years later the last of these was also destroyed or broken up. The bulk of this slaughter was done in the dozen years from 1872 to 1883; never before in all history were so many large wild animals of one species slain in so short a space of time.

The extermination of the buffalo has been a veritable tragedy of the animal world. Other races of animals have been destroyed within historic times, but these have been species of small size, local distribution, and limited numbers, usually found in some particular island or group of islands; while the huge buffalo, in countless myriads, ranged over the greater part of a continent. Its nearest relative, the Old World aurochs, formerly found all through the forests of Europe, is almost as near the verge of extinction, but with the latter the process has been slow and has extended over a period of a thousand years, instead of being compressed into a dozen. The destruction of the various larger species of South African game is much more local, and is proceeding at a much slower rate. It may truthfully be said that the sudden and complete extermination of the vast herds of the buffalo is without a parallel in historic times.

No sight is more common on the plains than that of a bleached buffalo skull; and their countless numbers attest the abundance of the animal at a time not so very long past. On those portions where the herds made their last stand, the carcasses, dried in the clear, high air, or the mouldering skeletons, abound. Last year, in crossing the country around the heads of the Big Sandy, O'Fallon Creek, Little Beaver, and Box Alder, these skeletons or dried carcasses were in sight from every hillock, often lying over the ground so thickly that several score could be seen at once. A ranchman who at the same time had made a journey of a thousand miles across northern Montana, along the Milk River, told me that, to use his own expression, during the whole distance he was never out of sight of a dead buffalo, and never in sight of a live one.

Thus, though gone, the traces of the buffalo are still thick over the land. Their dried dung is found everywhere, and is in many places the only fuel afforded by the plains; their skulls, which last longer than any other part of the animal, are among the most familiar of objects to the plainsman; their bones are in many districts so plentiful that it has become a regular industry, followed by hundreds of men (christened "bonehunters" by the frontiersmen), to go out with wagons and collect them in great numbers for the sake of the phosphates they yield; and Bad Lands, plateaus, and prairies alike, are cut up in all directions by the deep ruts which were formerly buffalo trails.

These buffalo trails were made by the herds travelling strung out in single file, and invariably taking the same route each time they passed over the same piece of ground. As a consequence, many of the ruts are worn so deeply into the ground that a horseman riding along one strikes his stirrups on the earth. In moving through very broken country they are often good guides; for though buffalo can go easily over the roughest places, they prefer to travel where it is smooth, and have a remarkable knack at finding out the best passage down a steep ravine, over a broken cliff, or along a divide. In a pass, or, as it is called in the West, "draw," between two feeding-grounds, through which the buffalo were fond of going, fifteen or twenty deep trails may be seen; and often, where the great beasts have travelled in parallel files, two ruts will run side by side over the prairie for a mile's length. These old trails are frequently used by the cattle herds at the present time, or are even turned into pony paths by the ranchmen. For many long years after the buffalo die out from a place, their white skulls and well-worn roads remain as melancholy monuments of their former existence.

The rapid and complete extermination of the buffalo affords an excellent instance of how a race that has thriven and multiplied for ages under conditions of life to which it has slowly fitted itself by a process of natural selection continued for countless generations, may succumb at once when these surrounding conditions are varied by the introduction of one or more new elements, immediately becoming the chief forces with which it has to contend in the struggle for life. The most striking characteristics of the buffalo, and those which had been found most useful in maintaining the species until the white man entered upon the scene, were its phenomenal gregariousness—surpassed by no

other four-footed beast, and only equalled, if equalled
at all, by one or two kinds of South African antelope
—its massive bulk, and unwieldy strength. The fact
that it was a plains and not a forest or mountain animal
was at that time also greatly in its favor. Its tough-
ness and hardy endurance fitted it to contend with
purely natural forces: to resist cold and the winter
blasts, or the heat of a thirsty summer, to wander away
to new pastures when the feed on the old was exhausted,
to plunge over the broken ground, and to plough its
way through snowdrifts or quagmires. But one beast
of prey existed sufficiently powerful to conquer it when
full grown and in health; and this, the grizzly bear,
could only be considered an occasional foe. The Indians were its most dangerous enemies, but they were
without horses, and their weapons, bows and arrows,
were only available at close range; so that a slight degree of speed enabled a buffalo to get out of the way of
their human foes when discovered, and on the open
plains a moderate development of the senses was sufficient to warn them of the approach of the latter before
they had come up to the very close distance required
for their primitive weapons to take effect. Thus the
strength, size, and gregarious habits of the brute were
sufficient for a protection against most foes; and a
slight degree of speed and moderate development of
the senses served as adequate guards against the grizzlies and bow-bearing foot Indians. Concealment, and
the habit of seeking lonely and remote places for a
dwelling, would have been of no service.

But the introduction of the horse, and shortly afterward the incoming of white hunters carrying long-
range rifles, changed all this. The buffaloes' gregarious
habits simply rendered them certain to be seen and

made it a matter of perfect ease to follow them up; their keeping to the open plains heightened their conspicuousness, while their senses were too dull to discover their foes at such a distance as to nullify the effects of the long rifles; their speed was not such as to enable them to flee from a horseman; and their size and strength merely made them too clumsy either to escape from or to contend with their foes. Add to this the fact that their hides and flesh were valuable, and it is small wonder that, under the new order of things, they should have vanished with such rapidity.

The incoming of the cattlemen was another cause of the completeness of their destruction. Wherever there is good feed for a buffalo, there is good feed for a steer or cow; and so the latter have penetrated into all the pastures of the former; and of course the cowboys follow. A cowboy is not able to kill a deer or antelope unless in exceptional cases, for they are too fleet, too shy, or keep themselves too well hidden. But a buffalo neither tries nor is able to do much in the way of hiding itself; its senses are too dull to give it warning in time; and it is not so swift as a horse, so that a cowboy, riding round in the places where cattle, and therefore buffalo, are likely to be, is pretty sure to see any of the latter that may be about, and then can easily approach near enough to be able to overtake them when they begin running. The size and value of the animal make the chase after it very keen. Hunters will follow the trail of a band for days, when they would not follow that of deer or antelope for a half-hour.

Events have developed a race of this species, known either as the wood or mountain buffalo, which is acquiring, and has already largely acquired, habits widely different from those of the others of its kind. It is found in the wooded and most precipitous portions of the mountains, instead of on the level and open plains; it goes singly or in small parties, instead of in huge herds; and it is more agile and infinitely more wary than is its prairie cousin. The formation of this race is due solely to the extremely severe process of natural selection that has been going on among the buffalo herds for the last sixty or seventy years; the vast majority of the individuals were utterly unable to accommodate themselves to the sudden and complete change in the surrounding forces with which they had to cope, and therefore died out; while a very few of the more active and wary, and of those most given to wandering off into mountainous and out-of-the-way places, in each generation survived, and among these the wariness continually increased, partly by personal experience, and still more by inheriting an increasingly suspicious nature from their ancestors. The sense of smell always was excellent in the buffalo; the sense of hearing becomes much quicker in any woods animal than it is in one found on the plains; while in beasts of the forest the eyesight does not have to be as keen as is necessary for their protection in open country. On the mountains the hair grows longer and denser, and the form rather more thickset. As a result, a new race has been built up; and we have an animal far better fitted to "harmonize with the environment," to use the scientific cant of the day. Unfortunately, this race has developed too late. With the settlement of the country it will also disappear, unless very stringent laws are made for its protection; but at least its existence will for some years prevent the total extermination of the species as a whole. It must be kept in mind that even this shyer kind of buffalo has not got the keen senses of other large game, such as moose; and it is more easily followed and much more keenly and eagerly sought after than would be any other animal smaller and less valuable to the hunter than itself.

While the slaughter of the buffalo has been in places needless and brutal, and while it is greatly to be regretted that the species is likely to become extinct, and while, moreover, from a purely selfish standpoint, many, including myself, would rather see it continue to exist as the chief feature in the unchanged life of the Western wilderness; yet, on the other hand, it must be remembered that its continued existence in any numbers was absolutely incompatible with anything but a very sparse settlement of the country; and that its destruction was the condition precedent upon the advance of white civilization in the West, and was a positive boon to the more thrifty and industrious frontiersmen. Where the buffalo were plenty, they ate up all the grass that could have supported cattle. The country over which the huge herds grazed during the last year or two of their existence was cropped bare, and the grass did not grow to its normal height and become able to support cattle for in some cases two, in others three, seasons. Every buffalo needed as much food as an ox or cow; and if the former abounded, the latter perforce would have to be scarce. Above all, the extermination of the buffalo was the only way of solving the Indian question. As long as this large animal of the chase existed, the Indians simply could not be kept on reservations, and always had an ample supply of meat on hand to support them in the event of a war; and its disappearance was the only method of forcing them to at least partially abandon their savage mode of life. From the standpoint of humanity at large, the extermination of the buffalo has been a blessing. The many have been benefited by it; and I suppose the comparatively few of us who would have preferred the continuance of the old order of things, merely for the sake of our own selfish enjoyment, have no right to complain.

The buffalo is more easily killed than any other kind of plains game; but its chase is very far from being the tame amusement it has lately been represented. It is genuine sport; it needs skill, marksmanship, and hardihood in the man who follows it, and if he hunts on horseback, it needs also pluck and good riding. It is in no way akin to various forms of so-called sport in vogue in parts of the East, such as killing deer in a lake or by fire-hunting, or even by watching at a runway. No man who is not of an adventurous temper, and able to stand rough food and living, will penetrate to the haunts of the buffalo. The animal is so tough and tenacious of life that it must be hit in the right spot; and care must be used in approaching it, for its nose is very keen, and though its sight is dull, yet, on the other hand, the plains it frequents are singularly bare of cover; while, finally, there is just a faint spice of danger in the pursuit, for the bison, though the least dangerous of all bovine animals, will, on occasions, turn upon the hunter, and though its attack is, as a rule, easily avoided, yet in rare cases it manages to charge home. A ranchman of my acquaintance once, many years ago, went out buffalo-hunting on horseback, together with a friend who was unused to the sport, and who was mounted on a large, untrained, nervous horse. While chasing a bull, the friend's horse became unmanageable, and when the bull turned, proved too clumsy to get out of the way, and was caught on the horns, one of which entered its flank, while the other inflicted a huge, bruised gash across the man's thigh, tearing the muscles all out. Both horse and rider were flung to the ground with tremendous violence. The horse had to be killed, and the man died in a few hours from the shock, loss of blood, and internal injuries. Such an accident, however, is very exceptional.

My brother was in at the death of the great Southern herds in 1877, and had a good deal of experience in buffalo-hunting, and once or twice was charged by old bulls, but never had any difficulty in either evading the charge or else killing the brute as it came on. My cousin, John Roosevelt, also had one adventure with a buffalo, in which he received rather a fright. He had been out on foot with a dog and had severely wounded a buffalo bull, which nevertheless, with the wonderful tenacity of life and ability to go over apparently inaccessible places that this species shows, managed to clamber up a steep, almost perpendicular, cliff. My cousin climbed up after it, with some difficulty; on reaching the top he got his elbows over and drew himself up on them only to find the buffalo fronting him with lowered head, not a dozen feet off. Immediately upon seeing him it cocked up its tail and came forward. He was clinging with both hands to the edge and could not use his rifle; so, not relishing what was literally a tête-à-tête, he promptly let go and slid or rather rolled head over heels to the foot of the cliff, not hurting himself much in the sand, though of course a good deal jarred by the fall. The buffalo came on till its hoofs crumbled the earth at the brink, when the dog luckily got up and distracted its attention; meanwhile, my cousin, having bounced down to the bottom, picked himself up, shook himself, and finding that nothing was broken, promptly scrambled up the bluff at another place a few yards off and shot his antagonist.

When my cattle first came on the Little Missouri three of my men took a small bunch of them some fifty miles to the south and there wintered with them on what were then the outskirts of the buffalo range, the herds having been pressed up northward. In the intervals of tending the cattle—work which was then entirely new to them—they occupied themselves in hunting buffalo, killing during the winter sixty or seventy, some of them on horseback, but mostly by still-hunting them on foot. Once or twice the bulls, when wounded, turned to bay; and a couple of them on one occasion charged one of the men and forced him to take refuge upon a steep isolated butte. At another time the three of them wounded a cow so badly that she broke down and would run no farther, turning to bay in a small clump of thick trees. As this would have been a very bad place in which to skin the body, they wished to get her out and tried to tease her into charging; but she seemed too weak to make the effort. Emboldened by her apathy, one of the men came up close to her behind, while another was standing facing her; and the former finally entered the grove of trees and poked her with a long stick. This waked her up most effectually, and instead of turning on her assailant she went headlong at the man in front. He leaped to one side just in time, one of her horns grazing him, ripping away his clothes and knocking him over; as he lay she tried to jump on him with her forefeet, but he rolled to one side, and as she went past she kicked at him like a vicious mule. The effort exhausted her, however, and she fell before going a dozen yards farther. The man who was charged had rather a close shave; thanks to the rashness and contempt of the game's prowess which they all felt—for all three are very quiet men and not afraid of anything. It is always a good rule to be cautious in dealing with an apparently dead or dying buffalo. About the time the above incident occurred a party of hunters near my ranch killed a buffalo, as they thought, and tied a pony to its fore leg, to turn it over, as its position was a very bad one for skinning. Barely had the pony been tied when the buffalo came to with a jump, killed the unfortunate pony, and needed a dozen more balls before he fell for good.

At that time the buffalo would occasionally be scattered among the cattle, but, as a rule, avoided the latter and seemed to be afraid of them; while the cattle, on the contrary, had no apparent dread of the buffalo, unless it happened that on some occasion they got caught by a herd of the latter that had stampeded. A settler or small ranchman, not far from my place, was driving a team of oxen in a wagon one day three years since, when, in crossing a valley, he encountered a little herd of stampeded buffalo, who, in their blind and heedless terror, ran into him and knocked over the wagon and oxen. The oxen never got over the fright the rough handling caused them, and ever afterward became unmanageable and tore off at sight or smell of a buffalo. It is said that the few buffalo left in the country through which the headwaters of the Belle Fourche flow have practically joined themselves to the great herds of cattle now found all over that region.

Buffalo are very easily tamed. On a neighboring ranch there are four which were taken when very young calves. They wander about with the cattle, and are quite as familiar as any of them, and do not stray any farther away. One of them was captured when a yearling, by the help of a large yellow hound. The cowboy had been chasing it some time and, finally, fearing it might escape, hied on the hound, which dashed in, caught the buffalo by the ear, and finally brought it down to its knees, when the cowboy, by means of his lariat, secured it, and, with the help of a companion, managed to get it back to the ranch. Buffalo can be trained to draw a wagon, and are valuable for their great strength; but they are very headstrong and stupid. If thirsty, for instance, and they smell or see water, it is absolutely impossible to prevent their going to it, no matter if it is in such a place that they have to upset the wagon to get down to it, nor how deep the mud is. When tamed, they do not seem to be as ferocious as ordinary cattle that are allowed to go free; but they are such strong, blundering brutes that very few fences will hold them.

My men, in hunting buffalo, which was with them an occasional occupation and not a regular pursuit, used light Winchesters; but the professional buffalo-hunters carried either 40–90 or 45–120 Sharps, than which there are in the world no rifles more accurate or powerful; with the larger-calibered ones (45 or 50) a man could easily kill an elephant. These weapons are excellent for very long-range work, being good for half a mile and over; and sometimes the hunters were able to kill very many buffalo at a time, owing to their curious liability to fits of stupid, panic terror. Sometimes when these panics seize them they stampede and run off in headlong, heedless flight, going over anything in their way. Once, in midwinter, one of my men was lying out in the open, under a heavy roll of furs, the wagon-sheet over all. During the night a small herd of stampeded buffalo passed by, and one of them jumped on the bed, almost trampling on the sleeper, and then bounded off as the latter rose with a yell. The others of the herd passed almost within arm's length on each side.

Occasionally, these panic fits have the opposite effect, and make them run together and stand still in a stupid, frightened manner. This is now and then the result when a hunter fires at a herd while keeping himself concealed; and on rare occasions (for buffalo act very differently at different times, according to their moods) it occurs even when he is in full sight. When they are made to act thus it is called in hunters' parlance getting a "stand" on them; and often thirty or forty have been killed in one such stand, the hunter hardly shifting his position the whole time. Often, with their long-range heavy rifles, the hunters would fire a number of shots into a herd half a mile off, and on approaching would find that they had bagged several—for the Sharp's rifle has a very long range, and the narrow, heavy conical bullets will penetrate almost anything. Once, while coming in over the plains with an ox wagon, two of my cowboys surprised a band of buffaloes, which, on being fired at, ran clear round them and then made a stand in nearly their former position; and there they stood until the men had fired away most of their ammunition, but only half a dozen or so were killed, the Winchesters being too light for such a distance. Hunting on foot is much the most destructive way of pursuing buffaloes; but it lacks the excitement of chasing them with horses.

When in Texas my brother had several chances to hunt them on horseback, while making a trip as guest of a captain of United States cavalry. The country through which they hunted was rolling and well watered, the buffalo being scattered over it in bands of no great size. While riding out to look for the game they were mounted on large horses; when a band was spied they would dismount and get on the smaller buffalo ponies which the orderlies had been leading behind them. Then they would carefully approach from the leeward side, if possible keeping behind some hill or divide. When this was no longer possible they trotted gently toward the game, which usually gathered together and stood for a moment looking at them. The instant the buffalo turned, the spurs were put in and the ponies raced forward for all there was in them, it being an important point to close as soon as possible, as buffalo, though not swift, are very enduring. Usually a half a mile took the hunters up to the game, when each singled out his animal, rode alongside on its left flank, so close as almost to be able to touch it with the hand, and fired the heavy revolver into the loins or small of the back, the bullet ranging forward. At the instant of firing, the trained pony swerved off to the left, almost at right angles to its former course, so as to avoid the lunging charge sometimes made by the wounded brute. If the animal kept on, the hunter, having made a half-circle, again closed up and repeated the shot; very soon the buffalo came to a halt, then its head dropped, it straddled widely with its fore legs, swayed to and fro, and pitched heavily forward on its side. The secret of success in this sort of hunting is to go right up by the side of the buffalo; if a man stays off at a distance of fifteen or twenty feet he may fire a score of shots and not kill or cripple his game.

While hunting this, the largest of American animals, on horseback, is doubtless the most exciting way in which its chase can be carried on, we must beware of crying down its pursuit on foot. To be sure, in the latter case the actual stalking and shooting the buffalo does not need on the part of the hunter as much skill and as good marksmanship as is the case in hunting most other kinds of large game, and is but a trifle more risky; yet, on the other hand, the fatigue of following the game is much greater, and the country is usually so wild as to call for some hardihood and ability to stand rough work on the part of the man who penetrates it.

One September I determined to take a short trip after bison. At that time I was staying in a cow-camp a good many miles up the river from my ranch; there were then no cattle south of me, where there are now very many thousand head, and the buffalo had been plentiful in the country for a couple of winters past, but the last of the herds had been destroyed or driven out six months before, and there were only a few stragglers left. It was one of my first hunting trips; previously, I had shot with the rifle very little, and that only at deer or antelope. I took as a companion one of my best men, named Ferris (a brother of the Ferris already mentioned); we rode a couple of ponies, not very good ones, and each carried his roll of blankets and a very small store of food in a pack behind the saddle.

Leaving the cow-camp early in the morning, we crossed the Little Missouri and for the first ten miles threaded our way through the narrow defiles and along the tortuous divides of a great tract of Bad Lands. Although it was fall and the nights were cool, the sun was very hot in the middle of the day, and we jogged along at a slow pace, so as not to tire our ponies. Two or three blacktail deer were seen, some distance off, and, when we were a couple of hours on our journey, we came across the fresh track of a bull buffalo. Buffalo wander a great distance, for, though they do not go fast, yet they may keep travelling, as they graze, all day long; and though this one had evidently passed but a few hours before, we were not sure we would see him. His tracks were easily followed as long as he had kept to the soft creek bottom, crossing and recrossing the narrow wet ditch which wound its way through it; but when he left this and turned up a winding coulée that branched out in every direction, his hoofs scarcely made any marks in the hard ground. We rode up the ravine, carefully examining the soil for nearly half an hour, however; finally, as we passed the mouth of a little side coulée, there was a plunge and crackle through the bushes at its head, and a shabby-looking old bull bison galloped out of it and, without an instant's hesitation, plunged over a steep bank into a patch of rotten, broken ground which led around the base of a high butte. So quickly did he disappear that we had not time to dismount and fire. Spurring our horses we galloped up to the brink of the cliff down which he had plunged; it was remarkable that he should have gone down it unhurt. From where we stood we could see nothing; so, getting our horses over the broken ground as fast as possible, we ran to the butte and rode round it, only to see the buffalo come out of the broken land and climb up the side of another butte over a quarter of a mile off. In spite of his great weight and cumbersome, heavy-looking gait, he climbed up the steep bluff with ease and even agility, and when he had reached the ridge stood and looked back at us for a moment; while so doing he held his head high up, and at that distance his great shaggy mane and huge forequarter made him look like a lion. In another second

he again turned away and made off; and being evidently
very shy and accustomed to being harassed by hunters,
must have travelled a long distance before stopping,
for we followed his trail for some miles, until it got on
such hard, dry ground that his hoofs did not leave a
scrape in the soil, and yet did not again catch so much
as a glimpse of him.

Soon after leaving his trail we came out on the great
broken prairies that lie far back from the river. These
are by no means everywhere level. A flat space of a
mile or two will be bounded by a low cliff or a row of
small round-topped buttes; or will be interrupted by
a long, gently sloping ridge, the divide between two
creeks; or by a narrow canyon, perhaps thirty feet deep
and not a dozen wide, stretching for miles before there
is a crossing place. The smaller creeks were dried up,
and were merely sinuous hollows in the prairie; but one
or two of the larger ones held water here and there, and
cut down through the land in bold, semicircular sweeps,
the outside of each curve being often bounded by a
steep bluff with trees at its bottom, and occasionally
holding a miry pool. At one of these pools we halted,
about ten o'clock in the morning, and lunched; the
banks were so steep and rotten that we had to bring
water to the more clumsy of the two ponies in a hat.

Then we remounted and fared on our way, scanning
the country far and near from every divide, but seeing
no trace of game. The air was hot and still, and the
brown, barren land stretched out on every side for
leagues of dreary sameness. Once we came to a canyon which ran across our path, and followed along its
brink for a mile to find a place where we could get into
it; when we finally found such a place, we had to back
the horses down to the bottom and then lead them

along it for some hundred yards before finding a break through which we could climb out.

It was late in the afternoon before we saw any game; then we made out in the middle of a large plain three black specks, which proved to be buffalo—old bulls. Our horses had come a good distance, under a hot sun, and, as they had had no water except from the mud-hole in the morning, they were in no condition for running. They were not very fast, anyhow; so, though the ground was unfavorable, we made up our minds to try to creep up to the buffalo. We left the ponies in a hollow half a mile from the game, and started off on our hands and knees, taking advantage of every sage-brush as cover. After a while we had to lie flat on our bodies and wriggle like snakes; and while doing this I blundered into a bed of cactus, and filled my hands with the spines. After taking advantage of every hollow, hillock, or sage-brush, we got within about a hundred and twenty-five or fifty yards of where the three bulls were unconsciously feeding, and as all between was bare ground I drew up and fired. It was the first time I ever shot at buffalo, and, confused by the bulk and shaggy hair of the beast, I aimed too far back at one that was standing nearly broadside on toward me. The bullet told on his body with a loud crack, the dust flying up from his hide; but it did not work him any immediate harm, or in the least hinder him from making off; and away went all three, with their tails up, disappearing over a light rise in the ground.

Much disgusted, we trotted back to where the horses were picketed, jumped on them, a good deal out of breath, and rode after the flying game. We thought that the wounded one might turn out and leave the

others; and so followed them, though they had over a
mile's start. For seven or eight miles we loped our
jaded horses along at a brisk pace, occasionally seeing
the buffalo far ahead; and finally, when the sun had
just set, we saw that all three had come to a stand in
a gentle hollow. There was no cover anywhere near
them; and, as a last desperate resort, we concluded
to try to run them on our worn-out ponies.

As we cantered toward them they faced us for a second and then turned round and made off, while with
spurs and quirts we made the ponies put on a burst
that enabled us to close in with the wounded one just
about the time that the lessening twilight had almost
vanished; while the rim of the full moon rose above the
horizon. The pony I was on could barely hold his
own, after getting up within sixty or seventy yards of
the wounded bull; my companion, better mounted,
forged ahead, a little to one side. The bull saw him
coming and swerved from his course, and by cutting
across I was able to get nearly up to him. The ground
over which we were running was fearful, being broken
into holes and ditches, separated by hillocks; in the
dull light, and at the speed we were going, no attempt
could be made to guide the horses, and the latter, fagged
out by their exertions, floundered and pitched forward
at every stride, hardly keeping their legs. When up
within twenty feet I fired my rifle, but the darkness,
and especially the violent labored motion of my pony,
made me miss; I tried to get in closer, when suddenly
up went the bull's tail, and, wheeling, he charged me
with lowered horns. My pony, frightened into momentary activity, spun round and tossed up his head;
I was holding the rifle in both hands, and the pony's
head, striking it, knocked it violently against my fore-

head, cutting quite a gash, from which, heated as I was, the blood poured into my eyes. Meanwhile the buffalo, passing me, charged my companion, and followed him as he made off, and, as the ground was very bad, for some little distance his lowered head was unpleasantly near the tired pony's tail. I tried to run in on him again, but my pony stopped short, dead beat; and by no spurring could I force him out of a slow trot. My companion jumped off and took a couple of shots at the buffalo, which missed in the dim moonlight; and to our unutterable chagrin the wounded bull labored off and vanished in the darkness. I made after him on foot, in hopeless and helpless wrath, until he got out of sight.

Our horses were completely done out; we did not mount them again, but led them slowly along, trembling, foaming, and sweating. The ground was moist in places, and after an hour's search we found in a reedy hollow a little mud-pool with water so slimy that it was almost gelatinous. Thirsty though we were, for we had not drunk for twelve hours, neither man nor horse could swallow more than a mouthful or two of this water. We unsaddled the horses, and made our beds by the hollow, each eating a biscuit; there was not a twig with which to make a fire, nor anything to which we might fasten the horses. Spreading the saddle-blankets under us, and our own over us, we lay down, with the saddles as pillows, to which we had been obliged to lariat our steeds.

The ponies stood about, almost too tired to eat; but in spite of their fatigue they were very watchful and restless, continually snorting or standing with their ears forward, peering out into the night; wild beasts, or some such things, were about. The day before we had

had a false alarm from supposed hostile Indians, who turned out to be merely half-breed Crees; and, as we were in a perfectly lonely part of the wilderness, we knew we were in the domain of both white and red horse-thieves, and that the latter might, in addition to our horses, try to take our scalps. It was some time before we dozed off, waking up with a start whenever we heard the horses stop grazing and stand motionless with heads raised, looking out into the darkness. But at last, tired out, we fell sound asleep.

About midnight we were rudely wakened by having our pillows whipped out from under our heads; and as we started from the bed we saw, in the bright moonlight, the horses galloping madly off with the saddles, tied to the lariats, whose other ends were around their necks, bounding and trailing after them. Our first thought was that they had been stampeded by horse-thieves, and we rolled over and crouched down in the grass with our rifles; but nothing could be seen, except a shadowy four-footed form in the hollow, and in the end we found that the horses must have taken alarm at a wolf or wolves that had come up to the edge of the bank and looked over at us, not being able at first to make out what we were.

We did not expect to find the horses again that night, but nevertheless took up the broad trail made by the saddles as they dragged through the dewy grass, and followed it well in the moonlight. Our task proved easier than we had feared; for they had not run much over half a mile, and we found them standing close together and looking intently round when we came up. Leading them back we again went to sleep; but the weather was rapidly changing, and by three o'clock a fine rain began to come steadily down, and we cowered and shivered under our wet blankets till morning. At the first streak of dawn, having again eaten a couple of biscuits, we were off, glad to bid good-by to the inhospitable pool in whose neighborhood we had spent such a comfortless night. A fine, drizzling mist shrouded us and hid from sight all distant objects; and at times there were heavy downpours of rain. Before we had gone any distance we became what is termed by backwoodsmen or plainsmen "turned round," and the creeks suddenly seemed to be running the wrong way; after which we travelled purely by the compass.

For some hours we kept a nearly straight course over the formless, shapeless plain, drenched through and thoroughly uncomfortable; then, as we rose over a low divide, the fog lifted for a few minutes, and we saw several black objects slowly crossing some rolling country ahead of us, and a glance satisfied us they were buffalo. The horses were picketed at once, and we ran up as near the game as we dared, and then began to stalk them, creeping forward on our hands and knees through the soft, muddy prairie soil, while a smart shower of rain blew in our faces, as we advanced up wind. The country was favorable, and we got within less than a hundred yards of the nearest, a large cow, though we had to creep along so slowly that we were chilled through, and our teeth chattered behind our blue lips. To crown my misfortunes, I now made one of those misses which a man to his dying day always looks back upon with wonder and regret. The rain was beating in my eyes, and the drops stood out in the sights of the rifle so that I could hardly draw a bead; and I either overshot or else at the last moment must have given a nervous jerk and pulled the rifle clear off the mark. At any rate, I missed clean, and the whole band plunged down into a hollow and were off before, with my stiffened and numbed fingers, I could get another shot; and in wet, sullen misery we plodded back to the ponies.

All that day the rain continued, and we passed another wretched night. Next morning, however, it had cleared off, and as the sun rose brightly we forgot our hunger and sleepiness, and rode cheerily off up a large dry creek, in whose bottom pools of rain-water still stood. During the morning, however, our ill luck continued. My companion's horse almost trod on a rattlesnake, and narrowly escaped being bitten. While riding along the face of a steeply inclined bluff the sandy soil broke away under the ponies' hoofs, and we slid and rolled down to the bottom, where we came to in a heap, horses and men. Then while galloping through a brush-covered bottom my pony put both forefeet in a hole made by the falling and uprooting of a tree, and turned a complete somersault, pitching me a good ten feet beyond his head. And, finally, while crossing what looked like the hard bed of a dry creek, the earth gave way under my horse as if he had stepped on a trap-door and let him down to his withers in soft, sticky mud. I was off at once and floundered to the bank, loosening the lariat from the saddle-bow; and both of us turning to with a will and bringing the other pony into our aid, hauled him out by the rope, pretty nearly strangling him in so doing; and he looked rather a melancholy object as he stood up, trembling and shaking, and plastered with mire from head to tail.

So far the trip had certainly not been a success, although sufficiently varied as regards its incidents. We had been confined to moist biscuits for three days as our food; had been wet and cold at night, and sunburned until our faces peeled in the day; were hungry and tired, and had met with bad weather and all kinds of accidents; in addition to which I had shot badly. But a man who is fond of sport and yet is not naturally a good hunter, soon learns that if he wishes any success at all he must both keep in memory and put in practice Anthony Trollope's famous precept: "It's dogged as does it." And if he keeps doggedly on in his course the odds are heavy that in the end the longest lane will prove to have a turning. Such was the case on this occasion.

Shortly after midday we left the creek bottom, and skirted a ridge of broken buttes, cut up by gullies and winding ravines, in whose bottoms grew bunch-grass. While passing near the mouth, and to leeward of one of these ravines, both ponies threw up their heads and snuffed the air, turning their muzzles toward the head of the gully. Feeling sure that they had smelt some wild beast, either a bear or a buffalo, I slipped off my pony, and ran quickly but cautiously up along the valley. Before I had gone a hundred yards, I noticed in the soft soil at the bottom the round prints of a bison's hoofs; and immediately afterward got a glimpse of the animal himself, as he fed slowly up the course of the ravine, some distance ahead of me. The wind was just right, and no ground could have been better for stalking. Hardly needing to bend down, I walked up behind a small sharp-crested hillock and, peeping over, there below me, not fifty yards off, was a great bison bull. He was walking along, grazing as he walked. His glossy fall coat was in fine trim and shone in the rays of the sun, while his pride of bearing showed him to be in the lusty vigor of his prime. As I rose above the crest of the hill, he held up his head and cocked his tail in the air. Before he could go off, I put the bullet in behind his shoulder. The wound was an almost immediately fatal one, yet with surprising agility for so large and heavy an animal, he bounded up the opposite side of the ravine, heedless of two more balls, both of which went into his flank and ranged forward, and disappeared over the ridge at a lumbering gallop, the blood pouring from his mouth and nostrils. We knew he could not go far, and trotted leisurely along on his bloody trail; and in the next gully we found him stark dead, lying almost on his back, having pitched over the side when he tried to go down it. His head was a remarkably fine one, even for a fall buffalo. He was lying in a very bad position, and it was most tedious and tiresome work to cut it off and pack it out. The flesh of a cow or calf is better eating than is that of a bull; but the so-called hump meat—that is, the strip of steak on each side of the backbone—is excellent and tender and juicy. Buffalo meat is with difficulty to be distinguished from ordinary beef. At any rate, the flesh of this bull tasted uncommonly good to us, for we had been without fresh meat for a week; and until a healthy, active man has been without it for some little time, he does not know how positively and almost painfully hungry for flesh he becomes, no matter how much farinaceous food he may have. And the very toil I had been obliged to go through, in order to procure the head, made me feel all the prouder of it when at last it was in my possession.

A year later I made another trip, this time with a wagon, through what had once been a famous buffalo range, the divide between the Little Missouri and the Powder, at its northern end, where some of the creeks flowing into the Yellowstone also head up; but, though

in most places throughout the range the grass had not
yet grown from the time, a few months before, when it
had been cropped off down close to the roots by the
grazing herds, and though the ground was cut up in all
directions by buffalo trails, and covered by their innumerable skulls and skeletons, not a living one did we
see, and only one moderately fresh track, which we followed until we lost it.   Some of the sharper ridges were
of soft, crumbling sandstone, and when a buffalo trail
crossed such a one, it generally made a curious heart-
shaped cut, the feet of the animals sinking the narrow
path continually deeper and deeper, while their bodies
brushed out the sides.   The profile of a ridge across
which several trails led had rather a curious look when
seen against the sky.

Game was scarce on this broken plains country,
where the water-supply was very scanty and where the
dull brown grass that grew on the parched, sun-cracked
ground had already been cropped close; still we found
enough to keep us in fresh meat; and, though no buffalo
were seen, the trip was a pleasant one.   There was a
certain charm in the very vastness and the lonely, melancholy desolation of the land over which every day
we galloped far and wide from dawn till nightfall; while
the heavy canvas-covered wagon lumbered slowly along
to the appointed halting-place.   On such a trip one
soon gets to feel that the wagon is home; and after a
tiresome day it is pleasant just to lie still in the twilight
by the side of the smouldering fire and watch the men
as they busy themselves cooking or arranging the beds,
while the solemn old ponies graze around or stand
quietly by the great white-topped prairie-schooner.

The blankets and rubbers being arranged in a carefully chosen spot to leeward of the wagon, we were not

248

often bothered at night, even by quite heavy rainfalls; but once or twice, when in peculiarly exposed places, we were struck by such furious gusts of wind and rain that we were forced to gather up our bedding and hastily scramble into the wagon, where we would at least be dry, even though in pretty cramped quarters.

CHAPTER IX

STILL-HUNTING ELK ON THE MOUNTAINS

AFTER the buffalo, the elk are the first animals to disappear from a country when it is settled. This arises from their size and consequent conspicuousness, and the eagerness with which they are followed by hunters; and also because of their gregariousness and their occasional fits of stupid panic, during whose continuance hunters can now and then work great slaughter in a herd. Five years ago elk were abundant in the valley of the Little Missouri, and in fall were found wandering in great bands of over a hundred individuals each. But they have now vanished completely, except that one or two may still lurk in some of the most remote and broken places where there are deep, wooded ravines.

Formerly, the elk were plentiful all over the plains, coming down into them in great bands during the fall months and traversing their entire extent. But the incoming of hunters and cattlemen has driven them off the ground as completely as the buffalo; unlike the latter, however, they are still very common in the dense woods that cover the Rocky Mountains and the other great Western chains. In the old days, running elk on horseback was a highly esteemed form of plains sport; but now that it has become a beast of the timber and the craggy ground, instead of a beast of the open, level prairie, it is followed almost solely on foot and with the rifle. Its sense of smell is very acute, and it has good eyes and quick ears; and its wariness makes it under ordinary circumstances very difficult to approach. But it is subject to fits of panic folly, and during their continuance great numbers can be destroyed. A band places almost as much reliance upon the leaders as does a flock of sheep; and if the leaders are shot down, the others will huddle together in a terrified mass, seemingly unable to make up their minds in which direction to flee. When one, more bold than the rest, does at last step out, the hidden hunter's at once shooting it down will produce a fresh panic. I have known of twenty elk (or wapiti, as they are occasionally called) being thus procured out of one band. And at times they show a curious indifference to danger, running up on a hunter who is in plain sight, or standing still for a few fatal seconds to gaze at one that unexpectedly appears.

In spite of its size and strength and great branching antlers, the elk is but little more dangerous to the hunter than is an ordinary buck. Once, in coming up to a wounded one, I had it strike at me with its forefeet, bristling up the hair on the neck, and making a harsh, grating noise with its teeth; as its back was broken it could not get at me, but the savage glare in its eyes left me no doubt as to its intentions. Only in a single instance have I ever known of a hunter being regularly charged by one of these great deer. He had struck a band of elk and wounded an old bull, which, after going a couple of miles, received another ball and then separated from the rest of the herd and took refuge in a dense patch of small timber. The hunter went in on its trail and came upon it lying down; it jumped to its feet, and, with hair all bristling, made a regular charge upon its pursuer, who leaped out of the way behind a tree just in time to avoid it. It crashed past through the

251

undergrowth without turning, and he killed it with a third and last shot. But this was a very exceptional case, and in most instances the elk submits to death with hardly an effort at resistance; it is by no means as dangerous an antagonist as is a bull moose.

The elk is unfortunately one of those animals seemingly doomed to total destruction at no distant date. Already its range has shrunk to far less than one-half its former size. Originally it was found as far as the Atlantic seaboard; I have myself known of several sets of antlers preserved in the house of a Long Island gentleman, whose ancestors had killed the bearers shortly after the first settlement of New York. Even so late as the first years of this century, elk were found in many mountainous and densely wooded places east of the Mississippi: in New York, Pennsylvania, Virginia, Kentucky, Tennessee, and all of what were then the Northwestern States and Territories. The last individual of the race in the Adirondacks was killed in 1834; in Pennsylvania, not till nearly thirty years later; while a very few are still to be found in northern Michigan. Elsewhere they must now be sought far to the west of the Mississippi; and even there they are almost gone from the great plains, and are only numerous in the deep mountain forests. Wherever it exists the skin-hunters and meat-butchers wage the most relentless and unceasing war upon it for the sake of its hide and flesh, and their unremitting persecution is thinning out the herds with terrible rapidity.

The gradual extermination of this, the most stately and beautiful animal of the chase to be found in America, can be looked upon only with unmixed regret by every sportsman and lover of nature. Excepting the moose, it is the largest and, without exception, it is the noblest of the deer tribe. No other species of true deer, in either the Old or the New World, comes up to it in size and in the shape, length, and weight of its mighty antlers; while the grand, proud carriage and lordly bearing of an old bull make it perhaps the most majestic-looking of all the animal creation. The open plains have already lost one of their great attractions, now that we no more see the long lines of elk trotting across them; and it will be a sad day when the lordly, antlered beasts are no longer found in the wild, rocky glens and among the lonely woods of towering pines that cover the great Western mountain chains.

The elk has other foes besides man. The grizzly will always make a meal of one if he gets a chance; and against his ponderous weight and savage prowess hoofs and antlers avail but little. Still he is too clumsy and easily avoided ever to do very much damage in the herds. Cougars, where they exist, work more havoc. A bull elk in rutting season, if on his guard, would with ease beat off a cougar; but the sly, cunning cat takes its quarry unawares, and once the cruel fangs are fastened in the game's throat or neck, no plunging or struggling can shake it off. The gray timber-wolves also join in twos and threes to hunt down and hamstring the elk, if other game is scarce. But these great deer can hold their own and make head against all their brute foes; it is only when pitted against Man the Destroyer that they succumb in the struggle for life.

I have never shot any elk in the immediate neighborhood of where my cattle range; but I have had very good sport with them in a still wilder and more western region; and this I will now describe.

During last summer we found it necessary to leave

my ranch on the Little Missouri and take quite a long trip through the cattle country of southeastern Montana and northern Wyoming; and, having come to the foot of the Bighorn Mountains, we took a fortnight's hunt through them after elk and bear.

We went into the mountains with a pack-train, leaving the ranch wagon at the place where we began to go up the first steep rise. There were two others, besides myself, in the party; one of them, the teamster, a weather-beaten old plainsman, who possessed a most extraordinary stock of miscellaneous misinformation upon every conceivable subject, and the other my ranch foreman, Merrifield. None of us had ever been within two hundred miles of the Bighorn range before; so that our hunting trip had the added zest of being also an exploring expedition.

Each of us rode one pony, and the packs were carried on four others. We were not burdened by much baggage. Having no tent, we took the canvas wagon-sheet instead; our bedding, plenty of spare cartridges, some flour, bacon, coffee, sugar, and salt, and a few very primitive cooking utensils completed the outfit.

The Bighorn range is a chain of bare, rocky peaks stretching lengthwise along the middle of a table-land which is about thirty miles wide. At its edges this table-land falls sheer off into the rolling plains country. From the rocky peaks flow rapid brooks of clear, icy water, which take their way through deep gorges that they have channelled out in the surface of the plateau; a few miles from the heads of the streams these gorges become regular canyons, with sides so steep as to be almost perpendicular; in travelling, therefore, the trail has to keep well up toward timber-line, as lower down horses find it difficult or impossible to get across the valleys. In strong contrast to the treeless cattle plains extending to its foot, the sides of the table-land are densely wooded with tall pines. Its top forms what is called a park country; that is, it is covered with alternating groves of trees and open glades, each grove or glade varying in size from half a dozen to many hundred acres.

We went in with the pack-train two days' journey before pitching camp in what we intended to be our hunting-grounds, following an old Indian trail. No one who has not tried it can understand the work and worry that it is to drive a pack-train over rough ground and through timber. We were none of us very skilful at packing, and the loads were all the time slipping; sometimes the ponies would stampede with the pack half tied, or they would get caught among the fallen logs, or in a ticklish place would suddenly decline to follow the trail, or would commit some one of the thousand other tricks which seem to be all a pack-pony knows. Then at night they were a bother; if picketed out, they fed badly and got thin, and if they were not picketed they sometimes strayed away. The most valuable one of the lot was also the hardest to catch. Accordingly, we used to let him loose with a long lariat tied round his neck, and one night this lariat twisted up in a sage-brush, and in struggling to free himself the pony got a half-hitch round his hind leg, threw himself, and fell over a bank into a creek on a large stone. We found him in the morning very much the worse for wear and his hind legs swelled up so that his chief method of progression was by a series of awkward hops. Of course no load could be put upon him, but he managed to limp along behind the other horses, and actually in the end reached the ranch on the Little Missouri,

255

three hundred miles off. No sooner had he got there and been turned loose to rest than he fell down a big washout and broke his neck. Another time one of the mares—a homely beast with a head like a camel's—managed to flounder into the very centre of a mud-hole, and we spent the better part of the morning in fishing her out.

It was on the second day of our journey into the mountains, while leading the pack-ponies down the precipitous side of a steep valley, that I obtained my first sight of elk. The trail wound through a forest of tall, slender pines, standing very close together, and with dead trees lying in every direction. The narrow trunks or overhanging limbs threatened to scrape off the packs at every moment, as the ponies hopped and scrambled over the fallen trunks; and it was difficult work, and most trying to the temper, to keep them going along straight and prevent them from wandering off to one side or the other. At last we got out into a succession of small, open glades, with boggy spots in them; the lowest glade was of some size, and as we reached it we saw a small band of cow elk disappearing into the woods on its other edge. I was riding a restive horse, and when I tried to jump off to shoot, it reared and turned round before I could get my left foot out of the stirrup; when I at last got free I could get a glimpse of but one elk, vanishing behind a dead trunk, and my hasty shot missed. I was a good deal annoyed at this, my opening experience with mountain game, feeling that it was an omen of misfortune; but it did not prove so, for during the rest of my two weeks' stay, I with one exception got every animal I fired at.

A beautiful clear mountain brook ran through the bottom of the valley, and in an open space by its side we pitched camp. We were entirely out of fresh meat, and after lunch all three of us separated to hunt, each for his own hand. The teamster went upstream, Merrifield went down, while I followed the tracks of the band of cows and calves that we had started in the morning; their trail led along the wooded hill-crests parallel to the stream, and therefore to Merrifield's course. The crests of the hills formed a wavy-topped but continuous ridge between two canyon-like valleys, and the sides fell off steeper and steeper the farther downstream I went, until at last they were broken in places by sheer precipices and cliffs; the groves of trees, too, though with here and there open glades, formed a continuous forest of tall pines. There was a small growth of young spruce and other evergreen, thick enough to give cover, but not to interfere with seeing and shooting to some distance. The pine trunks rose like straight columns, standing quite close together; and at their bases the ground was carpeted with the sweet-scented needles, over which, in my moccasined feet, I trod without any noise. It was but a little past noon, and the sun in the open was very hot; yet underneath the great archways of the pine woods the air though still was cool, and the sunbeams that struggled down here and there through the interlacing branches and glinted on the rough trunks, only made bright spots in what was elsewhere the uniform, grayish half-light of the mountain forest. Game trails threaded the woods in all directions, made for the most part by the elk. These animals, when not disturbed, travel strung out in single file, each one stepping very nearly in the tracks of the one before it; they are great wanderers, going over an immense amount of country during the course of a day, and so they soon wear regular, well-

257

beaten paths in any place where they are at all plentiful.

The band I was following had, as is their custom, all run together into a wedge-shaped mass when I fired, and crashed off through the woods in a bunch during the first moments of alarm. The footprints in the soil showed that they had in the beginning taken a plunging gallop, but after a few strides had settled into the swinging, ground-covering trot that is the elk's most natural and characteristic gait. A band of elk, when alarmed, is likely to go twenty miles without halting; but these had probably been very little molested, and there was a chance that they would not go far without stopping. After getting through the first grove, the huddled herd had straightened itself out into single file, and trotted off in a nearly straight line. A mile or two of ground having been passed over in this way, the animals had slackened their pace into a walk, evidently making up their minds that they were out of danger. Soon afterward they had begun to go slower, and to scatter out on each side, browsing or grazing.

It was not difficult work to follow up the band at first. While trotting, their sharp hoofs came down with sufficient force to leave very distinct footprints, and, moreover, the trail was the more readily made out as all the animals trod nearly in each other's steps. But when the band spread out the tracking was much harder, as each single one, walking slowly along, merely made here and there a slight scrape in the soil or a faint indentation in the bed of pine-needles. Besides, I had to advance with the greatest caution, keeping the sharpest lookout in front and on all sides of me. Even as it was, though I got very close up to my game, they were on foot before I saw them and I did not get a standing shot. While carefully looking to my foot-steps I paid too little heed to the rifle which I held in my right hand, and let the barrel tap smartly on a tree-trunk. Instantly there was a stamp and movement among the bushes ahead and to one side of me; the elk had heard but had neither seen nor smelt me; and a second afterward I saw the indistinct, shadowy out-lines of the band as they trotted downhill, from where their beds had been made on the very summit of the crest, taking a course diagonal to mine. I raced for-ward and also downhill, behind some large mossy boulders, and cut them fairly off, the band passing di-rectly ahead of me and not twenty yards away, at a slashing trot, which a few of them changed for a wild gallop as I opened fire. I was so hemmed in by the thick tree-trunks, and it was so difficult to catch more than a fleeting glimpse of each animal, that though I fired four shots I only brought down one elk, a full-grown cow, with a broken neck, dead in its tracks; but I also broke the hind leg of a bull calf. Elk offer easy marks when in motion, much easier than deer, because of their trotting gait, and their regular, deliberate movements. They look very handsome as they trot through a wood, stepping lightly and easily over the dead trunks and crashing through the underbrush, with the head held up and nose pointing forward. In gal-loping, however, the neck is thrust straight out in front, and the animal moves with labored bounds which carry it along rapidly but soon tire it out.

After thrusting the hunting-knife into the throat of the cow, I followed the trail of the band; and in an open glade, filled with tall sage-brush, came across and finished the wounded calf. Meanwhile the others ran directly across Merrifield's path, and he shot two.

This gave us much more meat than we wished, nor would we have shot as many, but neither of us could reckon upon the other's getting as much game, and flesh was a necessity. Leaving Merrifield to skin and cut up the dead animals, I walked back to camp, where I found the teamster, who had brought in the hams and tongues of two deer he had shot, and sent him back with a pack-pony for the hides and meat of the elk. Elk tongues are most delicious eating, being juicy, tender, and well flavored; they are excellent to take out as a lunch on a long hunting trip.

We now had more than enough meat in camp, and did not shoot at another cow or calf elk while on the mountains, though we saw quite a number; the last day of my stay I was within fifty yards of two that were walking quietly through a very dense, swampy wood. But it took me some time longer before I got any fine heads.

The day after killing the cow and calf I went out in the morning by myself and hunted through the woods up toward the rocky peaks, going above timber-line, and not reaching camp until after nightfall. In hunting through a wild and unknown country a man must always take great care not to get lost. In the first place, he should never, under any conceivable circumstances, stir fifty yards from camp without a compass, plenty of matches, and his rifle; then he need never feel nervous, even if he is lost, for he can keep himself from cold and hunger, and can steer a straight course until he reaches some settlement. But he should not get lost at all. Old plainsmen or backwoodsmen get to have almost an instinct for finding their way, and are able to tell where they are and the way home in almost any place; probably they keep in their heads an accurate idea of their course and of the general lay of the land. But most men cannot do this. In hunting through a new country a man should, if possible, choose some prominent landmarks, and then should learn how they look from different sides—for they will with difficulty be recognized as the same objects if seen from different points of view. If he gets out of sight of these, he should choose another to work back to, as a kind of half-way point; and so on. He should keep looking back: it is wonderful how different a country looks when following back on one's trail. If possible, he should locate his camp, in his mind, with reference to a line and not a point; he should take a river or a long ridge, for example. Then at any time he can strike back to this line and follow it up or down till he gets home.

If possible, I always spend the first day, when on new ground, in hunting upstream. Then, so long as I am sure I do not wander off into the valleys or creeks of another watercourse, I am safe, for, no matter on what remote branch, all I have to do is to follow downstream until I reach camp; while if I was below camp, it would be difficult to tell which fork to follow up every time the stream branched. A man should always notice the position of the sun, the direction from which the wind blows, the slope of the watercourses, prominent features in the landscape, and so forth, and should keep in mind his own general course; and he had better err on the side of caution rather than on that of boldness. Getting lost is very uncomfortable, both for the man himself and for those who have to break up their work and hunt for him. Deep woods or perfectly flat, open country are almost equally easy places in which to get lost; while, if the country is moderately open and level, with only here and there a prominent and easily recognized hill or butte, a man can safely go where he wishes, hardly paying any heed to his course. But even here he should know his general direction from camp, so as to be able to steer for it with a compass if a fog comes up. And if he leaves his horse hidden in a gully or pocket while he goes off to hunt on foot, he must recollect to keep the place well in his mind; on one occasion when I feared that somebody might meddle with my horse, I hid him so successfully that I spent the better part of a day in finding him.

Keeping in mind the above given rules, when I left camp the morning after the breaking up of the band of cows and calves, I hunted upstream, and across and through the wooded spurs dividing the little brooks that formed its headwaters. No game was encountered, except some blue grouse, which I saw when near camp on my return, and shot for the pot. These blue grouse are the largest species found in America, except the sage-fowl. They are exclusively birds of the deep mountain forests, and in their manners remind one of the spruce-grouse of the Northeastern woods, being almost equally tame. When alarmed they fly at once into a tree, and several can often be shot before the remainder take fright and are off. On this trip we killed a good many, shooting off their heads with our rifles. They formed a most welcome addition to our bill of fare, the meat being white and excellent. A curious peculiarity in their flesh is that the breast meat has in it a layer of much darker color. They are very handsome birds and furnish dainty food to men wearied of venison; but, unless their heads are knocked off with a rifle, they do not furnish much sport, as they will not fly off when flushed, but simply rise into a fairly tall tree, and there sit, motionless, except that the head is twisted and bobbed around to observe the acts of the foe.

All of the sights and sounds in these pine woods that clothed the Bighorn Mountains reminded me of the similar ones seen and heard in the great sombre forests of Maine and the Adirondacks. The animals and birds were much the same. As in the East, there were red squirrels, chipmunks, red hares, and woodchucks, all of them differing but slightly from our common kinds; woodpeckers, chickadees, nuthatches, and whiskey-jacks came about camp; ravens and eagles flew over the rocky cliffs. There were some new forms, however. The nutcracker, a large, noisy, crow-like bird, with many of the habits of a woodpecker, was common, and in the rocks above timber-line we came upon the Little Chief hare, a wee animal, with a shrill, timorous squeak.

During our stay upon the mountains the weather was generally clear, but always cold—thin ice covering the dark waters of the small mountain tarns, and there were slight snowfalls every two or three days; but we were only kept in camp one day, when it sleeted, snowed, and rained from dawn till nightfall. We passed this day very comfortably, however. I had far too much forethought to go into the woods without a small supply of books for just such occasions. We had rigged the canvas wagon-sheet into a tent, at the bottom of the ravine, near the willow-covered brink of the brook that ran through it. The steep hillsides bounding the valley, which a little below us became sheer cliffs, were partly covered with great pines and spruces, and partly open ground grown up with tall grass and sage-brush. We were thus well sheltered from the wind; and when, one morning, we looked out and saw the wet snow lying on the ground, and with its weight bending down the willow bushes and loading the tall evergreens, while the freezing sleet rattled against the canvas, we simply started a roaring fire of pine logs in front of the tent, and passed a cosey day inside, cleaning guns, reading, and playing cards. Blue grouse, elk hams, and deer saddles hung from the trees around, so we had no fear of starvation. Still, toward evening we got a little tired, and I could not resist taking a couple of hours' brisk ride in the mist, through a chain of open glades that sloped off from our camp.

Later on we made a camp at the head of a great natural meadow where two streams joined together and in times long gone by had been dammed by the beaver. This had at first choked up the passage and made a small lake; then dams were built higher and higher up, making chains of little ponds. By degrees these filled up, and the whole valley became a broad, marshy meadow through which the brook wound between rows of willows and alders. These beaver meadows are very common, but are not usually of such large size. Around this camp there was very little game; but we got a fine mess of spotted trout by taking a long and most toilsome walk up to a little lake lying very near timberline. Our rods and lines were most primitive, consisting of two clumsy dead cedars (the only trees within reach), about six feet of string tied to one and a piece of catgut to the other, with preposterous hooks; yet the trout were so ravenous that we caught them at the rate of about one a minute; and they formed another welcome change in our camp fare. This lake lay in a valley whose sides were so steep and boulder-covered as to need hard climbing to get into and out of it. Every day in the cold, clear weather we tramped miles and miles through the woods and mountains, which, after a snow-storm, took on a really wintry look; while in the moonlight the snow-laden forests shone and sparkled like crystal. The dweller in cities has but a faint idea of the way we ate and slept.

One day Merrifield and I went out together and had a rather exciting chase after some bull elk. The previous evening, toward sunset, I had seen three bulls trotting off across an open glade toward a great stretch of forest and broken ground, up near the foot of the rocky peaks. Next morning, early, we started off to hunt through this country. The walking was hard work, especially up and down the steep cliffs, covered with slippery pine-needles; or among the windfalls, where the rows of dead trees lay piled up across one another in the wildest confusion. We saw nothing until we came to a large patch of burnt ground, where we at once found the soft, black soil marked up by elk hoofs; nor had we penetrated into it more than a few hundred yards before we came to tracks made but a few minutes before, and almost instantly afterward saw three bull elk, probably those I had seen on the preceding day. We had been running briskly uphill through the soft, heavy loam, in which our feet made no noise but slipped and sank deeply; as a consequence, I was all out of breath and my hand so unsteady that I missed my first shot. Elk, however, do not vanish with the instantaneous rapidity of frightened deer, and these three trotted off in a direction quartering to us. I doubt if I ever went through more violent exertion than in the next ten minutes. We raced after them at full speed, opening fire; I wounded all three, but none of the wounds were immediately disabling. They trotted on and we panted afterward, slipping on the wet earth, pitching headlong over charred stumps, leaping on dead logs that broke beneath our weight, more than once measuring our full length on the ground, halting and firing whenever we got a chance. At last one bull fell; we passed him by after the others, which were still running uphill. The sweat streamed into my eyes and made furrows in the sooty mud that covered my face, from having fallen full length down on the burnt earth; I sobbed for breath as I toiled at a shambling trot after them, as nearly done out as could well be. At this moment they turned downhill. It was a great relief; a man who is too done up to go a step uphill can still run fast enough down; with a last spurt I closed in near enough to fire again: one elk fell; the other went off at a walk. We passed the second elk and I kept on alone after the third, not able to go at more than a slow trot myself, and too much winded to dare risk a shot at any distance. He got out of the burnt patch, going into some thick timber in a deep ravine; I closed pretty well, and rushed after him into a thicket of young evergreens. Hardly was I in when there was a scramble and bounce among them and I caught a glimpse of a yellow body moving out to one side; I ran out toward the edge and fired through the twigs at the moving beast. Down it went, but when I ran up, to my disgust I found that I had jumped and killed, in my haste, a blacktail deer, which must have been already roused by the passage of the wounded elk. I at once took up the trail of the latter again, but after a little while the blood grew less, and ceased, and I lost the track; nor could I find it, hunt as hard as I might. The poor beast could not have gone five hundred yards; yet we never found the carcass.

Then I walked slowly back, past the deer I had slain

by so curious a mischance, to the elk. The first one shot down was already dead. The second was only wounded, though it could not rise. When it saw us coming it sought to hide from us by laying its neck flat on the ground, but when we came up close it raised its head and looked proudly at us, the heavy mane bristling up on the neck, while its eyes glared and its teeth grated together. I felt really sorry to kill it. Though these were both well-grown elks, their antlers, of ten points, were small, twisted, and ill shaped; in fact, hardly worth preserving, except to call to mind a chase in which during a few minutes I did as much downright hard work as it has not often fallen to my lot to do. The burnt earth had blackened our faces and hands till we looked like negroes.

The bull elk had at this time begun calling, and several times they were heard right round camp at night, challenging one another or calling to the cows. Their calling is known to hunters as "whistling"; but this is a most inappropriate name for it. It is a most singular and beautiful sound, and is very much the most musical cry uttered by any four-footed beast. When heard for the first time it is almost impossible to believe that it is the call of an animal; it sounds far more as if made by an æolian harp or some strange wind-instrument. It consists of quite a series of notes uttered continuously, in a most soft, musical, vibrant tone, so clearly that they can be heard half a mile off. Heard in the clear, frosty moonlight from the depths of the rugged and forest-clad mountains, the effect is most beautiful; for its charm is heightened by the wild and desolate surroundings. It has the sustained, varied melody of some bird songs, with, of course, a hundred-fold greater power. Now and then, however, the performance is

marred by the elk's apparently getting out of breath
toward the close, and winding up with two or three
gasping notes which have an unpleasantly mule-like
sound.

The great pine-clad mountains, their forests studded
with open glades, were the best of places for the still-
hunter's craft. Going noiselessly through them in our
dull-colored buckskin and noiseless moccasins, we kept
getting glimpses, as it were, of the inner life of the
mountains. Each animal that we saw had its own in-
dividuality. Aside from the thrill and tingle that a
hunter experiences at the sight of his game, I by degrees grew to feel as if I had a personal interest in the
different traits and habits of the wild creatures. The
characters of the animals differed widely, and the dif-
ferences were typified by their actions; and it was pleasant to watch them in their own homes, myself unseen,
when, after stealthy, silent progress through the sombre and soundless depths of the woods, I came upon
them going about the ordinary business of their lives.
The lumbering, self-confident gait of the bears, their
burly strength, and their half-humorous, half-ferocious
look, gave me a real insight into their character; and I
never was more impressed by the exhibition of vast,
physical power than when watching from an ambush a
grizzly burying or covering up an elk carcass. His motions looked awkward, but it was marvellous to see the
ease and absence of effort with which he would scoop
out great holes in the earth or twitch the heavy carcass
from side to side. And the proud, graceful, half-timid,
half-defiant bearing of the elk was in its own way quite
as noteworthy; they seemed to glory in their own power
and beauty, and yet to be ever on the watch for foes
against whom they knew they might not dare to con-

tend. The true still-hunter should be a lover of nature as well as of sport, or he will miss half the pleasure of being in the woods.

The finest bull, with the best head that I got, was killed in the midst of very beautiful and grand surroundings. We had been hunting through a great pine wood which ran up to the edge of a broad canyon-like valley, bounded by sheer walls of rock. There were fresh tracks of elk about, and we had been advancing up-wind with even more than our usual caution when, on stepping out into a patch of open ground, near the edge of the cliff, we came upon a great bull, beating and thrashing his antlers against a young tree, about eighty yards off. He stopped and faced us for a second, his mighty antlers thrown in the air, as he held his head aloft. Behind him towered the tall and sombre pines, while at his feet the jutting crags overhung the deep chasm below, that stretched off between high walls of barren and snow-streaked rocks, the evergreens clinging to their sides, while along the bottom the rapid torrent gathered in places into black and sullen mountain lakes. As the bull turned to run I struck him just behind the shoulder; he reeled to the death-blow, but staggered gamely on a few rods into the forest before sinking to the ground, with my second bullet through his lungs.

Two or three days later than this I killed another bull, nearly as large, in the same patch of woods in which I had slain the first. A bear had been feeding on the carcass of the latter, and, after a vain effort to find his den, we determined to beat through the woods and try to start him up. Accordingly, Merrifield, the teamster, and myself took parallel courses some three hundred yards apart, and started at one end to walk through to the other. I doubt if the teamster much wished to meet a bear alone (while nothing would have given Merrifield more hearty and unaffected enjoyment than to have encountered an entire family), and he gradually edged in pretty close to me. Where the woods became pretty open I saw him suddenly lift his rifle and fire, and immediately afterward a splendid bull elk trotted past in front of me, evidently untouched, the teamster having missed. The elk ran to the other side of two trees that stood close together some seventy yards off, and stopped for a moment to look round. Kneeling down I fired at the only part of his body I could see between the two trees, and sent a bullet into his flank. Away he went, and I after, running in my moccasins over the moss and pine-needles for all there was in me. If a wounded elk gets fairly started he will go at a measured trot for many hours, and even if mortally hurt may run twenty miles before falling; while at the same time he does not start off at full speed, and will often give an active hunter a chance for another shot as he turns and changes his course preparatory to taking a straight line. So I raced along after the elk at my very best speed for a few hundred feet, and then got another shot as he went across a little glade, injuring his hip somewhat. This made it all right for me, and another hundred yards' burst took me up to where I was able to put a ball in a fatal spot, and the grand old fellow sank down and fell over on his side.

No sportsman can ever feel much keener pleasure and self-satisfaction than when, after a successful stalk and good shot, he walks up to a grand elk lying dead in the cool shade of the great evergreens, and looks at the massive and yet finely moulded form, and at the mighty antlers which are to serve in the future as the trophy and proof of his successful skill. Still-hunting the elk on the mountains is as noble a kind of sport as can well be imagined; there is nothing more pleasant and enjoyable, and at the same time it demands that the hunter shall bring into play many manly qualities. There have been few days of my hunting life that were so full of unalloyed happiness as were those spent on the Bighorn range. From morning till night I was on foot, in cool, bracing air, now moving silently through the vast, melancholy pine forests, now treading the brink of high, rocky precipices, always amid the most grand and beautiful scenery; and always after as noble and lordly game as is to be found in the Western world.

Since writing the above, I killed an elk near my ranch; probably the last of his race that will ever be found in our neighborhood. It was just before the fall round-up. An old hunter, who was under some obligation to me, told me that he had shot a cow elk and had seen the tracks of one or two others not more than twenty-five miles off, in a place where the cattle rarely wandered. Such a chance was not to be neglected; and, on the first free day, one of my Elkhorn foremen, Will Dow by name, and myself took our hunting-horses and started off, accompanied by the ranch wagon, in the direction of the probable haunts of the doomed deer. Toward nightfall we struck a deep spring pool, near by the remains of an old Indian encampment. It was at the head of a great basin, several miles across, in which we believed the game to lie. The wagon was halted and we pitched camp; there was plenty of dead wood, and soon the venison-steaks were broiling over the coals raked from beneath the crackling cottonwood logs, while in the narrow valleys the ponies grazed almost within the circle of the flickering firelight. It was in the cool and pleasant month of September; and long after going to bed we lay awake under the blankets watching the stars that on clear nights always shine with such intense brightness over the lonely Western plains.

We were up and off by the gray of the morning. It was a beautiful hunting day; the sun-dogs hung in the red dawn; the wind hardly stirred over the crisp grass; and though the sky was cloudless yet the weather had that queer, smoky, hazy look that it is most apt to take on during the time of the Indian summer. From a high spur of the table-land we looked out far and wide over a great stretch of broken country, the brown of whose hills and valleys was varied everywhere by patches of dull red and vivid yellow, tokens that the trees were already putting on the dress with which they greet the mortal ripening of the year. The deep and narrow but smooth ravines running up toward the edges of the plateaus were heavily wooded, the bright-green tree-tops rising to a height they rarely reach in the barren plains country; and the rocky sides of the sheer gorges were clad with a thick growth of dwarfed cedars, while here and there the trailing Virginia creepers burned crimson among their sombre masses.

We hunted stealthily up-wind, across the line of the heavily timbered coulées. We soon saw traces of our quarry; old tracks at first, and then the fresh footprints of a single elk—a bull, judging by the size—which had come down to drink at the miry alkali pool, its feet slipping so as to leave the marks of the false hoofs in the soft soil. We hunted with painstaking and noiseless care for many hours; at last, as I led old Manitou up to look over the edge of a narrow ravine, there was a crash and movement in the timber below me, and immediately afterward I caught a glimpse of a great bull elk trotting up through the young trees as he gallantly breasted the steep hillside opposite. When clear of the woods, and directly across the valley from me, he stopped and turned half round, throwing his head in the air to gaze for a moment at the intruder. My bullet struck too far back, but, nevertheless, made a deadly wound, and the elk went over the crest of the hill at a wild, plunging gallop. We followed the bloody trail for a quarter of a mile, and found him dead in a thicket. Though of large size, he yet had but small antlers, with few points.

CHAPTER X

OLD EPHRAIM

But few bears are found in the immediate neighborhood of my ranch; and though I have once or twice seen their tracks in the Bad Lands, I have never had any experience with the animals themselves except during the elk-hunting trip on the Bighorn Mountains, described in the preceding chapter.

The grizzly bear undoubtedly comes in the category of dangerous game, and is, perhaps, the only animal in the United States that can be fairly so placed, unless we count the few jaguars found north of the Rio Grande. But the danger of hunting the grizzly has been greatly exaggerated, and the sport is certainly very much safer than it was at the beginning of this century. The first hunters who came into contact with this great bear were men belonging to that hardy and adventurous class of backwoodsmen which had filled the wild country between the Appalachian Mountains and the Mississippi. These men carried but one weapon: the long-barrelled, small-bored pea-rifle, whose bullets ran seventy to the pound, the amount of powder and lead being a little less than that contained in the cartridge of a 32-caliber Winchester. In the Eastern States almost all the hunting was done in the woodland; the shots were mostly obtained at short distance, and deer and black bear were the largest game; moreover, the pea-rifles were marvellously accurate for close range, and their owners were famed the world over for their skill as marksmen. Thus these rifles had so far proved plenty good enough for the work they had to do, and indeed had done excellent service as military weapons in the ferocious wars that the men of the border carried on with their Indian neighbors, and even in conflict with more civilized foes, as at the battles of King's Mountain and New Orleans. But when the restless frontiersmen pressed out over the Western plains, they encountered in the grizzly a beast of far greater bulk and more savage temper than any of those found in the Eastern woods, and their small-bore rifles were utterly inadequate weapons with which to cope with him. It is small wonder that he was considered by them to be almost invulnerable and extraordinarily tenacious of life. He would be a most unpleasant antagonist now to a man armed only with a 32-caliber rifle that carried but a single shot and was loaded at the muzzle. A rifle, to be of use in this sport, should carry a ball weighing from half an ounce to an ounce. With the old pea-rifles the shot had to be in the eye or heart; and accidents to the hunter were very common. But the introduction of heavy breech-loading repeaters has greatly lessened the danger, even in the very few and far-off places where the grizzlies are as ferocious as formerly. For nowadays these great bears are undoubtedly much better aware of the death-dealing power of men, and, as a consequence, much less fierce, than was the case with their forefathers, who so unhesitatingly attacked the early Western travellers and explorers. Constant contact with rifle-carrying hunters, for a period extending over many generations of bear life, has taught the grizzly by bitter experience that man is his undoubted overlord, as far as fighting goes; and this knowledge has become an hereditary characteristic. No grizzly will assail a man now unprovoked, and one will almost always rather run than fight; though if he is wounded or thinks himself cornered he will attack his foes with a headlong, reckless fury that renders him one of the most dangerous of wild beasts. The ferocity of all wild animals depends largely upon the amount of resistance they are accustomed to meet with, and the quantity of molestation to which they are subjected.

The change in the grizzly's character during the last half-century has been precisely paralleled by the change in the characters of its Northern cousin, the polar bear, and of the South African lion. When the Dutch and Scandinavian sailors first penetrated the arctic seas, they were kept in constant dread of the white bear, who regarded a man as simply an erect variety of seal, quite as good eating as the common kind. The records of these early explorers are filled with examples of the ferocious and man-eating propensities of the polar bears; but in the accounts of most of the later arctic expeditions, they are portrayed as having learned wisdom, and being now most anxious to keep out of the way of the hunters. A number of my sporting friends have killed white bears, and none of them were ever even charged. And in South Africa the English sportsmen and Dutch Boers have taught the lion to be a very different creature from what it was when the first white man reached that continent. If the Indian tiger had been a native of the United States, it would now be one of the most shy of beasts. Of late years our estimate of the grizzly's ferocity has been lowered, and we no longer accept the tales of uneducated hunters as being proper authority by which to judge it. But we should make a parallel reduction in the cases of many foreign animals and their describers. Take, for example, that purely melodramatic beast, the North African lion, as portrayed by Jules Gérard, who bombastically describes himself as "*le tueur des lions.*" Gérard's accounts are self-evidently in large part fictitious, while, if true, they would prove less for the bravery of the lion than for the phenomenal cowardice, incapacity, and bad marksmanship of the Algerian Arabs. Doubtless Gérard was a great hunter; but so is many a Western plainsman, whose account of the grizzlies he has killed would be wholly untrustworthy. Take, for instance, the following from page 223 of "La Chasse au Lion": "The inhabitants had assembled one day to the number of two or three hundred, with the object of killing [the lion] or driving it out of the country. The attack took place at sunrise; at midday five hundred cartridges had been expended; the Arabs carried off one of their number dead and six wounded, and the lion remained master of the field of battle." Now, if three hundred men could fire five hundred shots at a lion without hurting him, it merely shows that they were wholly incapable of hurting anything, or else that M. Gérard was more expert with the longbow than with the rifle. Gérard's whole book is filled with equally preposterous nonsense; yet a great many people seriously accept this same book as trustworthy authority for the manners and ferocity of the North African lion. It would be quite as sensible to accept M. Jules Verne's stories as being valuable contributions to science. A good deal of the lion's reputation is built upon just such stuff.

How the prowess of the grizzly compares with that of the lion or tiger would be hard to say; I have never shot either of the latter myself, and my brother, who has killed tigers in India, has never had a chance at a grizzly. Any one of the big bears we killed on the mountains would, I should think, have been able to make short work of either a lion or a tiger; for the grizzly is greatly superior in bulk and muscular power to either of the great cats, and its teeth are as large as theirs, while its claws, though blunter, are much longer; nevertheless, I believe that a lion or a tiger would be fully as dangerous to a hunter or other human being, on account of the superior speed of its charge, the lightning-like rapidity of its movements, and its apparently sharper senses. Still, after all is said, the man should have a thoroughly trustworthy weapon and a fairly cool head who would follow into its own haunts and slay grim Old Ephraim.

A grizzly will only fight if wounded or cornered, or, at least, if he thinks himself cornered. If a man by accident stumbles on to one close up, he is almost certain to be attacked really more from fear than from any other motive; exactly the same reason that makes a rattlesnake strike at a passer-by. I have personally known of but one instance of a grizzly turning on a hunter before being wounded. This happened to a friend of mine, a Californian ranchman, who, with two or three of his men, was following a bear that had carried off one of his sheep. They got the bear into a cleft in the mountain from which there was no escape, and he suddenly charged back through the line of his pursuers, struck down one of the horsemen, seized the arm of the man in his jaws and broke it as if it had been a pipe-stem, and was only killed after a most lively fight, in which, by repeated charges, he at one time drove every one of his assailants off the field.

But two instances have come to my personal knowledge where a man has been killed by a grizzly. One was that of a hunter at the foot of the Bighorn Mountains who had chased a large bear and finally wounded him. The animal turned at once and came straight at the man, whose second shot missed. The bear then closed and passed on, after striking only a single blow; yet that one blow, given with all the power of its thick, immensely muscular forearm, armed with nails as strong as so many hooked steel spikes, tore out the man's collar-bone and snapped through three or four ribs. He never recovered from the shock, and died that night.

The other instance occurred to a neighbor of mine— who has a small ranch on the Little Missouri—two or three years ago. He was out on a mining trip, and was prospecting with two other men near the headwater of the Little Missouri, in the Black Hills country. They were walking down along the river, and came to a point of land thrust out into it, which was densely covered with brush and fallen timber. Two of the party walked round by the edge of the stream; but the third, a German, and a very powerful fellow, followed a well-beaten game trail, leading through the bushy point. When they were some forty yards apart the two men heard an agonized shout from the German, and at the same time the loud coughing growl, or roar, of a bear. They turned just in time to see their companion struck a terrible blow on the head by a grizzly, which must have been roused from its lair by his almost stepping on it; so close was it that he had no time to fire his rifle, but merely held it up over his head as a guard. Of course it was struck down, the claws of the great brute at the same time shattering his skull like an egg-shell. Yet the man staggered on some ten feet before he fell; but when he did he never spoke or moved again. The two others killed the bear after a short, brisk struggle as he was in the midst of a most determined charge.

In 1872, near Fort Wingate, New Mexico, two soldiers of a cavalry regiment came to their death at the claws of a grizzly bear. The army surgeon who attended them told me the particulars, as far as they were known. The men were mail-carriers, and one day did not come in at the appointed time. Next day a relief party was sent out to look for them, and after some search found the bodies of both, as well as that of one of the horses. One of the men still showed signs of life; he came to his senses before dying, and told the story. They had seen a grizzly, and pursued it on horseback with their Spencer rifles. On coming close, one had fired into its side, when it turned with marvellous quickness for so large and unwieldy an animal, and struck down the horse, at the same time inflicting a ghastly wound on the rider. The other man dismounted and came up to the rescue of his companion. The bear then left the latter and attacked the other. Although hit by the bullet, it charged home and threw the man down, and then lay on him and deliberately bit him to death, while his groans and cries were frightful to hear. Afterward it walked off into the bushes without again offering to molest the already mortally wounded victim of its first assault.

At certain times the grizzly works a good deal of havoc among the herds of the stockmen. A friend of mine, a ranchman in Montana, told me that one fall bears became very plenty around his ranches, and caused him severe loss, killing with ease even full-grown beef-steers. But one of them once found his intended quarry too much for him. My friend had a stocky, rather vicious range stallion, which had been grazing one day near a small thicket of bushes, and, toward evening, came galloping in with three or four gashes in his haunch, that looked as if they had been cut with a dull axe. The cowboys knew at once that he had been assailed by a bear, and rode off to the thicket near which he had been feeding. Sure enough, a bear, evidently in a very bad temper, sallied out as soon as the thicket was surrounded, and, after a spirited fight and a succession of charges, was killed. On examination, it was found that his under jaw was broken, and part of his face smashed in, evidently by the stallion's hoofs. The horse had been feeding when the bear leaped out at him, but failed to kill at the first stroke; then the horse lashed out behind, and not only freed himself, but also severely damaged his opponent.

Doubtless the grizzly could be hunted to advantage with dogs, which would not, of course, be expected to seize him, but simply to find and bay him, and distract his attention by barking and nipping. Occasionally, a bear can be caught in the open and killed with the aid of horses. But nine times out of ten the only way to get one is to put on moccasins and still-hunt it in its own haunts, shooting it at close quarters. Either its tracks should be followed until the bed wherein it lies during the day is found, or a given locality in which it is known to exist should be carefully beaten through, or else a bait should be left out, and a watch kept on it to catch the bear when he has come to visit it.

For some days after our arrival on the Bighorn range we did not come across any grizzly.

Although it was still early in September, the weather was cool and pleasant, the nights being frosty; and every two or three days there was a flurry of light snow, which rendered the labor of tracking much more easy. Indeed, throughout our stay on the mountains, the peaks were snow-capped almost all the time. Our fare was excellent, consisting of elk venison, mountain grouse, and small trout—the last caught in one of the beautiful little lakes that lay almost up by timber-line. To us, who had for weeks been accustomed to make small fires from dried brush, or from sage-brush roots, which we dug out of the ground, it was a treat to sit at night before the roaring and crackling pine logs; as the old teamster quaintly put it, we had at last come to a land "where the wood grew on trees." There were plenty of blacktail deer in the woods, and we came across a number of bands of cow and calf elk, or of young bulls; but after several days' hunting we were still without any head worth taking home, and had seen no sign of grizzly, which was the game we were especially anxious to kill; for neither Merrifield nor I had ever seen a wild bear alive.

Sometimes we hunted in company; sometimes each of us went out alone; the teamster, of course, remaining in to guard camp and cook. One day we had separated; I reached camp early in the afternoon, and waited a couple of hours before Merrifield put in an appearance. At last I heard a shout—the familiar long-drawn *Eikoh-h-h* of the cattlemen—and he came in sight galloping at speed down an open glade, and waving his hat, evidently having had good luck; and when he reined in his small, wiry cow-pony, we saw that he had packed behind his saddle the fine glossy pelt of a black bear. Better still, he announced that he had been off about ten miles to a perfect tangle of ravines and valleys where bear sign was very thick; and not of black bear either, but of grizzly. The black bear (the only one we got on the mountains) he had run across by accident, while riding up a valley in which there was a patch of dead timber grown up with berry bushes. He noticed a black object which he first took to be a stump; for during the past few days we had each of us made one or two clever stalks up to charred logs, which our imagination converted into bears. On coming near, however, the object suddenly took to its heels; he followed over frightful ground at the pony's best pace, until it stumbled and fell down. By this time he was close on the bear, which had just reached the edge of the wood. Picking himself up, he rushed after it, hearing it growling ahead of him; after running some fifty yards the sound stopped, and he stood still listening. He saw and heard nothing, until he happened to cast his eyes upward, and there was the bear, almost overhead, and about twenty-five feet up a tree; and in as many seconds afterward it came down to the ground with a bounce, stone-dead. It was a young bear, in its second year, and had probably never before seen a man, which accounted for the ease with which it was treed and taken. One minor result of the encounter was to convince Merrifield—the list of whose faults did not include lack of self-confidence—that he could run down any bear; in consequence of which idea we on more than one subsequent occasion went through a good deal of violent exertion.

Merrifield's tale made me decide to shift camp at once, and go over to the spot where the bear tracks were so plenty. Next morning we were off, and by noon pitched camp by a clear brook, in a valley with steep, wooded sides, but with good feed for the horses in the open bottom. We rigged the canvas wagon-sheet into a small tent, sheltered by the trees from the wind, and piled great pine logs near by where we wished to place the fire; for a night camp in the sharp fall weather is cold and dreary unless there is a roaring blaze of flame in front of the tent.

That afternoon we again went out, and I shot a fine bull elk. I came home alone toward nightfall, walking through a reach of burnt forest, where there was nothing but charred tree-trunks and black mould. When nearly through it I came across the huge, half-human footprints of a great grizzly, which must have passed by within a few minutes. It gave me rather an eerie feeling in the silent, lonely woods, to see for the first time the unmistakable proofs that I was in the home of the mighty lord of the wilderness. I followed the tracks in the fading twilight until it became too dark to see them any longer, and then shouldered my rifle and walked back to camp.

That evening we almost had a visit from one of the animals we were after. Several times we had heard at night the musical calling of the bull elk—a sound to which no writer has as yet done justice. This particular night, when we were in bed and the fire was smouldering, we were roused by a ruder noise—a kind of grunting or roaring whine, answered by the frightened snorts of the ponies. It was a bear which had evidently not seen the fire, as it came from behind the bank, and had probably been attracted by the smell of the horses. After it made out what we were, it stayed round a short while, again uttered its peculiar roaring grunt, and went off; we had seized our rifles and had run out into the woods, but in the darkness could see nothing; indeed, it was rather lucky we did not stumble across the bear, as he could have made short work of us when we were at such a disadvantage.

Next day we went off on a long tramp through the woods and along the sides of the canyons. There were plenty of berry bushes growing in clusters; and all around these there were fresh tracks of bear. But the grizzly is also a flesh-eater, and has a great liking for carrion. On visiting the place where Merrifield had killed the black bear, we found that the grizzlies had been there before us, and had utterly devoured the carcass, with cannibal relish. Hardly a scrap was left, and we turned our steps toward where lay the bull elk I had killed. It was quite late in the afternoon when we reached the place. A grizzly had evidently been at the carcass during the preceding night, for his great footprints were in the ground all around it, and the carcass itself was gnawed and torn, and partially covered with earth and leaves—for the grizzly has a curious habit of burying all of his prey that he does not at the moment need. A great many ravens had been feeding on the body, and they wheeled about over the tree-tops above us, uttering their barking croaks.

The forest was composed mainly of what are called ridge-pole pines, which grow close together, and do not branch out until the stems are thirty or forty feet from the ground. Beneath these trees we walked over a carpet of pine-needles, upon which our moccasined feet made no sound. The woods seemed vast and lonely, and their silence was broken now and then by the strange noises always to be heard in the great forests, and which seem to mark the sad and everlasting unrest of the wilderness. We climbed up along the trunk of a dead tree which had toppled over until its upper branches struck in the limb crotch of another, that thus supported it at an angle half-way in its fall. When above the ground far enough to prevent the bear's smelling us, we sat still to wait for his approach, until, in the gathering gloom, we could no longer see the sights of our rifles, and could but dimly make out the carcass of the great elk. It was useless to wait longer; and we clambered down and stole out to the edge of the woods. The forest here covered one side of a steep, almost canyon-like ravine whose other side was bare except of rock and sage-brush. Once out from under the trees there was still plenty of light, although the sun had set, and we crossed over some fifty yards to the opposite hillside, and crouched down under a bush to see if, perchance, some animal might not also leave the cover. To our right the ravine sloped downward toward the valley of the Bighorn River, and far on its other side we could catch a glimpse of the great main chain of the Rockies, their snow-peaks glinting crimson in the light of the set sun. Again we waited quietly in the growing dusk until the pine-trees in our front blended into one dark, frowning mass. We saw nothing; but the wild creatures of the forest had begun to stir abroad. The owls hooted dismally from the tops of the tall trees, and two or three times a harsh wailing cry, probably the voice of some lynx or wolverine, arose from the depths of the woods. At last, as we were rising to leave, we heard the sound of the breaking of a dead stick from the spot where we knew the carcass lay. It was a sharp, sudden noise, perfectly distinct from the natural creaking and snapping of the branches; just such a sound as would be made by the tread of some heavy creature. Old Ephraim had come back to the carcass. A minute afterward, listening with strained ears, we heard him brush by some dry twigs. It was entirely too dark to go in after him; but we made up our minds that on the morrow he should be ours.

OLD EPHRAIM

Early next morning we were over at the elk carcass, and, as we expected, found that the bear had eaten his full at it during the night. His tracks showed him to be an immense fellow, and were so fresh that we doubted if he had left long before we arrived; and we made up our minds to follow him up and try to find his lair. The bears that lived on these mountains had evidently been little disturbed; indeed, the Indians and most of the white hunters are rather chary of meddling with Old Ephraim, as the mountain men style the grizzly, unless they get him at a disadvantage; for the sport is fraught with some danger and but small profit. The bears thus seemed to have very little fear of harm, and we thought it likely that the bed of the one who had fed on the elk would not be far away.

My companion was a skilful tracker, and we took up the trail at once. For some distance it led over the soft, yielding carpet of moss and pine-needles, and the footprints were quite easily made out, although we could follow them but slowly; for we had, of course, to keep a sharp lookout ahead and around us as we walked noiselessly on in the sombre half-light always prevailing under the great pine-trees, through whose thickly interlacing branches stray but few beams of light, no matter how bright the sun may be outside. We made no sound ourselves, and every little sudden noise sent a thrill through me as I peered about with each sense on the alert. Two or three of the ravens that we had scared from the carcass flew overhead, croaking hoarsely; and the pine-tops moaned and sighed in the slight breeze—for pine-trees seem to be ever in motion, no matter how light the wind.

After going a few hundred yards the tracks turned

off on a well-beaten path made by the elk; the woods
were in many places cut up by these game trails, which
had often become as distinct as ordinary footpaths.
The beast's footprints were perfectly plain in the dust,
and he had lumbered along up the path until near the
middle of the hillside, where the ground broke away
and there were hollows and boulders. Here there had
been a windfall, and the dead trees lay among the living, piled across one another in all directions; while between and around them sprouted up a thick growth of
young spruces and other evergreens. The trail turned
off into the tangled thicket, within which it was almost
certain we would find our quarry. We could still follow the tracks, by the slight scrapes of the claws on the
bark, or by the bent and broken twigs; and we advanced with noiseless caution, slowly climbing over the
dead tree-trunks and upturned stumps, and not letting
a branch rustle or catch on our clothes. When in the
middle of the thicket we crossed what was almost a
breastwork of fallen logs, and Merrifield, who was leading, passed by the upright stem of a great pine. As
soon as he was by it, he sank suddenly on one knee,
turning half round, his face fairly aflame with excitement; and as I strode past him, with my rifle at the
ready, there, not ten steps off, was the great bear,
slowly rising from his bed among the young spruces.
He had heard us, but apparently hardly knew exactly
where or what we were, for he reared up on his haunches
sideways to us. Then he saw us, and dropped down
again on all fours, the shaggy hair on his neck and
shoulders seeming to bristle as he turned toward us.
As he sank down on his forefeet I had raised the rifle;
his head was bent slightly down, and when I saw the
top of the white bead fairly between his small, glitter-

ing, evil eyes, I pulled trigger. Half rising up, the huge beast fell over on his side in the death throes, the ball having gone into his brain, striking as fairly between the eyes as if the distance had been measured by a carpenter's rule.

The whole thing was over in twenty seconds from the time I caught sight of the game; indeed, it was over so quickly that the grizzly did not have time to show fight at all or come a step toward us. It was the first I had ever seen, and I felt not a little proud as I stood over the great brindled bulk which lay stretched out at length in the cool shade of the evergreens. He was a monstrous fellow, much larger than any I have seen since, whether alive or brought in dead by the hunters. As near as we could estimate (for of course we had nothing with which to weigh more than very small portions) he must have weighed about twelve hundred pounds, and though this is not as large as some of his kind are said to grow in California, it is yet a very unusual size for a bear. He was a good deal heavier than any of our horses; and it was with the greatest difficulty that we were able to skin him. He must have been very old, his teeth and claws being all worn down and blunted; but nevertheless he had been living in plenty, for he was as fat as a prize hog, the layers on his back being a finger's length in thickness. He was still in the summer coat, his hair being short, and in color a curious brindled brown, somewhat like that of certain bulldogs; while all the bears we shot afterward had the long thick winter fur, cinnamon or yellowish brown. By the way, the name of this bear has reference to its character and not to its color, and should, I suppose, be properly spelt grisly—in the sense of horrible, exactly as we speak of a "grisly spectre"—and not grizzly; but perhaps the latter way of spelling it is too well established to be now changed.

In killing dangerous game, steadiness is more needed than good shooting. No game is dangerous unless a man is close up, for nowadays hardly any wild beast will charge from a distance of a hundred yards, but will rather try to run off; and if a man is close it is easy enough for him to shoot straight if he does not lose his head. A bear's brain is about the size of a pint bottle; and any one can hit a pint bottle offhand at thirty or forty feet. I have had two shots at bears at close quarters, and each time I fired into the brain, the bullet in one case striking fairly between the eyes, as told above, and in the other going in between the eye and ear. A novice at this kind of sport will find it best and safest to keep in mind the old Norse viking's advice in reference to a long sword: "If you go in close enough your sword will be long enough." If a poor shot goes in close enough he will find that he shoots straight enough.

I was very proud over my first bear; but Merrifield's chief feeling seemed to be disappointment that the animal had not had time to show fight. He was rather a reckless fellow, and very confident in his own skill with the rifle; and he really did not seem to have any more fear of the grizzlies than if they had been so many jack-rabbits. I did not at all share his feelings, having a hearty respect for my foes' prowess, and in following and attacking them always took all possible care to get the chances on my side. Merrifield was sincerely sorry that we never had to stand a regular charge; while on this trip we killed five grizzlies with seven bullets, and, except in the case of the she and cub spoken of farther on, each was shot about as quickly as it got sight of us. The last one we got was an old male, which was feeding on an elk carcass. We crept up to within about sixty feet, and as Merrifield had not yet killed a grizzly purely to his own gun, and I had killed three, I told him to take the shot. He at once whispered gleefully: "I'll break his leg, and we'll see what he'll do!" Having no ambition to be a participator in the antics of a three-legged bear, I hastily interposed a most emphatic veto; and with a rather injured air he fired, the bullet going through the neck just back of the head. The bear fell to the shot, and could not get up from the ground, dying in a few minutes; but first he seized his left wrist in his teeth and bit clean through it, completely separating the bones of the paw and arm. Although a smaller bear than the big one I first shot, he would probably have proved a much more ugly foe, for he was less unwieldy, and had much longer and sharper teeth and claws. I think that if my companion had merely broken the beast's leg, he would have had his curiosity as to its probable conduct more than gratified.

We tried eating the grizzly's flesh, but it was not good, being coarse and not well flavored; and, besides, we could not get over the feeling that it had belonged to a carrion-feeder. The flesh of the little black bear, on the other hand, was excellent; it tasted like that of a young pig. Doubtless, if a young grizzly, which had fed merely upon fruits, berries, and acorns, was killed, its flesh would prove good eating; but even then it would probably not be equal to a black bear.

A day or two after the death of the big bear, we went out one afternoon on horseback, intending merely to ride down to see a great canyon lying some six miles west of our camp; indeed, we went more to look at the

scenery than for any other reason, though, of course,
neither of us ever stirred out of camp without his rifle.
We rode down the valley in which we had camped,
through alternate pine groves and open glades, until
we reached the canyon, and then skirted its brink for
a mile or so. It was a great chasm, many miles in
length, as if the table-land had been rent asunder by
some terrible and unknown force; its sides were sheer
walls of rock, rising three or four hundred feet straight
up in the air, and worn by the weather till they looked
like the towers and battlements of some vast fortress.
Between them, at the bottom, was a space, in some
places nearly a quarter of a mile wide, in others very
narrow, through whose middle foamed a deep, rapid
torrent, of which the sources lay far back among the
snow-topped mountains around Cloud Peak. In this
valley, dark green, sombre pines stood in groups, stiff
and erect; and here and there among them were groves
of poplar and cottonwood, with slender branches and
trembling leaves, their bright green already changing
to yellow in the sharp fall weather. We went down to
where the mouth of the canyon opened out, and rode
our horses to the end of a great jutting promontory of
rock, thrust out into the plain; and in the cold, clear
air we looked far over the broad valley of the Bighorn
as it lay at our very feet, walled in on the other side
by the distant chain of the Rocky Mountains.

Turning our horses, we rode back along the edge of
another canyon-like valley, with a brook flowing down
its centre, and its rocky sides covered with an uninterrupted pine forest—the place of all others in whose inaccessible wildness and ruggedness a bear would find a
safe retreat. After some time we came to where other
valleys, with steep, grass-grown sides, covered with

sage-brush, branched out from it, and we followed one of these out. There was plenty of elk sign about, and we saw several blacktail deer. These last were very common on the mountains, but we had not hunted them at all, as we were in no need of meat. But this afternoon we came across a buck with remarkably fine antlers, and accordingly I shot it, and we stopped to cut off and skin out the horns, throwing the reins over the heads of the horses, and leaving them to graze by themselves. The body lay near the crest of one side of a deep valley, or ravine, which headed up on the plateau a mile to our left. Except for scattered trees and bushes the valley was bare; but there was heavy timber along the crests of the hills on its opposite side. It took some time to fix the head properly, and we were just ending when Merrifield sprang to his feet and exclaimed: "Look at the bears!" pointing down into the valley below us. Sure enough, there were two bears (which afterward proved to be an old she and a nearly full-grown cub) travelling up the bottom of the valley, much too far off for us to shoot. Grasping our rifles and throwing off our hats, we started off as hard as we could run, diagonally down the hillside, so as to cut them off. It was some little time before they saw us, when they made off at a lumbering gallop up the valley. It would seem impossible to run into two grizzlies in the open, but they were going up hill and we down, and, moreover, the old one kept stopping. The cub would forge ahead and could probably have escaped us, but the mother now and then stopped to sit up on her haunches and look round at us, when the cub would run back to her. The upshot was that we got ahead of them, when they turned and went straight up one hillside as we ran straight down the other behind them.

By this time I was pretty nearly done out, for running along the steep ground through the sage-brush was most exhausting work; and Merrifield kept gaining on me and was well in front. Just as he disappeared over a bank, almost at the bottom of the valley, I tripped over a bush and fell full length. When I got up I knew I could never make up the ground I had lost, and, besides, could hardly run any longer; Merrifield was out of sight below, and the bears were laboring up the steep hillside directly opposite and about three hundred yards off, so I sat down and began to shoot over Merrifield's head, aiming at the big bear. She was going very steadily and in a straight line, and each bullet sent up a puff of dust where it struck the dry soil, so that I could keep correcting my aim; and the fourth ball crashed into the old bear's flank. She lurched heavily forward, but recovered herself and reached the timber, while Merrifield, who had put on a spurt, was not far behind.

I toiled up the hill at a sort of trot, fairly gasping and sobbing for breath; but before I got to the top I heard a couple of shots and a shout. The old bear had turned as soon as she was in the timber, and came toward Merrifield, but he gave her the death wound by firing into her chest, and then shot at the young one, knocking it over. When I came up he was just walking toward the latter to finish it with the revolver, but it suddenly jumped up as lively as ever and made off at a great pace—for it was nearly full grown. It was impossible to fire where the tree-trunks were so thick, but there was a small opening across which it would have to pass, and, collecting all my energies, I made a last run, got into position, and covered the opening with my rifle. The instant the bear appeared I fired, and it turned a dozen somersaults downhill, rolling over and over; the ball had struck it near the tail, and had ranged forward through the hollow of the body. Each of us had thus given the fatal wound to the bear into which the other had fired the first bullet. The run, though short, had been very sharp, and over such awful country that we were completely fagged out, and could hardly speak for lack of breath. The sun had already set, and it was too late to skin the animals; so we merely dressed them, caught the ponies—with some trouble, for they were frightened at the smell of the bear's blood on our hands—and rode home through the darkening woods. Next day we brought the teamster and two of the steadiest pack-horses to the carcasses, and took the skins into camp.

The feed for the horses was excellent in the valley in which we were camped, and the rest after their long journey across the plains did them good. They had picked up wonderfully in condition during our stay on the mountains; but they were apt to wander very far during the night, for there were so many bears and other wild beasts around, that they kept getting frightened and running off. We were very loath to leave our hunting-grounds, but time was pressing, and we had already many more trophies than we could carry; so one cool morning, when the branches of the evergreens were laden with the feathery snow that had fallen overnight, we struck camp and started out of the mountains, each of us taking his own bedding behind his saddle, while the pack-ponies were loaded down with bearskins, elk and deer antlers, and the hides and furs of other game. In single file we moved through the woods, and across the canyons to the edge of the great table-land, and then slowly down the steep slope to its foot, where we found our canvas-topped wagon; and next day saw us setting out on our long journey homeward, across the three hundred weary miles of treeless and barren-looking plains country.

Last spring, since the above was written, a bear killed a man not very far from my ranch. It was at the time of the floods. Two hunters came down the river, by our ranch, on a raft, stopping to take dinner. A score or so of miles below, as we afterward heard from the survivor, they landed, and found a bear in a small patch of brushwood. After waiting in vain for it to come out, one of the men rashly attempted to enter the thicket, and was instantly struck down by the beast, before he could so much as fire his rifle. It broke in his skull with a blow of its great paw, and then seized his arm in its jaws, biting it through and through in three places, but leaving the body and retreating into the bushes as soon as the unfortunate man's companion approached. We did not hear of the accident until too late to go after the bear, as we were just about starting to join the spring round-up.

ADDENDUM

In speaking of the trust antelope place in their eyesight as a guard against danger, I do not mean to imply that their noses are not also very acute; it is as important with them as with all other game to prevent their getting the hunter's wind. So with deer; while their eyes are not as sharp as those of bighorn and pronghorn, they are yet quite keen enough to make it necessary for the still-hunter to take every precaution to avoid being seen.

Although with us antelope display the most rooted

296

objection to entering broken or wooded ground, yet a friend of mine, whose experience in the hunting-field is many times as great as my own, tells me that in certain parts of the country they seem by preference to go among the steepest and roughest places (of course, in so doing, being obliged to make vertical as well as horizontal leaps), and even penetrate into thick woods. Indeed, no other species seems to show such peculiar "freakiness" of character, both individually and locally.

GAME–SHOOTING IN THE WEST

BIBLIOGRAPHICAL NOTE

GAME-SHOOTING IN THE WEST

This series of six illustrated articles originally appeared in *Outing,* March to August, 1886, under the title RANCH LIFE AND GAME-SHOOTING IN THE WEST, and has never been reprinted. The illustrations are from drawings by J. R. Chapin, R. Swain Gifford, McDougall, J. B. Sword, and J. Carter Beard.

CONTENTS

GAME–SHOOTING IN THE WEST

CHAPTER I

THE RANCH

To see the rapidity with which the larger kinds of game animals are being exterminated throughout the United States is really melancholy. Twenty-five years ago, or even fifteen years ago, the Western plains and mountains were in places fairly thronged with deer, elk, antelope, and buffalo; indeed there was then no other part of the world save South Africa where the number of individuals of large game animals was so large. All this has now been changed, or else is being changed at a really remarkable rate of speed. The buffalo are already gone; a few straggling individuals, and perhaps here and there a herd so small that it can hardly be called more than a squad, are all that remain. Over four-fifths of their former range the same fate has befallen the elk; and their number, even among the mountainous haunts which still afford them a refuge, is greatly decreased. The shrinkage among deer and antelope has been relatively nearly as serious. There are but few places left now where it is profitable for a man to take to hunting as a profession; the brutal skin-hunters and meat-butchers of the woods and prairies have done their work; and these buckskin-clad and greasy Nimrods are now themselves sharing the fate of the game that has disappeared from before their rifles.

Still, however, there is plenty of sport to be had by men who are of a more or less adventurous turn of mind, and sufficiently hardy and resolute to be willing to stand rough work and scant fare; and of course, excepting men who go out to spend some months in travelling solely for purposes of sport, no class has as much chance to get it as is the case with the ranchmen, whose herds now cover the great plains of the West, and even range well up on the foot-hills of the mighty central chain of the Rocky Mountains. All of my own hunting has been done simply in the intervals of the numerous duties of ranch life; and in order to understand the way we set out on a trip after game it is necessary also to understand a little about the nature of our homes and surroundings.

Many of the ranches are mere mud hovels or log shanties, stuck down in any raw, treeless spot where there happen to be water and grass; but many others are really beautifully situated, and though very rude in construction, are still large enough and solid enough to yield ample comfort to the inmates. One such, now in my mind, which is placed in a bend of the Heart River, could not possibly be surpassed as regards the romantic beauty of its surroundings. My own house stands on a bottom of the Little Missouri nearly two miles in length, and perhaps half a mile or over in width, from the brink of the current to the line of steep and jagged buttes that rise sharply up to bound it on the side farthest from the river. Part of this bottom is open, covered only with rank grass and sprawling sagebrush; but there are patches of dense woodland, where the brittle cottonwood-trees grow close together and stretch their heads high in the air. The house itself, made out of hewn logs, is in a large open glade many acres in extent. It fronts the river with its length of sixty feet, and along the front runs a broad veranda, where we sit in our rocking-chairs in the summer-time when the day's work is done. Within it is divided into several rooms; one of these is where we spend the winter evenings at the time when the cold has set in with a bitter intensity hardly known in any other part of the United States. A huge fireplace contains the great logs of cedar and cottonwood; skins of elk and deer cover the floor, while wolf and fox furs hang from the walls; antlers and horns are thrust into the rafters to serve as pegs on which to hang coats and caps.

In the glade, besides the house, there are several other buildings—a stable, a smithy, and two or three sheds and outhouses, besides a high, circular horse corral, with a snubbing-post in the centre, and a fenced-in patch of garden land. The river itself is usually a shallow, rapid stream that a man can wade across but that cannot carry the lightest boat; but when the snows melt, or after heavy rains, it is changed into a boiling, muddy torrent that cannot be crossed by man or beast and that will bear huge rafts. It is at all times dangerous to cross on account of the quicksands; but after a series of freshets the whole river can be described as simply four or five feet of turbulent water running down over a moving mass of quicksand three feet in depth, that fills the entire bed of the stream. In ordinary floods there will remain certain fords and rapids that can be crossed; but at times any horse that dared to attempt a passage, no matter where, would be almost certainly lost.

Back from the river for several miles extends a stretch of broken and intensely rugged country, known in plains parlance as "Bad Lands." It consists of chains of steep buttes or hills, often spreading out into table-lands, and separated by a network of deep ravines and winding valleys, which branch out in every direction. When we pass these Bad Lands we come to the open prairie, which stretches out on every side in level or undulating expanse as far as the eye can reach. In a few of the gorges in the Bad Lands there are groves of wind-beaten pines, or dwarfed cedars, favorite haunts of the black-tail deer.

A hunting expedition from the ranch needs but scant preparation, because all of our business is carried on in the open air, and our whole outfit is such as is best suited for an outdoor life. After cattle the most conspicuous adjuncts of a cow-ranch are horses. Everything is done, and almost all of each day is spent, in the saddle. The horses run free in a band, which is driven to the corral every day or two, when the animals needed at the moment are roped (no plainsman, by the way, ever on any occasion uses the word "lasso"; in its place he uses the verb "to rope"; it is sure sign of being a "tenderfoot" to use the former), and the rest of the band again turned loose. Every day some rider goes out among the neighboring cattle; and from May to November most of the hands are away from the ranch-house on the different round-ups. For a short expedition only three or four men may go, taking a pack outfit; that is, each man taking a spare horse, on which his bedding, food, and the indispensable branding-irons are packed. On a longer trip a wagon is needed. The regular plains wagon is perforce a stout, rather heavy affair, or it would not stand the rough usage to which it is exposed. It needs a team of at least four horses to handle it properly, can carry a very large load, and with its hooped canvas top offers a good shelter to a small number of men in the event of a sudden night storm of rain. This is the wagon we take when going on a trip of any duration; but for quick, light work we use the buckboard. This will carry a couple of men and their traps in good style, can go almost everywhere, and moreover can travel nearly as fast as can a man on horseback. A pair can drag a buckboard perfectly, although if merely going up to a neighboring ranch or to some definite point we often put in a team of four, who bowl us along over the prairie at a great rate— trotting or galloping. The stock-saddles used throughout the cow country are admirably suited for a hunting trip, as they have pockets in which various articles can be stowed, and things can be tied on them almost everywhere, thanks to the rawhide strings with which they are plentifully provided. Thus a couple of antelope, or a brace of young deer, or a big buck can be carried behind the saddle with perfect ease. Both ranchmen and cowboys habitually spend their days in the very costume in which they hunt—broad hat, flannel shirt, trousers tucked into top-boots. In winter the biting gales render it necessary to take to fur caps and coats, great mittens, and the warmest wool-lined shoes. Leathern overalls or "chaps" (the cowboy abbreviation for the Spanish word *chaparajos*) are very useful when riding through thorns or to keep out the wet. The same blankets and bedding that are taken on a round-up of course do for a hunting expedition. Though we have a tent we do not often use it, shielding ourselves from wet weather by sleeping under the canvas wagon-sheet. The cooking utensils need not be very numerous; a kettle and a frying-pan, a "Dutch oven," so called, and a half-dozen tin plates and cups, with knives and forks, make up the not overextensive assortment. Flour, bacon, salt, sugar, and tea or coffee are the only provisions that need be taken along. Of course I am now speaking merely of short trips made from the ranch. If we make longer ones, such as an expedition after bear and elk to the Big Horn Mountains,* which would take a couple of months, we would need to make much more ample preparations.

Almost every cowboy carries on his hip a heavy Colt or Smith & Wesson revolver; but this is of very little use for game. The regular hunters use rifles, for the most part Winchesters, although many of them still carry the ponderous Sharps, of 40 or 45 caliber, carrying a long, narrow, heavy ball, an ounce or so in weight; weapons which are relics of the days when a war of extermination was waged on the herds of the buffalo, and than which no hunting-rifles in the world possess greater accuracy, range, and penetration. They are, however, very cumbersome, have but one shot, and, now that the larger kinds of game have grown so scarce, are giving way to the handier Winchester. A ranchman, however, with whom hunting is of secondary importance, and who cannot be bothered by carrying a long rifle always round with him on horseback, but who, nevertheless, wishes to have some weapon with which he can kill what game he runs across, usually adopts a short, light saddle gun, a carbine, weighing but five or six pounds, and of such convenient shape that it can be hung under his thigh alongside the saddle. A 40–60 Winchester is perhaps the best for such a purpose, as it carries far and straight and hits hard, and is a first-rate weapon for deer and antelope, and can also be used with effect against sheep, elk, and even bear, although for these last a heavier weapon is of course preferable.

There is thus very little need of preparation indeed when one starts off to hunt from his own ranch: horse, dress, outfit, and weapon are already all there. Our

* Described in my "Hunting Trips of a Ranchman" (Putnam: New York).

supply of fresh meat depends entirely upon what we ourselves kill; and even now we can generally get a deer in an afternoon's walk from the house, without having to make a regular trip; but, to insure the capture of anything else, it is now necessary to go prepared to spend a night or two out on the hunting-grounds.

CHAPTER II

ANTELOPE–SHOOTING ON THE CATTLE TRAIL

EARLY last May I had to take a thousand head of young cattle, mostly of Eastern origin, from the railroad down to my range. Ordinarily we drive cattle down along the river-bottom, but at that time there had been a series of freshets which had turned the stream itself into a raging torrent and its bed into a mass of treacherous quicksands, and as the cattle were for the most part young and, as is always the case in the spring, weak, we did not dare to trust them at the crossings, and indeed, had we done so, we would have run serious risk of losing the greater number. Accordingly we drove down along the great divide between the Little Missouri and the Beaver, making a six days' trail.

Owing to a variety of causes, our preparations had been very inadequate. The ranch wagon with a team of four accompanied us to carry our food and bedding. To work the cattle there were five men and myself, each with two horses, none of the latter being very well broken, by the way. All of the five men were originally Easterners, backwoodsmen, stout, hardy fellows, but with only one cowboy in the lot, the others being raw hands at the cattle business. I had intended said cowboy to assume control of the whole outfit on the trail, but though a first-rate cow-hand, he very shortly proved himself to be wholly incapable of acting as head, and after the first morning's work, during the course of which we got into inexplicable confusion, I was forced to take direct charge myself.

312

ANTELOPE-SHOOTING

Our course lay for the most part through the Bad
Lands, which enormously increased the difficulty of
driving the cattle. A herd of cattle always travels
strung out in lines, so that a thousand head, thus going
almost in single file, stretch out to a very great distance. The strong, speedy animals occupy the front,
while the weak and sluggish fall naturally to the rear.
On the march, I put two of the men at the head, a
couple more to ride along the flanks, and the other two
to hurry up the phalanx of reluctant beasts that hope-
lessly plodded along in the rear. In travelling through
a tangled mass of rugged hills and winding defiles, it
can readily be imagined that it was no easy task for
six men to keep the cattle from breaking off in many
different directions and to prevent the stronger beasts
that formed the vanguard from entirely outstripping
and leaving behind their weaker brethren. In addition,
one of our number had always to keep an eye upon
the band of our spare saddled ponies, which ran loose.

Driving cattle is at all times most tediously irritating
work. To get the animals to string out and to begin
walking is often a task of no mean difficulty, and when
it is once done, it becomes almost as hard to keep the
wedge-shaped bunch that always forms in the rear from
dropping altogether out of connection with the front
animals. The horses have to be perpetually ridden to
and fro and hither and thither, to head off a refractory
steer, to keep the line from making a break down into
a valley, to hurry up the loiterers, or to prevent the
thirsty brutes from making a rush toward some quak-
ing quagmire. The progress of a herd, such as this
was, is always slow, and we could make but a few miles
a day, generally dividing the distance into a morning
and an afternoon march, so as to give the cattle feed

and rest at midday, when we ourselves would drive the spare ponies into an improvised rope corral by the wagon and catch up the horses for the change.

The weather during the course of the trip went through a gamut of changes with that extraordinary and inconsequential rapidity that characterizes atmospheric variations on the plains. The second day out there was a light snow falling all day, the wind blew so furiously that early in the afternoon we were obliged to drive the cattle down into a sheltered valley to keep them overnight, and the cold was so intense that even in the sun the water froze at noon. Forty-eight hours afterward we really suffered from extreme heat.

Owing to the slowness with which the cattle travelled, we were obliged to make one dry night camp. This was on the night of the third day. After watering the cattle at noon, we had driven them along the very backbone of the divide through a grimly barren and forbidding country across which ran lines of buttes wrought into the most fantastic shapes of the peculiar Bad Lands formation. Night came on while we were still many miles from the string of deep spring pools which held the nearest water. The fagged-out condition of the cattle forced us to go into camp even before the sun set. The animals were already very thirsty, and it was evident that we would have hard work to keep them closed up during the hours of darkness.

Our usual course at night had been for all hands, about six o'clock, or shortly after, to bed the cattle down; that is, by keeping the bunch close together and by continuously riding round and round it to finally persuade the animals to lie down in a comparatively small space. Most of them being pretty tired, the odds were that they would not try to break out until morning, and the night hours were divided into four watches of two hours each, two of the six men taking each watch; thus every man had two watches one night and one the next.

On the night in question, however, it was evident that no two men would be able to hold the cattle, and practically all six of us were up all night long, part of the time lying or sitting on the grass by our horses, watching the slumbering beasts, but for almost as much of it galloping furiously around the cattle in the darkness, every rider receiving one or more severe falls before morning, while heading back the strings of thirsty animals that continually tried to break out first from one side and then from the other of the bedding-ground. Of course had they once succeeded in breaking out in such stretch of rough country as we were in, it would have been an impossibility to have gotten them together again.

The next morning we made a very early start, as soon as the cattle began to grow restive again, for it is much easier to drive restive beasts than to keep them together while stationary, and after a long and very tiresome journey, during the course of which the herd spread out to an even greater extent than ordinary, the thirst making the stronger animals travel faster than usual, while the weaker ones, becoming exhausted, could hardly be moved along at all, we finally reached, in the middle of the afternoon, the line of spring pools spoken of. Our own fare had so far been very rough. We had slept under our blankets in the open with our oilskin slickers to shelter us at least partially from rain and snow, and our food had consisted simply of coffee, pork, and rather soggy biscuits.

Both the horses and cattle were so exhausted that I

thought we had better make a thirty-six hours' halt where we were, especially as there was excellent water, very good feed, and as the country was admirably adapted for keeping a guard over the herd with little trouble to the men or exhaustion to the ponies. All our work had not ended yet, however, for at least a score of the steers and cows managed to get firmly stuck in the mud-holes along the edges of the pool, and we spent until well on into the evening drawing them out.

The land here was a rolling prairie with a few rounded hills. We camped in the bottom of a winding valley whose sides sloped steeply down, their lower portions covered here and there with groves of tall cottonwood-trees. Near one of these groves we drew up the wagon, a deep pool of icy water being but a few yards distant. A more beautiful place for a camp cannot be imagined, and we were ourselves almost as glad to be free from the worry and labor of the drive as was the unfortunate herd. But one drawback to our complete happiness still existed in the fact that we did not have, and had not for some time had, any fresh meat, and it is wonderful how men leading an active out-of-door life get to feel their carnivorous tastes develop.

Next day, accordingly, I determined to devote to going after antelope, one or two bands of which we had seen near the trail. The cattle were more than content to feed quietly on the thick bunch-grass and, from the nature of the ground, two men at a time were amply able to watch them and to head off any bunch which seemed inclined to wander far away.

I started soon after breakfast, for antelope are the only game which can be hunted as well in the middle of the day as early or late. I was riding a well-trained hunting-pony, and had with me the little 40–60 Winchester saddle gun. Before I had left the wagon camp a mile behind me, I came across a little band of pronghorns, catching a glimpse of them as they lay sunning themselves on the side of a hill, a very long distance off. Tying my pony to a sage-bush, I executed a most careful stalk up a shallow dry watercourse to a point from which I deemed I could get a shot, only to find to my chagrin that the band had left the place. I suppose they had seen me in the distance and had promptly run off the instant that I began the approach—a favorite trick with antelopes.

I made one other unsuccessful stalk in the morning, and spent nearly half an hour in trying to flag an old buck up to me, lying behind a ridge and waving a handkerchief fixed to the end of a rifle to and fro over its top. Curiosity is with antelope a perfect disease, and they will often be unable to resist the temptation to find out what an unknown object, or one going through singular motions, means, even if the price of gratifying their mania for information has to be paid with their lives. This particular old buck, however, although greatly interested and excited by the motions of the handkerchief, could not make up his mind to approach close enough to give me a fair shot, and after cantering to and fro, snorting and stamping his feet, advancing a few yards toward me, suddenly bolting back as many, and then returning, he eventually evidently came to the conclusion that there was something uncanny about the whole affair, and took to his heels for good.

I went back to the pony and rode on several miles farther to where the country became less prairie-like in character, the valleys being somewhat deeper and the ridges closer together, when I again dismounted and began to hunt over the ground on foot; and this time my perseverance was rewarded. As I was topping one ridge, I saw a little band of five bucks slowly walking over the crest of the one directly across. I had come up very cautiously, and felt certain that I had not been seen. The instant that the last of the animals disappeared I raced forward at a sharp gait, pulling up as I breasted the hillside opposite, so that I should not be blown when I came to shoot. The antelope had been proceeding in a very leisurely manner, stopping to indulge in mock combats with each other, or to nibble a mouthful of grass now and then; and when I came to the top of the ridge, they had halted for good, perhaps one hundred and fifty yards off.

I was out for meat, not for trophies, and so I took the one that offered me the fairest shot, a young buck which stood broadside to me; he was fat and in good condition for an antelope, but with small horns. The bullet went fairly in behind the shoulder, and though he galloped off with the rest of the band for a couple of hundred yards, his pace gradually slackened, he came to a halt, then walked backward in a curious manner for a few feet, fell over, and was dead when I came to him.

After dressing him, and I may remark parenthetically that this work of butchering, especially when far from water, is one of the disagreeable sides of a hunter's life, I got him on the pony (it was a quiet little beast, used to packing all sorts of strange things behind its rider) and started toward the camp. The shadows had begun to lengthen out well before I got there, to receive a very real and cordial welcome from my hungry associates. Before long the venison-steaks were frying or broiling over the mass of glowing coals raked out from beneath the roaring and crackling cottonwood logs, and I should be almost afraid to state how much we ate. Suffice it to say that there was very little indeed left of that antelope after next morning's breakfast.

The following day we took the somewhat refreshed cattle away from our resting-ground and, after two rather long and irksome drives, were able to head them out upon the great river-bottom where the ranch-house stands.

CHAPTER III

SHOOTING NEAR THE RANCH-HOUSE—THE WHITE-TAIL DEER

But a few years ago any ranchman in the wilder portions of the great Western plains country was able to get a large variety of game without having to travel very far from the immediate neighborhood of his own ranch-house. When my cattle first came to the Little Missouri almost every kind of plains game was to be found along the river; but circumstances have widely changed now. Antelope, mountain-sheep, and two species of deer are still to be found in greater or less numbers scattered through the country over which my cattle ranch, and occasionally not so very far from the house; thus, last winter one of my foremen shot a mountain ram on a ragged bluff crest but half a mile away; and I have myself killed antelope on the bottom directly across the river, while, but a year or two ago, the blacktail deer were more plentiful in my immediate neighborhood than were all the other kinds of game put together, and even last fall I more than once shot them but a mile or so from the house. These are now, however, but exceptional instances, and if we have time to go off for but two or three hours with the rifle we cannot reckon with any certainty upon the chance of a shot at any game, excepting the whitetail deer. Of some forty-odd deer killed last season (for meat, not sport, and not while on any regular wagon trip) at least nine out of ten belonged to this species. The white-tail, partly from its superior cunning, from a kind of shrewd common sense with which it is gifted to a preeminent degree, and partly from the nature of its haunts, survives in a locality long after all others of the larger game animals have been driven out by the hunters. It is pre-eminently the deer of the river-bottoms, dwelling among the dense, swampy thickets that form in the bends of the streams and in the larger patches of woodlands. It is mainly nocturnal in its habits, spending the day in impenetrable depths and tangled recesses, where it is practically entirely secure from the approach of the hunter. Its chase is thus very tedious, as in the localities where it is found it is almost impossible for a man to walk at all, and even with the most painstaking caution, he will hardly be able to avoid making a noise. The whitetail relies alike on ears, nose, and eyes to warn it of danger; and, indeed, it is almost impossible to still-hunt it successfully while lying or feeding in an extensive belt of woodland, and usually the only way to get an animal living in such a locality is to catch it on the outskirts in the very early morning or late evening. Such a meeting is more or less accidental.

At times, however, the deer will be found in the smaller, though still moderately extensive, patches of brushwood and dwarf trees that stud the winding bottoms of the larger creeks for miles up their courses, away from the river. In these localities a man runs a much better chance of getting his game, both because he can frequently "jump" it, getting a close running shot; and also because if out still-hunting at eventide or in early morning he is almost certain of having a chance to see the deer feeding along the edges of the brush. I have hardly ever been successful in single-handed still-hunting and killing the whitetail among the timber of the river-bottoms, and though I have

321

tried often enough, most of my shots have been taken when it was so dark that it was impossible to fire with any accuracy. When there is snow on the ground, however, we can often kill them along the river-bottom, by dividing forces and sending one or two men to beat down through a good locality while the others watch the probable places for the deer to pass.

As is the case with some other kinds of game, a man is not unapt to run across a deer by accident while riding about among the cattle, or while on one of the hundred errands that keep a ranchman perpetually on horseback. Accordingly, it is very rare for me to go off for any distance from the ranch-house without carrying the little saddle gun with me. Once, early last September, when we had been out of meat for nearly a week, owing to the stress of work having been so severe as not to give any of us time from our duties in which to go hunting, this custom of mine procured us a welcome addition to our exceedingly monotonous and scanty bill of fare. A small band of horses had strayed away from the rest, and I had ridden out with one of the cowboys to look for them. A ranchman's horses are, as might be expected, perpetually astray, and one of the most necessary, and at the same time one of the most irksome, parts of his business is to look them up. They may wander one or more hundred miles if not found, and as to have plenty of good horses is the condition precedent for the successful carrying on of the cattle industry, it may be readily imagined that a plainsman takes peculiar care of his saddle band. Often all the horses will keep well together, but frequently they will show a tendency to split into little groups, whose individuals are never found far from each other; and at times there will be some one horse that shows a marked inclination to wander off by himself. If one of these individuals or little groups is absent when the bunch is rounded up and driven into the corral, which happens every day or two, some man has to start out immediately and look it up.

This seems at first a good deal like looking for a needle in a haystack; and, indeed, at times it does possess a most painful similarity to such a feat; but if a man knows the country as well as the habits of the horse he is looking for, his work is greatly simplified. Time and again horses have been absent from my ranch for an amount of time varying from a week to six months, but with only two exceptions I have always hitherto recovered them in the end. As already said, it is particularly dreary and tiresome work to look after them, as one has to ride along at a slow jog, continually straining one's eyes in every direction and minutely examining every patch of broken ground or timber that could contain the missing animals. After a rain it is much easier, as then their tracks can be followed pretty readily, while on hard, dry ground they leave no trace; an immense amount of land has to be covered each day, and the probability is that several days' fruitless search will have to be gone through before the animals are really found. One gets gradually to have a certain hopeless and irritated feeling that makes this kind of duty rank as one of the least attractive of a ranchman's life.

On the particular day in question, which was the second one of our search, I and my companion were riding along about noon in the somewhat sullen silence that comes to be one's natural mood after a long course of monotonous exercise in a land whose general aspect is as same as it is barren. We travelled mostly along the higher ridges, whence we could survey the landscape far and near, but finally we came to a place where a creek headed up, and where the ravines twisted to and fro, their beds being filled with underbrush and young trees, and where, in consequence, horses might easily remain hidden in the thickets or in the clefts in the side of the hill without our observing them from the distance. Accordingly we descended to hunt them through more carefully; coming down into a smooth open valley, through whose bottom extended a dry watercourse, filled up with a dense growth of wild plums, ash, and chunk cherries, with a few trees of larger growth. We started to ride down along the side of, and some little distance from, this thicket, which was several hundred yards in length and only thirty or forty in breadth; as the thicket lay in the bottom of the valley, while we were on considerably higher ground, we could look down into it. While the horses were jogging along with their heads down, I was suddenly aroused from my condition of listless apathy by the sudden mashing of dead branches among the underbrush but a rod or two from where I was passing. My blood tingled with that thrill of excitement known only to the man who has a genuine and intense fondness for the nobler kinds of field-sports. I was off my horse in a second, running down with the rifle to where the valley sloped abruptly downward to its brush-covered bottom. After the first plunge a deer will often run almost noiselessly through places where it seems marvellous that animals should go at all, and I could not tell for a minute which way the game had gone; hearing, however, a twig snap farther down, I raced along to where the valley turned round a shoulder of the bluff and then again peered over into the dry watercourse.

For a second I then experienced a keen disappointment, for a long distance off I saw a yearling whitetail break out of the brush and canter off out of sight round a bend of the valley. I concluded that I had run down the wrong way from that in which the game had been going, but staying still for a second, I again heard a twig break beneath me, and in another minute a white-tail stole out and stood in a little opening in the brush; it was evidently, from its size, a this year's fawn, just out of the spotted coat, and I gathered at once that there must be a third deer somewhere near, it being not at all an uncommon thing for a doe, a yearling fawn, and a this year's fawn to be together. As we were in need of fresh meat, I levelled on the fawn, which stood facing me, offering a beautiful mark; at the report it plunged wildly forward a few feet and turned a somer-sault over a small bank. Immediately afterward the doe, which I had not previously seen, broke out within twenty yards of me. I fired three shots at her with the repeater, and with the last one hit her very far back, injuring her hips and causing her to turn round and run back into the brush. It seems a curious thing, doubtless, to those who have not tried, that a man should, at twenty yards, need three shots to disable, and even then not to kill, a deer; but unless one is a real expert with the rifle, he soon finds that he makes an unusually large percentage of misses on running shots, even when close up, and it is peculiarly difficult to remember to hold far enough ahead. The doe was evidently badly hurt; and by running on rapidly down the creek and taking up my station at a point where the watercourse was narrow, I headed her off; then the cowboy rode down through the bottom, and, when frightened by his approach, she tried to break by me,

I killed her. Each of us took one of the deer behind his saddle and, abandoning for that day our search for the strayed horses, we rode back to the ranch-house.

Although these deer were killed while on horseback, yet as a rule we hunt whitetail on foot, and this is especially the case if we go out merely for an afternoon or morning's work near the ranch. As a sample of such work may be mentioned a hunt I made a week or so after the above-mentioned incident.

About three o'clock in the afternoon I shouldered my rifle and walked away from the ranch, intending to strike back over the hills to a part of the divide some eight miles distant and from thence to hunt slowly back against the wind through a stretch of broken country, where toward evening one would be not unlikely to find deer. When I had reached the divide and started homeward the shadows had already begun to lengthen out, the heat of the day was well over, and the fall air was already cool enough to make walking pleasant. The country consisted of little else than a series of chains of steep, rounded hills, separated from each other by narrow valleys that split up and wound around in every direction. For the purpose of commanding as extensive a view as possible, I kept near the summits of the hills, avoiding, however, walking on the very crest, as that would throw my body out so sharply in relief against the sky as to attract almost of necessity the attention of any animal within the ken of whose vision I might be. The walking was very rough, the grassy hilltops and hillsides being exceedingly steep and slippery, nor did I at first see anything. But at last, when the sun was so near setting that the bottoms of the valleys had already almost begun to be in shadow, I crept out on the face of a great cliff shoulder that jutted over the broad bed of a long ravine, and my eye was at once caught by five or six objects below me in the valley, and probably nearly half a mile off. A second glance convinced me they were deer, and I drew back to make a rapid calculation as to the best means of getting near them, for I had to be quick about it if I wished to get a shot before the light failed. Running back at speed nearly half a mile, I crossed the ridge on which I was and slid down into a little washout that opened into a small ravine, whose mouth, I had seen, joined the larger valley not very far from where the deer were. This ravine was entirely bare of underbrush, and I had to clamber along one of its sides in spite of the steepness of the ground, as I did not dare to run the risk of an outlying deer catching a glimpse of me if I came openly down the bottom. Nor was my caution thrown away. I found that the animals I was after, having grazed slowly down the main valley, had come directly opposite the mouth of the cleft in which I was. Wriggling along, however, flat on my face, and taking advantage of every boulder or patch of sage-brush, I managed to get down near the very mouth. The wind was perfectly favorable, and after a few minutes' patient and motionless watching I saw four or five deer slowly moving along past the other side of a thicket but a couple of hundred yards away, and leaving between me and them a kind of natural embankment, just on the other side of which they halted. I was now able to walk rapidly and quietly up without danger of detection; throwing off my cap, I peered over the edge of the bank, to see them feeding in perfect unsuspicion forty or fifty yards away. They were all does or yearling bucks; one of the latter, a fine fat young fellow, stood broadside to me. There was still plenty of light to shoot, and I was able to put the bullet within a hair's breadth of the right place behind the shoulder. Taking off the saddle, hams, and forequarters, and cutting thongs out of his hide to tie them with, I slung them over my back and started off at a rapid rate for home, which I did not reach until long after the moon was well up above the horizon; for even if one knows the country fairly well, he soon finds that he makes but slow progress at night-time over broken, difficult ground.

CHAPTER IV

THE DEER OF THE UPLAND AND THE BROKEN GROUND

TILL very recently the blacktail deer was the most plentiful of all plains game, and it is still common in many localities; but after the extermination of the buffalo and the elk, it became itself the chief object of the chase with the professional hunters, and their ceaseless persecution has in many places totally destroyed it, and elsewhere has terribly thinned its ranks. It differs widely in haunts, habits, and gait from its white-tailed relative, which in form and size it so closely resembles, although rather larger. It is fond of very rough, open ground, and although in many places, as, for example, in the great chains of the Rockies, it is found in dense timber, yet it is also frequently found where there are hardly any trees, or else where they are so sparse and scattered as to afford but the scantiest cover.

It is, with us, the rarest thing in the world to find blacktail on the timbered river-bottoms, and it never penetrates into the tangled swamps in which the white-tail delights. The brushy coulées and the heads of the ravines are its favorite resorts, and it also ranges into the most sterile and desolate portions of the Bad Lands, intruding upon the domains of the mountain-sheep. The cover in which it is found is almost always too scanty to, of itself, afford the deer adequate protection; it cannot, therefore, as is the case with its white-tailed relative, often escape by hiding and remaining motionless and unobserved while the hunter passes through

329

the locality where it is found; nor can it, like its more fortunate cousin, skulk around without breaking cover and thus bid defiance to its pursuers. Whitetail deer may abound in a locality, and yet a man may never so much as catch a glimpse of them; but if black-tail exist they are far more commonly seen. The nature of their haunts, too, renders them much more easily approached. Out in the open country the hunter can advance far more noiselessly than in the woods, can take advantage of inequalities of ground for cover much more readily, and can also shoot at a longer distance; then, again, the blacktail, although with fully as keen senses as the whitetail, is put at a disadvantage in the struggle for life by his much greater curiosity. He has a habit, when alarmed, of almost invariably stopping, after having galloped a hundred yards or so, to stand still and look round at the object that has frightened him, and this pause gives the hunter time to make a successful shot. A blacktail is, on the other hand, more difficult to hit while running than is the case with the whitetail. The latter runs more as a horse does, with a succession of long bounds, going at a rolling or almost even pace, while a blacktail progresses by a series of stiff-legged buck jumps, all four feet seeming as if they left the ground together. This gives him a most irregular and awkward-looking gait, but yet one which carries him along, for a short time, at a great speed, and which enables him to get over broken, craggy country in a manner that can only be surpassed by the astounding feats of the mountain-sheep in simi-lar localities.

Most of my plains shooting has been done after black-tail, and, indeed, I have killed nearly as many of them as of all other large game put together; but they are now pretty well thinned out from round the immediate neighborhood of my ranch, and if I wish to get them I generally have to take a wagon and make a general trip of two or three days' duration. There is no locality nearer than ten or twelve miles where they can really be considered at all plenty, and as the best time for hunting them is in the early morning or late evening, one should be able to camp out directly on or by the ground he intends to hunt over, if he wishes to be even moderately certain of success. At times, however, when the blacktail have gathered in bands of eight or ten or more individuals, they will wander away from their usual haunts, and then may be put up in rather unexpected places. On one occasion last fall, when I had walked eight or ten miles away from the ranch, preparatory to beginning an afternoon's hunt after whitetail, I unexpectedly came across such a small band. I had struck the trail that we follow with our wagon in going in toward the settlement when the river is too high to permit us to travel along the river-bottom, and was walking quietly along it, following the faint scrapes made in the dry ground by the wagon wheels (for the trail is a blind one at best), when, as I came over the crest of a little hill, I saw a deer jump up out of a thicket, about two hundred yards off to one side of the trail, take two or three of the jumps so characteristic of the blacktail, and then turn around to look at me with his great ears thrown forward. In another second a dozen others also rose up and stood in a clump around him. I fired at them as they thus stood clustered together, and more by good luck than by anything else my bullet broke the back of a fine fat young doe.

Only twice last fall did I make a regular trip after

blacktail; in each case taking one of my men, himself a very good hunter, with me, and camping out all night right by the ground through which we intended to search. On the first of these occasions I killed a young buck by the side of a shallow pool in a deep gorge, almost as soon as we had left camp, and half an hour afterward my companion and I killed a doe and one well-grown fawn, as the result of an immense expenditure of cartridges. The doe and fawn were down in the bottom of a valley; we saw them as we were riding along the ridge above. They were in ground where it would have been almost impossible to have gotten near them, as almost the only piece of brush was that in which the two were standing; and as they both offered fair broadside marks, although at least four hundred yards off, we opened fire on them, I with a Winchester, my companion with a 40-90 Sharp's rifle. The deer, not seeing us, seemed to be perfectly confused by the firing and the echoes, and after each shot merely jumped a few paces and again stood still. I fired much more often than my companion, but without any success, and just as I had emptied my magazine he brought down the doe. The fawn then ran down the valley half a mile or so and entered a deep thicket, in which, after a somewhat careful stalk, I killed it. My companion was a really good shot, and he had killed the doe fairly at about four hundred yards; but even for him to kill at such a distance as this is an exceptional feat, and almost invariably represents the expenditure of a large number of cartridges.

On our next hunt, however, he made one shot that was even better. We had, as before, camped out all night, and started off early in the morning through as rugged and precipitous a tract of country as could be found anywhere, the sheer cliffs, deep gorges, and towering ragged hills rendering the walking very difficult, and in some places even dangerous. Game was plenty, however, and during the course of the morning we killed five blacktail deer, three bucks and two does. One of these, a very fine buck with unusually large antlers and as fat as a prize sheep, I shot in a rather unusual locality. We had been following up three mountain-sheep, which, however, having caught a glimpse of us, went off for good and were seen no more. The course led over and across a succession of knife-like ridges of rock and sandstone, separated by sheer narrow gorges of great depth, and with their sides almost overhanging. On coming to the edge of one of these, and, as usual, peering cautiously over, I was astonished to see a great buck lying out on a narrow ledge along the face of the cliff wall opposite; the gorge must have been at least a couple of hundred feet deep and less than one-half as much across. He was lying below, diagonally across from me, with his legs spread out and his head turned round so as to give me a fair shot for the centre of his forehead, and as in the position where I was I could not be sure of killing him instantly with a bullet elsewhere, I fired between his eyes, and, beyond a convulsive motion of one of his hind legs, he did not move an inch out of the place where he was lying. So steep was the cliff, and so narrow the ledge where he had made his bed, that it was a long and really difficult climb before we could get to him, and it was then no mean labor to get him out unharmed to where we could dress him. The time when he was shot was near midday, and he had evidently chosen the cliff for the purpose of getting a regular sun-bath. It is a rare thing even for this bold and rock-loving species, however, to take its noonday siesta in such an exceedingly open place. The locality had probably not before been visited by hunters that season, and the deer had gotten very bold, as the result of being unmolested. Three of the other deer that were killed on this day were shot without any special or unusual incident attending their death; but the fifth represented another piece of good marksmanship on the part of my companion, whose name, by the way, was Will Dow. We were going back to camp, not intending to shoot anything more, but to fetch out the ponies in order to pack back to camp the game we had already gotten. While walking along a line of hills, bounding one side of a broad valley, we saw on the face of the steep bluff-side opposite two deer standing near a patch of cedars; owing to the difficulty of the intervening ground I was unable afterward to pace off accurately the distance, a thing I usually do in the case of an unusually long shot; but it must certainly have been close upon five hundred yards. We sat down and began to fire at them. With his fourth shot Dow apparently touched one, and both went off up the hill; immediately afterward, however, another rose up from a thicket by which they went and stood looking around. We transferred our attention to this one; again I missed three or four times, and again my companion (thanks doubtless in part to his own superior skill, and in part also to the superior efficacy of his weapon for long-range shooting), after having wasted two or three bullets, sent one ball home, breaking a hind leg, and, after a rather long and tedious chase, we succeeded in overtaking and killing the animal. As a rule, I may explain, I do not shoot at anything but bucks; but during the past season, when game had become so scarce, and when our entire supply of fresh meat depended upon our prowess with the rifle, it was no longer possible to choose what we would kill, and, after the first of September, when we could keep deer hanging up for a long time, we did not spare either buck or doe if we were able to get one within range of our rifles.

CHAPTER V

THE LAST OF THE ELK

FROM that portion of the plains country over which my cattle range, the elk have disappeared almost as completely as the buffalo; but in the more remote and inaccessible fastnesses one or two scattered individuals still linger. A year ago a couple of cowboys, while on the round-up, killed an elk near the head of a very long and almost dry creek, up which they had gone in search of a small bunch of cattle; and the last individual of the species seen on the Little Missouri was shot by myself last September.

An old hunter, who had been under some obligations to me, brought me word, shortly before the fall round-up began, that he had come across unmistakable fresh elk sign in a piece of wild broken land, some thirty miles from my ranch-house. My informant was perfectly trustworthy, and was able to describe to me the position of the probable haunt of the game with great accuracy, and as the chance was too rare a one to be lightly thrown aside, I at once prepared to start the following morning in search of the doomed deer, it being more than doubtful whether we would be able to strike the trail of the beast for a day or two. I took along the ranch wagon, drawn by four shaggy horses, and driven by a weather-beaten old plainsman, who had been teaming for me during the summer; while I and one of my men, Will Dow, rode our hunting-horses, I taking old Manitou, who for speed, strength, good-tempered courage, and downright common sense surpasses any horse I have ever been on. There was, of course, no wagon trail for us to follow, and as the country was very wild and broken, one of the horsemen had continually to be riding ahead of the wagon, to choose the easiest and most practicable routes. Even thus, it seemed incredible that the wagon should be able to go through and over the incredibly rough places that we had to pass, and no man less expert than the old California stage-driver who was guiding it could have carried a four-horse team, or, indeed, any wheeled vehicle whatsoever, through such a country. The day's march had its monotony, varied by the usual incidents and accidents attendant upon plains travel. Across some of the steep canyon-like gullies the wagon had to be brought by the help of the saddle-horses, all the team pulling together; often the ground being so steep as to render it necessary to unharness the hauling horses, and slip a rope from the end of the pole to the high ground upon which the animals could get good footing. There was little water, and when we finally struck an alkali pool, my own horse got mired in trying to reach it to drink.

We had started very early in the morning, and had pushed on at as fast a pace as possible, but it was well toward sunset before we reached the curious cluster of conical red scoria buttes which the old hunter had told us to take as a landmark; and not far from their foot, in a winding valley, closed in by low hills, with steep sloping sides, we found, as we had expected, the three essentials for a camp in the plains country—wood, water, and grass. There were two or three deep spring pools of cool clear water; clumps of small scattered cottonwood-trees grew along here and there through the valley, whose bottom was covered with rich grass. A better spot for a camp could not have been imagined, and that its beauties had been appreciated by others before us was shown by the presence of the remains of half a dozen old Indian teepees. We had taken no tent with us, making our beds under the protection of the canvas wagon-sheet. Soon after reaching camp the sun went down, and by the time supper was ready, darkness had fallen. The tired horses grazed on the luscious grass almost within the circle of the flickering firelight, while we sat before the roaring logs, as the venison-steak simmered over the hot coals that had been raked out to one side. Men living all the time in the open air are willing enough to go to bed early, and soon after supper we crept in under the heavy blankets, which the chill fall night already rendered so comfortable. But long after going to bed I lay awake, looking up at the myriads of stars that were shining overhead with that peculiar and intense brilliancy so well known to the wanderer over the lonely Western plains.

We were up by the first streak of dawn, and were ready to start after the shortest preparation. It was a beautiful hunting morning—the sun-dogs hung in the red dawn, the wind moved gently over the crisp brown grass, and the weather had that peculiar smoky, hazy look so often seen about the time of the Indian Summer. We moved off along toward the edge of a great plateau, and by the time the sun was well up had reached the hunting-grounds. From the jutting shoulder on which we stood we looked off far and wide over a great stretch of barren brown country, broken into countless valleys and ravines, which were separated by ridges of low, round hills. Although it was early fall, the touch of the frost had already changed the leaves of the trees, and the sameness of the landscape was relieved by the patches of vivid color that marked where the thickets of ash, cherries, and wild plums were scattered along the hillsides, or where the tall cottonwood-trees grew in the bottoms of the larger valleys.

Before long we, ourselves, came upon the fresh sign of large game, finding a small muddy pool, at which one or more elk had evidently drunk but a day or two previous. After this we proceeded with great caution, hunting silently and stealthily through every locality where we deemed it possible that the animals we were in search of might be found. An elk, from his greater size, needs, of course, much more cover than does a deer, and we expected to find our quarry in one of the heavy timber coulées. A "coulée," I may explain, is a plains word, derived from the old-time French trappers and hunters, who traversed the basins of the upper Missouri and Saskatchewan before the men of the Anglo-Saxon race had penetrated even to their borders. The term is used to denote any small ravine or side valley, usually up near the head of a creek or water system, through which the snow or rain runs at certain seasons, but which does not contain a regular water-course.

Near the base of the great plateau in whose neighborhood we were hunting, the creeks forked and branched again and again, and finally resolved themselves into a multitude of deep, narrow coulées, in many of whose bottoms grew groves of cottonwood-trees, which, favored by the shelter and moisture, reached a height that they rarely attain in the barren plains country. The look of the land, and our knowledge of the habits of the elk, led us to suppose that if we found one of the latter at all, we would be most apt to find it in one of these timber coulées, nor were we disappointed. After some hours of patient and fruitless search, mostly conducted on foot, I rode Manitou up to the edge of a deep and narrow defile, in whose bottom grew a band or grove of tall trees. As I peered over the edge, there was a crash and a scramble in the woods beneath me, and immediately afterward I saw dimly through the scanty tree-tops the glistening light-colored hide of a great bull elk as he gallantly breasted the steep hillside opposite. I was off the horse in a minute, and, kneeling on one knee, waited for him to come above the tree-tops into plain sight. In another moment he stood out on the bare hillside over against me, and turning round, half faced us, throwing his head up into the air. Although less than a hundred yards off, and offering a splendid side shot, I yet, for some cause or other, pulled too far back on him. Nevertheless, the bullet inflicted a fatal wound; for the moment, however, he hardly seemed as if he were hurt, but breaking from the long ground-covering trot which is so characteristic a gait for this species, and at which he had been going, he went off over the hill crest at a wild plunging gallop. Mounting old Manitou, I scrambled down into the ravine at a breakneck pace, then strained up the other side, the old fellow going over the rough ground at a speed that would be impossible for any horse not well accustomed to such country. On reaching the top of the crest, the elk was not in sight, and I feared I had lost him; with much labor, however, we followed his footprints, marked by an occasional drop of blood, for a half-mile or so, till we came to a broader, shallower valley, with brushwood thick in its bottom. With increasing difficulty, we followed the trail that was ever growing fainter, and finally found where the great beast, changing his pace to a trot, had entered the thicket; and but a few rods within it, close to the opposite side, we found the elk himself already stone-dead. He was a fine large one, in excellent condition, but his antlers were small, with few points.

This was an unexpectedly early and successful termination to our hunt, for although, from the sign, there must have been one or two other elk about, yet the latter were evidently much smaller, probably cows, and I did not wish to molest them, especially as the one we had killed furnished us with all the meat that we then needed. Accordingly the animal was skinned and cut up, and carried back on our horses to the wagon, by which time it was already late in the afternoon; and early next morning we broke camp and started home to the ranch. It is possible that other elk may be killed in our neighborhood hereafter, but I doubt this myself; and unless I am mistaken, the bull I shot will be the last of his kind to be shot in the immediate vicinity of the ground over which our cattle range.

CHAPTER VI

WATER–FOWL AND PRAIRIE–FOWL

ORDINARILY the Little Missouri is not navigable for the lightest craft, but in the season of the floods it will bear an even large boat; and as these floods come at the times when there are apt to be many wild duck and a few geese on the river, I keep at the ranch-house a small light boat especially for use in shooting water-fowl; my usual course being to send it up the river to a convenient point some time when the wagon happens to be going empty toward the settlement, and then coming downstream in it when the water is high enough. The current is altogether too swift to make it possible to paddle against it; and it would be most slow and tedious work to pole upstream over such a bad bottom as that of the Little Missouri. Accordingly, whatever shooting I get must be done while drifting down the river. The course of the latter is very winding, and in coming round the points one can often get close up to a flock of ducks or a couple of geese without being observed.

It is pretty good fun to go down the stream, even apart from the shooting, the scenery in the Bad Lands having for me a great attraction from its strange, *bizarre* wildness; although I suppose it could hardly be called really beautiful. In many places the river has cut its way through lines of hills, making sheer bluffs that rise straight out of the water, and whose faces show the lines of parallel strata, of which they are composed, with most abrupt clearness. These strata are

342

composed of lignites, marls, chalks, and clays, and exposure to the weather causes them to turn most extraordinary colors; and the face of the cliff is thus often marked by broad horizontal bands of black, red, purple, brown, and yellow. Floating downstream one will thus first be passing between banks overgrown with tall cottonwood-trees, then going through a region of barren sage plains, then again winding and twisting through bluffs and hills that are as fantastic in color as they are in shape.

The shooting itself is never as good for water-fowl on the Little Missouri or elsewhere throughout the cattle country as it is in the more fertile farm-land prairies to the eastward. Still, occasionally, we can make fair bags. The little teal are the commonest and least shy of the water-fowl. As they sit out on a sand-bar, they often let a boat drift close up to them, and it is quite easy also to creep within gunshot from the bank. I have killed eleven of them with a single barrel. The mallard duck, shoveller duck, and broadbill are also common, and afford excellent sport. These, however, are shyer, and will rarely let a boat drift down upon them, unless one is able to take advantage of some cover, or come quickly round the point. Geese are more wary still. Quite a number of these breed with us; sometimes in the river, sometimes in the reedy slews or pools far up in the creeks, out in the Bad Lands, or on the prairie. When they are moulting, it is not difficult to get them if one cares to; and on such occasions, although there cannot be said to be any sport to be obtained from them, yet I have shot the young birds for the table; for there can be no better eating than a fat, three-parts grown young goose. When their feathers are grown, however, the geese show themselves most amply fit for self-protection, and it needs then very careful stalking, indeed, before one can come up to them.

In addition to the water-fowl proper, to be obtained while drifting or paddling down the river, there are also, at times, flocks of waders at which one can get a shot. Avocets, stilts, yelper, marlin, and yellowlegs are all occasionally found, although not plenty. They are not apt to be very shy, and if a shot is taken just as they rise or as they wheel, the expenditure of a single cartridge loaded with small shot will often suffice to bring down a dozen birds, which may prove a pleasant change to the ranchman's somewhat monotonous diet.

To make any large bag of water-fowl, however, it is necessary to take a trip of several days and get over in the farming country, whose western edge lies many miles to the eastward of the broad pastoral belt whose easternmost border comes within the Dakota Territory. In this farm region there are many hills, lakes, and ponds, with reed-grown borders, branching out into large slews, and connected by winding, often sluggish streams. A man with a light boat can even by himself make a really very large bag in localities such as these, and his bag will be greatly increased if he is able to take with him a good dog. Out in the West, of course, a sportsman cannot be by any means so particular in reference to the fine points of his animal as is the case in the East; and many a mongrel does duty as a duck-retriever which an Eastern sportsman would scorn to look at, and I may mention, by the way, that these ill-looking beasts often do their work uncommonly well. The usual course for a sportsman to follow in such a locality is to find out where the flight of ducks passes in the evening or morning. A reedy passageway between two lakes, or the borders of a favorite feeding-ground are especially good stations. The gunner has his boat in the lake, and paddles over its broad, shallow surface, or pushes it through the reeds until he finds a spot where there is plenty of cover, and where he will be in the line of the flight. There he remains until the flight begins; once the ducks have begun to come in, if the place is a good one, he may expect almost continuous shooting, as flock follows flock with really remarkable rapidity. A strong close-shooting gun is a necessity for one who wishes to make a big bag. Personally, I have never done anything to speak of at duck-shooting, my practice with the shotgun having been comparatively limited. Still I know a number of places where even an indifferent shot may get ten or fifteen couple of birds in an afternoon.

Besides water-fowl, the devotee of the shotgun can also have some sport, in the cattle country, with prairie-chickens. The proper name of the prairie-chicken found with us is the sharp-tailed grouse. It is a somewhat different bird from the pinnated grouse, or prairie-chicken of Illinois and Iowa, being a little smaller, and affording hardly as good eating. The sharptails are pretty common with us, and, unlike the larger game, seem to be growing more plenty yearly, owing to the fact that the cattlemen, with their firearms, and still more with their poison, destroy numbers of the wolves, wildcats, skunks, and other carnivorous animals, who are the chief foes of ground-living birds. For many years to come, the plains will afford fine sport to those fond of wing-shooting. Average ranchmen, whose favorite weapon is invariably the rifle, are not apt to go out much after prairie-chickens. Still, I every now

345

and then take a day after them, both for the sake of the sport and also for the sake of the addition they make to our bill of fare. Of course the best way of proceeding is to take a buckboard and a couple of good, far-ranging pointers, but usually we simply go out on horseback, or else take a stroll on foot through ground which we know contains one or more coveys. Last August we were cutting hay on a great plateau, and noticed that every afternoon numbers of prairie-fowl, in small coveys, each one probably consisting of an old hen and her nearly grown brood of chicks, came up round the edges of the plateau. Toward eventide, accordingly, one afternoon, an hour before sunset, I took the No. 10 choke-bore and strolled off to the plateau, which the haymakers had left some days before. Walking around its edge, across the spurs and the heads of the little brush coulées, I came across plenty of grouse. Some were very shy, and would not let me get anywhere near them; others, again, would squat down in the brush or long grass at my approach, and permit themselves to be walked up to, offering easy marks as they flew off, sometimes the whole covey rising together, while on other occasions the birds rose one by one. Although the time was short, I yet had as many plump grouse as I could carry by the time the sun had sunk, and that, too, in spite of making many more misses than should have been the case with such very easy shooting.

In the wild and more barren part of the plains country we find another kind of grouse, the largest species inhabiting America. This is the great sage-cock, a bird of fine appearance, and one which, contrary to the generally received opinion, affords excellent eating. Its food consists, at different times of the year, of sage-leaves or of grasshoppers. Young birds, in August or

September, that have been feeding mainly upon grass-hoppers, are exceedingly tender and well flavored, quite as good as any other grouse. An old cock or hen that has been feeding exclusively upon sage, of course, would offer very poor eating. In shooting these large and fine birds, it is almost impossible to go on foot or with a dog, owing to the dryness and remoteness of the haunts which they mostly affect; and those that I have gotten have almost invariably been procured while riding on horseback through ground containing them, and, when I came across a covey, dismounting to do what execution I could, while my companion held the horses.

GOOD HUNTING

IN PURSUIT OF BIG
GAME IN THE WEST

Good hunting all
That keep the Jungle law.
RUDYARD KIPLING

BIBLIOGRAPHICAL NOTE

GOOD HUNTING IN PURSUIT OF BIG GAME IN THE WEST. By Theodore Roosevelt. Illustrated. New York and London: Harper & Brothers, Publishers (1907). 107 *pp., illus., 12mo, brown buckram.*

The seven chapters of this volume were originally published in *Harper's Round Table*, April 7, 1896; January 19, April 27, May 25, June 22, July 27, and August 31, 1897. The illustrations are from drawings by Frederic Remington, Tappan Adney, and A. B. Frost, and from photographs.

PUBLISHER'S NOTE TO THE FIRST EDITION

THIS book offers to younger readers a series of pictures of outdoor life and big-game hunting in the West. More than this, the author makes us feel not only the zest of sport and adventure, but also the interest attaching to the habits and peculiarities of the remarkable animals which he describes. It is a field-book, since it is written by a true sportsman out of his own experiences, and its general spirit tends to a better appreciation of the value of close observation of animal life. The elk, bear, goats, deer, and other animals which are described represent the most remarkable large fauna of our country. These descriptions, by one whose acquaintance with them has been so intimate, have an added value in view of the diminution in their number.

It is interesting, also, to remember that the influence of the author has been constantly exerted in favor of the preservation of big game and the maintenance of national parks and forest reserves, which, in addition to other advantages, include the protection of these noble forms of animal life.

This series of articles upon big-game hunting was written for *Harper's Round Table*, and published therein in 1897. The picture of ranch life which forms the closing chapter appeared in *Harper's Round Table* in 1896. These articles are now presented together in book form for the first time after consultation with the author. For the title of the book and the proof-reading the publishers are responsible.

CONTENTS

GOOD HUNTING

CHAPTER I

THE WAPITI, OR ROUND-HORNED ELK

No country of the temperate zone can begin to compare with south Asia, and, above all, tropical and subtropical Africa, in the number and size of those great beasts of the chase which are known to hunters as big game; but after the Indian and African hunting-grounds, the best are still those of North America. Until a few years before 1897 there were large regions, even in the United States, where the teeming myriads of wild game, though of far fewer and less varied species, almost equalled the multitudes found in South Africa, and much surpassed those found anywhere else in point of numbers, though inferior in variety to those of India.

This, however, is now a thing of the past. The bison, which was the most characteristic animal of the American fauna, has been practically exterminated There remained in 1897, however, a fair abundance of all other kinds of game. Perhaps, on the whole, the one affording most sport from the standpoint of the hardy and skilful hunter is the bighorn, though in size and in magnificence of horn it is surpassed by some of the wild sheep of Asia.

There is a spice of danger in the pursuit of the grizzly bear—the largest of all the land bears—especially in Alaska, where it is even larger than its Kamchatkan brother. The moose and the wapiti—ordinarily called the elk—are closely related to the Old World representatives of their kind; but the moose is a little larger and the wapiti very much larger than any of their

357

European or Asiatic kinsfolk. In particular, the elk, or wapiti, is the stateliest of all deer, and the most beautiful of American game beasts.

It is a pity we cannot always call the wapiti by its right name, but the hunters and settlers never know him as anything but the elk, and I fear it would be pedantry to try to establish his rightful title. In former days the elk ranged to tide-water on the Atlantic coast. A few lingered in Pennsylvania until 1869, and throughout the middle of the century they were abundant on the great plains. In 1888 I shot one on the Little Missouri, however. In many parts of the Rocky Mountains and of the Coast Range the species is still as abundant as ever, and this is especially true of northwestern Wyoming, since that great animal preserve the Yellowstone Park swarms with elk, and is their natural nursery and breeding-ground.

The elk is the lordliest of his kind throughout the world. The Scotch stag is a pigmy but a fourth his size. The stags of eastern Europe are larger than those of Scotland, and in Asia larger still, approaching in size a small wapiti. They are all substantially alike except in size.

The wapiti is rather easier to kill than the deer, because his size makes it easier to see him, and he is slower in his movements, so that he is easier to hit. When pressed he can gallop very hard for a few hundred yards, but soon becomes tired. The trot is his natural gait, and this he can keep up for hours at a time, going at a pace which makes it necessary for a horse to gallop smartly to overtake him, and clearing great logs in his stride, while he dodges among the thick timber in a really marvellous way, when one comes to think of the difficulty he must have in handling his great antlers.

Late in September the rut begins, and then the elk gather in huge bands, while the great bulls fight vicious battles for leadership. Hunters call this the whistling-time, because throughout its continuance the bulls are very noisy, continually challenging one another. Their note is really not much like a whistle. It consists of two or three bars, rising and then falling, ending with a succession of grunts; the tone of voice varies greatly in different individuals; but when heard at a little distance in the heart of the great wooded wilderness the sound is very musical, and to me—and, I suppose, to most hunters—it is one of the most attractive sounds in all nature.

At this season the big bulls are quite easy to approach by any man at all skilled in still-hunting, for their incessant challenging betrays their whereabouts, and they are so angry and excited as to be less watchful than usual. Some of my most pleasurable memories of hunting are connected with stalking some great bull elk in frosty weather, when the woods rang with his challenges.

One evening in early October I was camped high among the mountains of western Montana. We were travelling with a pack-train, and had pitched our small tent among some firs by a brook, while the horses grazed in the little park or meadow close by. Elk were plentiful round about. We had seen their trails everywhere, and late in the afternoon we had caught a glimpse of a band of cows as they disappeared among the pines.

Toward morning I was awakened by hearing a bull challenge not very far from camp. The sound of the challenge kept coming nearer and nearer, and finally I heard one of the horses snort loudly in response; evidently the elk saw them, and, not making out exactly what they were, was coming down to join them. Sometimes horses will stampede when thus approached; but our ponies were veterans, and were very tired, and evidently had no intention of leaving their good pasture.

Sitting up in my blankets, I could tell from the sound that they were still in the park, and then the challenge of the bull came pealing up not three hundred yards from the tent. This was more than I could stand, and I jumped up and put on my shoes and jacket. The moon was bright, but shooting by moonlight is very deceptive, and I doubt whether I would have hit him even had I got down to the park in time. However, he had moved on before I got down, and I heard his challenge in the woods beyond.

Looking at my watch, I saw that it was nearly dawn. I returned to the tent and lay down as I was under the blankets, and shivered and dozed for half an hour, then I came back to the meadow, where the pack-ponies stood motionless. In the brightening light the moon paled, and I was very soon able to pick out the bull's trail on the frost-covered ground, where it was almost as plain as if he had been walking in snow. I saw that he had struck up a long valley, from which a pass led into a wooded basin. At the top of the pass I lost the trail entirely, and as it was almost impossible to see for any distance through the woods, I came to the conclusion that the best thing to do was to sit down and await events.

I did not have long to wait. In a couple of minutes the bugle of a bull came echoing across the basin through the frosty morning. Evidently my friend was still travelling, hunting for some possibly weaker rival. Almost immediately I heard far off another answering the challenge, and I stood up and meditated what to do. There was very little air, but such as there was blew to one side of the spot from which the last challenge seemed to come, and I immediately struck off at a trot through the woods to get below the wind.

The answer to the challenge had evidently greatly excited the bull whose trail I had been following; he called every two or three minutes. The other answer was somewhat more irregular, and as I drew nearer I could tell from the volume of sound that the second challenge was from some big master-bull, who probably had his herd around him, and was roaring defiance at his would-be despoiler, for the single bull was doubtless on the lookout for some weaker one whom he could supplant as master of a herd.

It was likely that the second bull, being a herd-master, would have the larger antlers, and I therefore preferred to get a shot at him. However, I was doomed to disappointment. As I groped toward the herd, and was within a couple of hundred yards, as I knew by the volume of sound, I almost stumbled upon a small spike-bull, who was evidently loitering about the outskirts of the herd, not daring to go too near the bad-tempered old chief. This little bull dashed away, giving the alarm, and a clash in the bushes soon told that the herd was following him.

But luck favored me. The master-bull, being absorbed in thoughts of his rival, evidently suspected that the cows had some thought of fleeing from him, and, as they ran, tried to hold them together. I ran too, going at full speed, with the hope of cutting him off; in this I failed, but I came almost face to face with the very bull which I had been following from camp, and which had evidently followed the herd at full speed as soon as they ran.

Great was his astonishment when he saw me. He pulled up so suddenly to wheel round that he almost fell on his side; then off he went in a plunging gallop of terror; but he was near by, and stepping to one side I covered an opening between two trees, firing the minute he appeared. A convulsive leap showed that the bullet had struck, and after him I went at full speed. In a short time I saw him again, walking along with drooping head, and again I fired into his flank; he seemed to pay no attention to the shot, but walked forward a few steps, then halted, faltered, and fell on his side. In another second I had placed my rifle against a tree, and was admiring his shapely form and massive antlers.

CHAPTER II

A CATTLE–KILLING BEAR

THERE were, in 1897, a few grizzlies left here and there along the Little Missouri, usually in large bottoms covered with an almost impenetrable jungle of timber and thorny brush. In the old days they used to be very plentiful in this region, and ventured boldly out on the prairie. The Little Missouri region was a famous hunting-ground for both the white trappers and the Indian hunters in those old days when the far West was still a wilderness, and the men who trapped beaver would wander for years over the plains and mountains and see no white faces save those of their companions.

Indeed, at that time the Little Missouri was very dangerous country, as it was the debatable ground between many powerful Indian tribes, and was only visited by formidable war-parties and hunting-parties. In consequence of nobody daring to live there, game swarmed—buffalo, elk, deer, antelope, mountain-sheep, and bear. The bears were then very bold, and the hunters had little difficulty in getting up to them, for they were quite as apt to attack as to run away.

But when, in 1880, the Northern Pacific Railroad reached the neighborhood of the Little Missouri, all this changed forever. The game that for untold ages had trodden out their paths over the prairies and along the river-bottoms vanished, as the Indians that had hunted it also vanished. The bold white hunters also passed away with the bears they had chased and the red foes against whom they had warred. In their places the ranchmen came in with great herds of cattle and horses and flocks of sheep, and built their log cabins and tilled their scanty garden-patches, and cut down the wild hay for winter fodder. Now bears are as shy as they are scarce. No grizzly in such a settled region would dream of attacking a man unprovoked, and they pass their days in the deepest thickets, so that it is almost impossible to get at them. I never killed a bear in the neighborhood of my former ranch, though I have shot quite a number some hundreds of miles to the west in the Rocky Mountains.

Usually the bears live almost exclusively on roots, berries, insects, and the like. In fact, there is always something grotesque and incongruous in comparing the bear's vast size, and his formidable claws and teeth, with the uses to which those claws and teeth are normally put. At the end of the season the claws, which are very long in spring, sometimes become so much blunted as to be tender, because the bear has worked on hard ground digging roots and the like.

Bears often graze on the fresh, tender spring grass. Berries form their especial delight, and they eat them so greedily when in season as to become inordinately fat. Indeed, a bear in a berry-patch frequently grows so absorbed in his work as to lose his wariness, and as he makes a good deal of noise himself in breaking branches and gobbling down the fruit, he is exposed to much danger from the hunter.

Besides roots and berries, the bear will feed on any small living thing he encounters. If in plundering a squirrel's *cache* he comes upon some young squirrels, down they go in company with the hoarded nuts. He is continually knocking to pieces and overturning old dead logs for the sake of devouring the insects living beneath them. If, when such a log is overturned, mice, shrews, or chipmunks are found underneath, the bear promptly scoops them into his mouth while they are still dazed by the sudden inrush of light. All this seems rather ludicrous as the life-work of an animal of such huge proportions and such vast strength.

Sometimes, however, a bear will take to killing fresh meat for itself. Indeed, I think it is only its clumsiness that prevents it from becoming an habitual flesh-eater. Deer are so agile that bears can rarely get them; yet on occasions not only deer but moose, buffalo, and elk fall victims to them. Wild game, however, are so shy, so agile, and so alert that it is only rarely they afford meals to Old Ephraim—as the mountain hunters call the grizzly.

Domestic animals are slower, more timid, more clumsy, and with far duller senses. It is on these that the bear by preference preys when he needs fresh meat. I have never, myself, known one to kill horses; but I have been informed that the feat is sometimes performed, usually in spring; and the ranchman who told me insisted that when a bear made his rush he went with such astonishing speed that the horse was usually overtaken before it got well under way.

The favorite food of a bear, however, if he really wants fresh meat, is a hog or sheep—by preference the former. If a bear once gets into the habit of visiting a sheepfold or pig-pen, it requires no slight skill and watchfulness to keep him out. As for swine, they dread bears more than anything else. A drove of half-wild swine will make head against a wolf or panther; but the bear scatters them in a panic. This feat is entirely justifiable, for a bear has a peculiar knack in knocking down a hog and then literally eating him alive, in spite of his fearful squealing.

Every now and then bears take to killing cattle regularly. Sometimes the criminal is a female with cubs; sometimes an old male in spring, when he is lean and has the flesh hunger upon him. But on one occasion a very large and cunning bear, some twenty-five miles below my ranch, took to cattle-killing early in the summer and continued it through the fall. He made his home in a very densely wooded bottom; but he wandered far and wide, and I have myself frequently seen his great, half-human footprints leading along some narrow divide, or across some great plateau, where there was no cover whatever, and where he must have gone at night. During the daytime, when on one of these expeditions, he would lie up in some timber coulée, and return to the river-bottoms after dark, so that no one ever saw him; but his tracks were seen very frequently.

He began operations on the bottom where he had his den. He at first took to lying in wait for the cattle as they came down to drink, when he would seize some animal, usually a fat young steer or heifer, knocking it over by sheer force. In his furious rush he sometimes broke the back with a terrific blow from his fore paw; at other times he threw the animal over and bit it to death. The rest of the herd never made any effort to retaliate, but fled in terror. Very soon the cattle would not go down on this bottom at all; then he began to wander over the adjoining bottoms, and finally to make excursions far off in the broken country. Evidently he would sometimes at night steal along a coulée until he found cattle lying down on the hillside, and then approach cautiously and seize his prey.

Usually the animals he killed were cows or steers;

and noticing this, a certain ranchman in the neighborhood used to boast that a favorite bull on his ranch, of which he was particularly proud, would surely account for the bear if the latter dared to attack him. The boast proved vain. One day a cowboy riding down a lonely coulée came upon the scene of what had evidently been a very hard conflict. There were deep marks of hoofs and claws in the soft soil, bushes were smashed down where the struggling combatants had pressed against and over them, and a little farther on lay the remains of the bull.

He must have been seized by surprise; probably the great bear rushed at him from behind, or at one side, and fastened upon him so that he had no fair chance to use his horns. Nevertheless, he made a gallant struggle for his life, staggering to and fro trying to shake off his murderous antagonist, and endeavoring in vain to strike back over his shoulder; but all was useless. Even his strength could not avail against the might of his foe, and the cruel claws and teeth tore out his life. At last the gallant bull fell and breathed his last, and the bear feasted on the carcass.

The angry ranchman swore vengeance, and set a trap for the bear, hoping it would return. The sly old beast, however, doubtless was aware that the body had been visited, for he never came back, but returned to the river-bottom, and again from time to time was heard of as slaying some animal. However, at last his fate overtook him. Early one morning a cow was discovered just killed and not yet eaten, the bear having probably been scared off. Immediately the ranchman put poison in the bait which the bear had thus himself left, and twenty-four hours later the shaggy beast was found lying dead within a dozen yards of his last victim.

CHAPTER III

A CHRISTMAS BUCK

THROUGHOUT most of the ranch country there are two kinds of deer, the blacktail and the whitetail. The whitetail is the same as the deer of the East; it is a beautiful creature, a marvel of lightness and grace in all its movements, and it loves to dwell in thick timber, so that in the plains country it is almost confined to the heavily wooded river-bottoms. The blacktail is somewhat larger, with a different and very peculiar gait, consisting of a succession of stiff-legged bounds, all four feet striking the earth at the same time. Its habits are likewise very different, as it is a bolder animal and much fonder of the open country. Among the Rockies it is found in the deep forests, but it prefers scantily wooded regions, and in the plains country it dwells by choice in the rough hills, spending the day in the patches of ash or cedar among the ravines. In 1882 the blacktail was very much more abundant than the whitetail almost everywhere in the West, but owing to the nature of its haunts it is more easily killed out, and in 1897, though both species had decreased in numbers, the whitetail was on the whole the more common.

My ranch-house was situated on a heavily wooded bottom, one of the places where the whitetail were found. On one occasion I killed one from the ranch veranda, and two or three times I shot them within half a mile of the house. Nevertheless, they are so cunning and stealthy in their ways, and the cover is so dense, that usually, although one may know of their existence right in one's neighborhood, there is more chance of getting game by going off eight or ten miles into the broken country of the blacktail.

One Christmas I was to be at the ranch, and I made up my mind that I would try to get a good buck for our Christmas dinner; for I had not had much time to hunt that fall, and Christmas was almost upon us before we started to lay in our stock of winter meat. So I arranged with one of the cowboys to make an all-day's hunt through some rugged hills on the other side of the river, where we knew there were blacktail.

We were up soon after three o'clock, when it was yet as dark as at midnight. We had a long day's work before us, and so we ate a substantial breakfast, then put on our fur caps, coats, and mittens, and walked out into the cold night. The air was still, but it was biting weather, and we pulled our caps down over our ears as we walked toward the rough, low stable where the two hunting-ponies had been put overnight. In a few minutes we were jogging along on our journey.

There was a powder of snow over the ground, and this and the brilliant starlight enabled us to see our way without difficulty. The river was frozen hard, and the hoofs of the horses rang on the ice as they crossed. For a while we followed the wagon road, and then struck off into a cattle trail which led up into a long coulée. After a while this faded out, and we began to work our way along the divide, not without caution, for in broken countries it is hard to take a horse during darkness. Indeed, we found we had left a little too early, for there was hardly a glimmer of dawn when we reached our proposed hunting-grounds. We left the horses in a sheltered nook where there was abundance of grass, and strode off on foot, numb after the ride.

The dawn brightened rapidly, and there was almost light enough for shooting when we reached a spur overlooking a large basin around whose edges there were several wooded coulées. Here we sat down to wait and watch. We did not have to wait long, for just as the sun was coming up on our right hand we caught a glimpse of something moving at the mouth of one of the little ravines some hundreds of yards distant. Another glance showed us that it was a deer feeding, while another behind it was walking leisurely in our direction.

There was no time to be lost, and, sliding back over the crest, we trotted off around a spur until we were in line with the quarry, and then walked rapidly toward them. Our only fear was lest they should move into some position where they would see us; and this fear was justified. While still one hundred yards from the mouth of the coulée in which we had seen the feeding deer, the second one, which all the time had been walking slowly in our direction, came out on a ridge crest to one side of our course. It saw us at once and halted short; it was only a spike buck, but there was no time to lose, for we needed meat, and in another moment it would have gone off, giving the alarm to its companion. So I dropped on one knee, and fired just as it turned.

From the jump it gave I was sure it was hit, but it disappeared over the hill, and at the same time the big buck, its companion, dashed out of the coulée in front, across the basin. It was broadside to me, and not more than one hundred yards distant; but a running deer is difficult to hit, and though I took two shots, both missed, and it disappeared behind another spur.

This looked pretty bad, and I felt rather blue as I climbed up to look at the trail of the spike. I was cheered to find blood, and as there was a good deal of snow here and there it was easy to follow it; nor was it long before we saw the buck moving forward slowly, evidently very sick. We did not disturb him, but watched him until he turned down into a short ravine a quarter of a mile off; he did not come out, and we sat down and waited nearly an hour to give him time to get stiff. When we reached the valley, one went down each side so as to be sure to get him when he jumped up. Our caution was needless, however, for we failed to start him; and on hunting through some of the patches of brush we found him stretched out already dead.

This was satisfactory; but still it was not the big buck, and we started out again after dressing and hanging up the deer. For many hours we saw nothing, and we had swung around within a couple of miles of the horses before we sat down behind a screen of stunted cedars for a last look. After attentively scanning every patch of brush in sight, we were about to go on when the attention of both of us was caught at the same moment by seeing a big buck deliberately get up, turn round, and then lie down again in a grove of small, leafless trees lying opposite to us on a hillside with a southern exposure. He had evidently very nearly finished his day's rest, but was not quite ready to go out to feed; and his restlessness cost him his life.

As we now knew just where he was, the work was easy. We marked a place on the hilltop a little above and to one side of him; and while the cowboy remained to watch him, I drew back and walked leisurely round to where I could get a shot. When nearly up to the crest I crawled into view of the patch of brush, rested my elbows on the ground, and gently tapped two stones together. The buck rose nimbly to his feet, and at seventy yards afforded me a standing shot, which I could not fail to turn to good account.

A winter day is short, and twilight had come before we had packed both bucks on the horses; but with our game behind our saddles we did not feel either fatigue or hunger or cold while the horses trotted steadily homeward. The moon was a few days old, and it gave us light until we reached the top of the bluffs by the river and saw across the frozen stream the gleam from the firelit windows of the ranch-house.

CHAPTER IV

THE TIMBER–WOLF

THERE are two kinds of wolves found in the United States. One is the little coyote, or prairie-wolf, or barking wolf, which never was found in the Eastern States, being an animal of the open country; the other is the big wolf, sometimes called the buffalo-wolf, and sometimes the timber-wolf, or gray wolf, which was formerly found everywhere from the Atlantic to the Pacific. In some districts it runs to color varieties of different kinds—red, black, or white.

The coyote is not at all a formidable beast, and holds its own quite persistently until civilization is well advanced in a country. Coyotes are not dangerous to either man or the larger domestic animals. Lambs, young pigs, hens, and cats often become their prey, and if very hungry several of them will combine to attack a young calf. In consequence, farmers and ranchers kill them whenever the chance offers; but they do not do damage which is even appreciable when compared with the ravages of their grim big brother, the gray wolf, which in many sections of the West is a veritable scourge of the stockmen.

The big wolves shrink back before the growth of the thickly settled districts, and in the Eastern States they often tend to disappear even from districts that are uninhabited save by a few wilderness hunters. They have thus disappeared almost entirely from Maine, the Adirondacks, and the Alleghanies, although here and there they are said to be returning to their old haunts.

373

Their disappearance is rather mysterious in some instances, for they are certainly not all killed off. The black bear is much more easily killed, yet the black bear holds its own in many parts of the land from which the wolf has vanished. No animal is quite so difficult to kill as is the wolf, whether by poison or rifle or hound. Yet, after a comparatively few have been slain, the entire species will perhaps vanish from certain localities.

But with all wild animals it is a noticeable fact that a course of contact with man continuing over many generations of animal life causes a species so to adapt itself to its new surroundings that it ceases to diminish in numbers. When white men take up a new country, the game, and especially the big game, being entirely unused to contend with the new foe, succumbs easily, and is almost completely killed out. If any individuals survive at all, however, the succeeding generations are far more difficult to exterminate than were their ancestors, and they cling much more tenaciously to their old homes.

The game to be found in old and long-settled countries is much more wary and able to take care of itself than the game of an untrodden wilderness. It is a very difficult matter to kill a Swiss chamois; but it is a very easy matter to kill a white goat after a hunter has once penetrated among the almost unknown peaks of the mountains of British Columbia. When the ranchmen first drove their cattle to the Little Missouri they found the deer tame and easy to kill, but the deer of Maine and the Adirondacks test to the full the highest skill of the hunter.

In consequence, after a time, game may even increase in certain districts where settlements are thin. This has been true of the wolves throughout the northern cattle country in Montana, Wyoming, and the western ends of the Dakotas. In the old days wolves were very plentiful throughout this region, closely following the huge herds of buffaloes. The white men who followed these herds as professional buffalo-hunters were often accompanied by other men, known as "wolfers," who poisoned these wolves for the sake of their furs. With the disappearance of the buffalo the wolves seemed so to diminish in numbers that they also seemed to disappear. During the last ten years their numbers have steadily increased, and now they seem to be as numerous as they ever were in the region in question, and they are infinitely more wary and more difficult to kill.

Along the Little Missouri their ravages were so serious from 1893 to 1897 as to cause heavy damage to the stockmen. Not only colts and calves, but young trail stock, and in midwinter even full-grown horses and steers, are continually slain; and in some seasons their losses have been so serious as to more than eat up all the profits of the ranchman. The county authorities put a bounty on wolf scalps of three dollars each, and in my own neighborhood the ranchmen of their own accord put on a further bounty of five dollars. This made eight dollars for every wolf, and as the skin is also worth something, the business of killing wolves was quite profitable.

Wolves are very shy, and show extraordinary cunning both in hiding themselves and in slinking out of the way of the hunter. They are rarely killed with the rifle. I have never shot but one myself. They are occasionally trapped, but after a very few have been procured in this way the survivors become so wary that it is almost impossible even for a master of the art to do much with them, while an ordinary man can never get one into a trap except by accident.

More can be done with poison, but even in this case the animal speedily learns caution by experience. When poison is first used in a district wolves are very easily killed, and perhaps almost all of them will be slain, but nowadays it is difficult to catch any but young ones in this way. Occasionally an old one will succumb, but there are always some who cannot be persuaded to touch a bait. The old she wolves teach their cubs, as soon as they are able to walk, to avoid man's trace in every way, and to look out for traps and poison.

In consequence, though most cow-punchers carry poison with them, and are continually laying out baits, and though some men devote most of their time to poisoning for the sake of the bounty and the fur, the results are not very remunerative.

The most successful wolf-hunter on the Little Missouri in 1896 was a man who did not rely on poison at all, but on dogs. He was a hunter named Massingale, and he always had a pack of at least twenty hounds. The number varied, for a wolf at bay is a terrible fighter, with jaws like those of a steel trap and teeth that cut like knives, so that the dogs were continually disabled and sometimes killed, and the hunter had always to be on the watch to add animals to his pack.

It was not a pack that would appeal, as far as looks go, to an old huntsman, but it was thoroughly fitted for its own work. Most of the dogs were greyhounds, either rough or smooth haired, but many of them were big mongrels, and part some other breed, such as bulldog, mastiff, Newfoundland, bloodhound, or collie.

The only two necessary requisites were that the dogs

should run fast and fight gamely; and in consequence they formed as wicked, hard-biting a crew as ever ran down and throttled a wolf. They were usually taken out ten at a time, and by their aid Massingale killed two hundred wolves in the course of the year.

Of course there was no pretense of giving the game fair play. The wolves were killed as vermin, not for sport. The greatest havoc was in the springtime, when the she wolves were followed to their dens, which were sometimes holes in the earth and sometimes natural caves. There were from three to nine whelps in each litter. Some of the hounds were very fast, and they could usually overtake a young or weak wolf; but an old wolf, with a good start, unless run into at once, would surely get away if he were in running trim. Frequently, however, he was caught when he was not in running trim, for the hunter was apt to find him when he had killed a calf or taken part in dragging down a horse or steer. Under these circumstances he could not run long before the pack.

If possible, as with all such packs, the hunter himself would get up in time to end the worry by a stab of his hunting-knife; but unless he was quick he would have nothing to do, for the pack was thoroughly competent to do its own killing. Grim fighter though a great wolf is, he stands no show before the onslaught of ten such dogs, agile and powerful, who rush on their antagonist in a body. They possessed great power in their jaws, and unless Massingale was up within two or three minutes after the wolf was taken, the dogs literally tore him to pieces, though one or more of their number might be killed or crippled in the fight.

Other hunters were striving to get together packs thoroughly organized, and the wolves may be thinned out; they were certainly altogether too plentiful. During the fall of 1896 I saw a number myself, although I was not looking for them. I frequently came upon the remains of sheep and young stock which they had killed, and once, on the top of a small plateau, I found the body of a large steer, while the torn and trodden ground showed that he had fought hard for his life before succumbing. There were apparently two wolves engaged in the work, and the cunning beasts had evidently acted in concert. While one attracted the steer's attention, the other, according to the invariable wolf habit, attacked him from behind, hamstringing him and tearing out his flanks. His body was still warm when I came up, but his murderers had slunk off, either seeing or smelling me. Their handiwork was unmistakable, however, for, unlike bears and cougars, wolves invariably attack their victim at the hind quarters, and begin their feast on the hams or flanks if the animal is of any size.

CHAPTER V

SHOOTING THE PRONGBUCK

FOR a few years before 1897, when I visited my cattle-range I spent most of my time out on the great plains, where almost the only game that can be found is the prong-horned antelope; and as on such trips the party depends for fresh meat upon the rifle, I have on each occasion done a certain amount of antelope-shooting.

In the old days, when antelope were far more plentiful than they are now, they could often be procured by luring them with a red flag—for they are very inquisitive beasts—but now they have grown wary, and must usually be either stalked, which is very difficult, owing to their extreme keenness of vision and the absence of cover on the prairies, or else must be ridden into.

With first-class greyhounds and good horses they can often be run down in fair chase; but ordinarily the rider can hope for nothing more than to get within fair shooting range, and this only by taking advantage of their peculiarity of running straight ahead in the direction in which they are pointed when once they have settled to their pace. Usually antelope, as soon as they see a hunter, run straight away from him; but sometimes they make their flight at an angle, and as they do not like to change their course when once started, it is occasionally possible to cut them off from the point toward which they are headed, and get a reasonably close shot.

In the fall of 1896 I spent a fortnight on the range

with the ranch wagon. I was using for the first time one of the then new small-caliber, smokeless-powder rifles, a 30–30–160 Winchester. I had a half-jacketed bullet, the butt being cased in hard metal, while the nose was of pure lead.

While travelling to and fro across the range we usually broke camp each day, not putting up the tent at all during the trip; but at one spot we spent three nights. It was in a creek bottom, bounded on either side by rows of grassy hills, beyond which stretched the rolling prairie. The creek bed, which at this season was of course dry in most places, wound in S-shaped curves, with here and there a pool and here and there a fringe of stunted, wind-beaten timber. We were camped near a little grove of ash, box-alder, and willow, which gave us shade at noonday; and there were two or three pools of good water in the creek bed—one so deep that I made it my swimming-bath.

The first day that I was able to make a hunt I rode out with my foreman, Sylvane Ferris. I was mounted on Muley. Twelve years before, when Muley was my favorite cutting-pony on the round-up, he never seemed to tire or to lose his dash, but Muley was now sixteen years old, and on ordinary occasions he liked to go as soberly as possible; yet the good old pony still had the fire latent in his blood, and at the sight of game—or, indeed, of cattle or horses—he seemed to regain for the time being all the headlong courage of his vigorous and supple youth.

On the morning in question it was two or three hours before Sylvane and I saw any game. Our two ponies went steadily forward at a single-foot or shack, as the cow-punchers term what Easterners call "a fox-trot." Most of the time we were passing over immense grassy flats, where the mats of short curled blades lay brown and parched under the bright sunlight. Occasionally we came to ranges of low, barren hills, which sent off gently rounding spurs into the plain.

It was on one of these ranges that we first saw our game. As we were travelling along the divide we spied eight antelope far ahead of us. They saw us as soon as we saw them, and the chance of getting to them seemed small; but it was worth an effort, for by humoring them when they start to run, and galloping toward them at an oblique angle to their line of flight, there is always some little chance of getting a shot. Sylvane was on a light buckskin horse, and I left him on the ridge crest to occupy their time while I cantered off to one side.

The pronghorns became uneasy as I galloped off, and ran off the ridge crest in a line nearly parallel to mine. They did not go very fast, and I held Muley in, who was all on fire at the sight of the game. After crossing two or three spurs, the antelope going at half speed, they found I had come closer to them, and, turning, they ran up one of the valleys between two spurs.

Now was my chance, and, wheeling at right angles to my former course, I galloped Muley as hard as I knew how up the valley nearest and parallel to where the antelope had gone. The good old fellow ran like a quarter-horse, and when we were almost at the main ridge crest I leaped off, and ran ahead with my rifle at the ready, crouching down as I came to the sky-line. Usually on such occasions I find that the antelope have gone on and merely catch a glimpse of them half a mile distant, but on this occasion everything went right. The band had just reached the ridge crest about two hundred and twenty yards from me across the head of the valley, and I halted for a moment to look around. They were starting as I raised my rifle, but the trajectory is very flat with these small-bore smokeless-powder weapons, and taking a coarse front sight I fired at a young buck which stood broadside to me. There was no smoke, and as the band raced away I saw him sink backward, the ball having broken his hip.

We packed him bodily behind Sylvane on the buckskin and continued our ride, as there was no fresh meat in camp, and we wished to bring in a couple of bucks if possible. For two or three hours we saw nothing. The unshod feet of the horses made hardly any noise on the stretches of sun-cured grass, but now and then we passed through patches of thin weeds, their dry stalks rattling curiously, making a sound like that of a rattlesnake. At last, coming over a gentle rise of ground, we spied two more antelopes, half a mile ahead of us and to our right.

Again there seemed small chance of bagging our quarry, but again fortune favored us. I at once cantered Muley ahead, not toward them, so as to pass them well on one side. After some hesitation they started, not straightaway, but at an angle to my own course. For some moments I kept at a hand-gallop, until they got thoroughly settled in their line of flight; then I touched Muley, and he went as hard as he knew how.

Immediately the two panic-stricken and foolish beasts seemed to feel that I was cutting off their line of retreat, and raced forward at mad speed. They went much faster than I did, but I had the shorter course, and when they crossed me they were not fifty yards ahead —by which time I had come nearly a mile. Muley stopped short, like the trained cow-pony he was; I leaped off, and held well ahead of the rearmost and largest buck. At the crack of the little rifle down he went with his neck broken. In a minute or two he was packed behind me on Muley, and we bent our steps toward camp.

During the remainder of my trip we were never out of fresh meat, for I shot three other bucks—one after a smart chase on horseback, and the other two after careful stalks.

The game being both scarce and shy, I had to exercise much care, and after sighting a band I would sometimes have to wait and crawl round for two or three hours before they would get into a position where I had any chance of approaching. Even then they were more apt to see me and go off than I was to get near them.

Antelope are the only game that can be hunted as well at noonday as in the morning or evening, for their times for sleeping and feeding are irregular. They never seek shelter from the sun, and when they lie down for a noonday nap they are apt to choose a hollow, so as to be out of the wind; in consequence, if the band is seen at all at this time, it is easier to approach them than when they are up and feeding.

They sometimes come down to water in the middle of the day, sometimes in the morning or evening. On this trip I came across bands feeding and resting at almost every time of the day. They seemed usually to feed for a couple of hours, then rest for a couple of hours, then begin feeding again.

The last shot I got was when I was out with Joe Ferris, in whose company I had killed my first buffalo, just thirteen years before, and not very far from the spot I then was at. We had seen two or three bands that morning, and in each case, after a couple of hours of useless effort, I failed to get near enough. At last, toward midday, we got within range of a small band lying down in a little cup-shaped hollow in the middle of a great flat. I did not have a close shot, for they were running about one hundred and eighty yards off. The buck was rearmost, and at him I aimed; the bullet struck him in the flank, coming out of the opposite shoulder, and he fell in his next bound. As we stood over him, Joe shook his head, and said, "I guess that little 30–30 is the ace"; and I told him I guessed so too.

CHAPTER VI

A TAME WHITE GOAT

ONE of the queerest wild beasts in North America is the so-called white goat. It is found all along the highest peaks of the Rocky Mountains from Alaska into Montana, Idaho, and Washington. Really it is not a goat at all, but a kind of mountain-antelope, whose nearest kinsfolk are certain Asiatic antelopes found in the Himalayas. It is a squat, powerfully built, and rather clumsy-looking animal, about as heavy as a good-sized deer, but not as tall. It is pure white in color, except that its hoofs, horns, and muzzle are jet black. In winter its fleece is very long, and at that time it wears a long beard, which makes it look still more like a goat. It has a very distinct hump on the shoulders, and the head is usually carried low.

White goats are quite as queer in their habits as in their looks. They delight in cold, and, except in the northernmost portion of their range, they keep to the very tops of the mountains; and at midday, if the sun is at all powerful, retire to caves to rest themselves. They have the very curious habit of sitting up on their haunches, in the attitude of a dog begging, when looking about for any foe whose presence they suspect. They are wonderful climbers, although they have no liveliness or agility of movement; their surefootedness and remarkable strength enable them to go up or down seemingly impossible places. Their great round hoofs, with sharp-cut edges, can grip the slightest projection in the rocks, and no precipice or ice-wall has any terror

385

for them. At times they come quite low toward the foot-hills, usually to visit some mineral lick, but generally they are found only in the very high broken ground, among stupendous crags and precipices. They are self-confident, rather stupid beasts, and as they are accustomed to look for danger only from below, it is an easy matter to approach them if once the hunter is able to get above them; but they live in such inaccessible places that their pursuit entails great labor and hardship.

Their sharp black horns are eight or ten inches long, with points like needles, and their necks are thick and muscular, so that they are dangerous enemies for any foe to handle at close quarters; and they know their capacities very well and are confident in their prowess, often preferring to stand and fight a dog or wolf rather than to try to run. Nevertheless, though they are such wicked and resolute fighters, they have not a few enemies. The young kids are frequently carried off by eagles; and mountain-lions, wolves, and occasionally even wolverenes prey on the grown animals whenever they venture down out of their inaccessible resting-places to prowl along the upper edges of the timber or on the open terraces of grass and shrubby mountain plants. If a goat is on its guard, and can get its back to a rock, both wolf and panther will fight shy of facing the thrust of the dagger-like horns; but the beasts of prey are so much more agile and stealthy that if they can get a goat in the open or take it by surprise, they can readily pull it down.

I have several times shot white goats for the sake of the trophies afforded by the horns and skins, but I have never gone after them much, as the work is very severe, and the flesh usually affords poor eating, being musky, as there is a big musk-pod situated between the ear and the horn. Only a few of the old-time hunters knew anything about white goats; and even nowadays there are not very many men who go into their haunts as a steady thing; but the settlers who live high up in the mountains do come across them now and then, and they occasionally have odd stories to relate about them.

One was told to me by an old fellow who had a cabin on one of the tributaries that ran into Flathead Lake. He had been off prospecting for gold in the mountains early one spring. The life of a prospector is very hard. He goes alone, and in these northern mountains he cannot take with him the donkey which toward the south is his almost invariable companion and beast of burden; the tangled forests of the northern ranges make it necessary for him to trust only to his own power as a pack-bearer, and he carries merely what he takes on his own shoulders.

The old fellow in question had been out for a month before the snow was all gone, and his dog, a large and rather vicious hound, to which he was greatly attached, accompanied him. When his food gave out he was working his way back toward Flathead Lake, and struck a stream, on which he found an old dugout canoe, deserted the previous fall by some other prospector or prospectors. Into this he got, with his traps and his dog, and started downstream.

On the morning of the second day, while rounding a point of land, he suddenly came upon two white goats, a female and a little kid, evidently but a few weeks old, standing right by the stream. As soon as they saw him they turned and galloped clumsily off toward the foot of the precipice. As he was in need of meat, he shoved ashore and ran after the fleeing animals with his rifle, while the dog galloped in front. Just before reaching the precipice the dog overtook the goats. When he was almost up, however, the mother goat turned suddenly around, while the kid stopped short behind her, and she threatened the dog with lowered head. After a second's hesitation the dog once more resumed his gallop, and flung himself full on the quarry. It was a fatal move. As he gave his last leap, the goat, bending her head down sideways, struck viciously, so that one horn slipped right up to the root into the dog's chest. The blow was mortal, and the dog barely had time to give one yelp before his life passed.

It was, however, several seconds before the goat could disengage its head from its adversary, and by that time the enraged hunter was close at hand, and with a single bullet avenged the loss of his dog. When the goat fell, however, he began to feel a little ashamed, thinking of the gallant fight she had made for herself and kid, and he did not wish to harm the latter. So he walked forward, trying to scare it away; but the little thing stood obstinately near its dead mother, and butted angrily at him as he came up. It was far too young to hurt him in any way, and he was bound not to hurt it, so he sat down beside it and smoked a pipe.

When he got up it seemed to have become used to his presence, and no longer showed any hostility. For some seconds he debated what to do, fearing lest it might die if left alone; then he came to the conclusion that it was probably old enough to do without its mother's milk, and would have at least a chance for its life if left to itself. Accordingly, he walked toward the boat; but he soon found it was following him. He tried to frighten it back, but it belonged to much too stout-hearted a race to yield to pretense, and on it came after him. When he reached the boat, after some hesitation he put the little thing in and started downstream. At first the motion of the boat startled it, and it jumped right out into the water. When he got it back, it again jumped out, on to a boulder. On being replaced the second time, it made no further effort to escape; but it puzzled him now and then by suddenly standing up with its forefeet on the very rim of the ticklish dug-out, so that he had to be very careful how he balanced. Finally, however, it got used to the motion of the canoe, and it was then a very contented and amusing passenger.

The last part of the journey, after its owner abandoned the canoe, was performed with the kid slung on his back. Of course it again at first objected strenuously to this new mode of progress, but in time it became quite reconciled, and accepted the situation philosophically. When the prospector reached his cabin his difficulties were at an end. The little goat had fallen off very much in flesh; for though it would browse of its own accord around the camp at night, it was evidently too young to take to the change kindly.

Before reaching the cabin, however, it began to pick up again, and it soon became thoroughly at home amid its new surroundings. It was very familiar, not only with the prospector, but with strangers, and evidently regarded the cabin as a kind of safety spot. Though it would stray off into the surrounding woods, it never ventured farther than two or three hundred yards, and after an absence of half an hour or so at the longest, it would grow alarmed, and come back at full speed, bounding along like a wild buck through the woods, until it reached what it evidently deemed its haven of refuge.

Its favorite abode was the roof of the cabin, at one corner of which, where the projecting ends of the logs were uneven, it speedily found a kind of ladder, up which it would climb until the roof was reached. Sometimes it would promenade along the ridge, and at other times mount the chimney, which it would hastily abandon, however, when a fire was lit. The presence of a dog always resulted in immediate flight, first to the roof, and then to the chimney; and when it came inside the cabin it was fond of jumping on a big wooden shelf above the fireplace, which served as a mantelpiece.

If teased it was decidedly truculent; but its tameness and confidence, and the quickness with which it recognized any friend, made it a great favorite, not only with the prospector, but with his few neighbors. However, the little thing did not live very long. Whether it was the change of climate or something wrong with its food, when the hot weather came on it pined gradually away, and one morning it was found dead, lying on its beloved rooftree. The prospector had grown so fond of it that, as he told me, he gave it a burial "just as if it were a Christian."

CHAPTER VII

RANCHING

THERE are in every community young men to whom life at the desk or behind the counter is unutterably dreary and unattractive, and who long for some out-of-door occupation which shall, if possible, contain a spice of excitement. These young men can be divided into two classes—first, those who, if they get a chance to try the life for which they long, will speedily betray their utter inability to lead it; and, secondly, those who possess the physical capacity and the peculiar mental make-up necessary for success in an employment far out of the usual paths of civilized occupations. A great many of these young men think of ranching as a business which they might possibly take up, and what I am about to say* is meant as much for a warning to one class as for advice to the other.

Ranching is a rather indefinite term. In a good many parts of the West a ranch simply means a farm; but I shall not use it in this sense, since the advantages and disadvantages of a farmer's life, whether it be led in New Jersey or Iowa, have often been dwelt upon by men infinitely more competent than I am to pass judgment. Accordingly, when I speak of ranching I shall mean some form of stock-raising or sheep-farming as practised now in the wilder parts of the United States, where there is still plenty of land which, because of the lack of rainfall, is not very productive for agricultural purposes.

* Written in 1896.

391

GOOD HUNTING

The first thing to be remembered by any boy or young man who wishes to go West and start life on a cattle-ranch, horse-ranch, or sheep-ranch is that he must know the business thoroughly before he can earn any salary to speak of, still less start out on his own accord. A great many young fellows apparently think that a cowboy is born and not made, and that in order to become one all they have to do is to wish very hard to be one. Now, as a matter of fact, a young fellow trained as a bookkeeper would take quite as long to learn the trade of a cowboy as the average cowboy would take to learn the trade of bookkeeper. The first thing that the beginner anywhere in the wilder parts of the West has to learn is the capacity to stand monotony, fatigue, and hardship; the next thing is to learn the nature of the country.

A young fellow from the East who has been brought up on a farm, or who has done hard manual labor as a machinist, need not go through a novitiate of manual labor in order to get accustomed to the roughness that such labor implies; but a boy just out of a high school, or a young clerk, will have to go through just such a novitiate before he will be able to command a dollar's pay. Both alike will have to learn the nature of the country, and this can only be learned by actual experience on the ground.

Again, the beginner must remember that, though there is occasional excitement and danger in a ranchman's life, it is only occasional, while the monotony of hard and regular toil is not often broken. Except in the matter of fresh air and freedom from crowding, a small ranchman often leads a life of as grinding hardness as the average dweller in a New York tenement-house. His shelter is a small log hut, or possibly a

392

dugout in the side of a bank, or in summer a shabby tent. For food he will have to depend mainly on the bread of his own baking, on fried fat pork, and on coffee or tea with sugar and no milk. Of course he will occasionally have some canned stuff or potatoes. The furniture of the hut is of the roughest description—a roll of blankets for bedding, a bucket, a tin wash-basin, and a tin mug, with perhaps a cracked looking-glass four inches square.

He will not have much society of any kind, and the society he does have is not apt to be overrefined. If he is a lad of a delicate, shrinking nature and fastidious habits, he will find much that is uncomfortable, and will need to show no small amount of pluck and fortitude if he is to hold his own. The work, too, is often hard and often wearisome from mere sameness. It is generally done on horseback even on a sheep-ranch, and always on a cow-ranch. The beginner must learn to ride with indifference all kinds of rough and dangerous horses before he will be worth his keep.

With all this before him, the beginner will speedily find out that life on a Western ranch is very far from being a mere holiday. A young man who desires to start in the life ought, if possible, to have with him a little money—just enough to keep body and soul together—until he can gain a foothold somewhere.

No specific directions can be given him as to where to start. Wyoming, most of Montana, the western edge of the Dakotas, western Texas, and some portions of the Rocky Mountain States still offer chances for a man to go into the ranch business. In different seasons in the different localities business may be good or bad, and it would be impossible to tell where was the best place to start.

Wherever the beginner goes, he ought to make up his mind at the outset to start by doing any kind of work he can. Let him chop wood, hoe, do any chore that will bring him in twenty-five cents. If he is once able to start by showing that he is willing to work hard and do something, he can probably get employment of some kind, although this employment will almost certainly be very ill paid and not attractive. Perhaps it will be to dig in a garden, or to help one of the men drive oxen, or to do the heavy work around camp for some party of cow-punchers or lumberers. Whatever it is, let the boy go at it with all his might, and at the same time take every opportunity to get acquainted with the kind of life which he intends ultimately to lead. If he wishes to try to ride a horse, he will have every chance, if for no other reason than that he will continually meet men whose ideas of fun are met by the spectacle of a tenderfoot on a bucking bronco.

By degrees he will learn a good deal of the ways of the life and of the country. Then he must snatch the first chance that offers itself to take a position in connection with the regular work of a ranch. He may be employed as a regular hand to help cook on the ranch wagon, or taken by a shepherd to do the hard and dirty work which the shepherd would like to put off on somebody else. When he has once got as far as this his rise is certain, if he is not afraid of labor and keeps a lookout for the opportunities that offer. After a while he will have a horse himself, and he will be employed as a second-rate man to do the ordinary ranch work.

Work on a sheep-ranch is less attractive but more profitable than on any other. A good deal of skill must be shown by the shepherd in managing his flock and in handling the sheep-dogs; but ordinarily it is

appallingly dreary to sit all day long in the sun, or loll
about in the saddle, watching the flocks of fleecy idiots.
In time of storm he must work like a demon and know
exactly what to do, or his whole flock will die before his
eyes, sheep being as tender as horses and cattle are
tough.

With the work of a cow-ranch or horse-ranch there
comes more excitement. Every man on such a ranch
has a string of eight or ten horses for his own riding,
and there is a great deal of exciting galloping and hot
riding across the plains; and the work in a stampede at
night, or in line-riding during the winter, or in breaking
the fierce little horses to the saddle, is as exciting as it
is hard and dangerous.

The wilder phases of the life, however, are steadily
passing away. Almost everywhere great wire fences
are being put up, and no small part of the cowboy's
duty nowadays is to ride along the line of a fence and
repair it wherever broken. Moreover, at present [1896]
the business of cattle or horse raising on the plains does
not pay well, and, except in peculiar cases, can hardly
be recommended to a boy ambitious for his future.

So much for the unattractive reality of ranch life.
It would be unfair not to point out that it has a very
attractive side also. If the boy is fond of open-air
exercise, and willing to risk tumbles that may break
an occasional bone, and to endure at need heat and
cold, hunger and thirst, he will find much that is pleasant in the early mornings on the great plains, particularly on the rare days when he is able to take a few
hours' holiday to go with his shotgun after prairie-
chickens or ducks, or, perchance, to ride out with a
Winchester rifle to a locality where on one of his working days he has seen a small band of antelope standing

in the open, or caught a glimpse of a deer bounding through the brush. There is little temptation to spend money, unless he is addicted to the coarsest kind of dissipation, and after a few years the young fellow ought to have some hundreds of dollars laid aside. By this time he should know all about the business and the locality, and should be able to gauge just what he can accomplish.

For a year or two perhaps he can try to run a little outfit of his own in connection with his work on a big ranch. Then he will abandon the latter and start out entirely on his own account. Disaster may overtake him, as it may overtake any business man; but if he wins success, even though of a moderate kind, he has a pleasant life before him, riding about over the prairie among his own horses or cattle or sheep, occasionally taking a day off to go after game, and, while working hard, not having to face the mere drudgery which he had to encounter as a tyro.

The chances are very small that he will ever gain great wealth; and when he marries and has children of his own there are many uncomfortable problems to face, the chief being that of schools; but for a young man in good health and of adventurous temper the life is certainly pleasanter than that of one cooped up in the counting-room, and while it is not one to be sought save by the very few who have a natural liking for it and a natural capacity to enjoy it and profit by it, still for these few people it remains one of the most attractive forms of existence in America.